23.38

THE
IMPOSSIBLE
MUSICAL

Dale Wasserman

APPLAUSE
THEATRE & CINEMA BOOKS

Library of Congress Cataloging-in-Publication Data
Wasserman, Dale.
The impossible musical : the Man of La Mancha
story / Dale Wasserman.
p. cm.
ISBN 1-55783-515-2
1. Wasserman, Dale. Man of La Mancha. I. Title.

ML423.W315W37 2003
782.1′4—dc21
2003005154

APPLAUSE THEATRE & CINEMA BOOKS
151 West 46th Street, 8th Floor
New York, NY 10036
Phone: (212) 575-9265
Fax: (646) 562-5852
Email: info@applausepub.com
Internet: www.applausepub.com

Sales & Distribution

NORTH AMERICA:
Hal Leonard Corp.
7777 West Bluemound Road
P. O. Box 13819
Milwaukee, WI 53213
Phone: (414) 774-3630
Fax: (414) 774-3259
Email: halinfo@halleonard.com
Internet: www.halleonard.com

UNITED KINGDOM:
Roundhouse Publishing Ltd.
Millstone, Limers Lane
Northam, North Devon
Ex 39 2RG
Phone: 01237-474474
Fax: 01237-474774
Email: roundhouse.group@ukgateway.net

Dedicated to:
Martha Nelly Garza
Wife, partner, good companion.
Siempre fiel y cariñosa.
DW

ACKNOWLEDGMENTS

Robert S. Sennett, for unstinting assistance and the use of quotations from our joint history of *Man of La Mancha.*

Brian J. Folkes, whose collection of Cervantiana is greatly superior to my own.

Beatrice Williams-Rude, for invaluable research in New York.

The Association for Hispanic Classical Theatre, Inc., and Donald T. Dietz, its president, for unique insights into Spain's Age of Gold.

The Cervantes magazine, Bulletin of the Cervantes Society of America, and its editor, Daniel Eisenberg, for publication of *A Diary for 'I, Don Quixote'* and of its complete script.

The Estate of W. H. Auden, Edward Mendelsohn, Executor.

Robbie Lantz, agent extraordinaire.

Michelle Calta, my assistant, conqueror of recalcitrant computers.

Richard Warren, playwright and friend, for critical comment.

Nicholas Salerno, Ph.D., connoisseur of cinema.

My editor, Greg Collins, and publisher, Glenn Young, for persistent but priceless harassment.

Note: The epigraphs that head each chapter are quotations from one draft or another of *Man of La Mancha.*

CONTENTS

CHAPTER ONE

Facts are the enemy of truth.

Man of La Mancha was born in November, 1965, as a production nobody wanted, booked into a theatre nobody else would have, and ignored by everyone except the public. Prior to opening and during its tryout it had been adjudged by the wise men of Broadway as bearing a certain shy charm but a dim future, incapable of competing against the heavyweights. Certainly not, as *Life* magazine proclaimed, A METAPHYSICAL SMASHEROO. Metaphysical it surely was, but certainly none of those wise men — or anyone else, in fact — could conceive that it would become a "smasheroo."

Observe the epigraph that opens this account: "Facts are the enemy of truth," spoken by the chief actor in the drama, and that I believe absolutely. Facts cannot explain the success of *Man of La Mancha*. Something more was at work, a something that I neither planned nor tried to define. Facts in their guise as statistics might explain the "smasheroo" part of the equation, but they are surely impotent in dealing with the "metaphysical" aspect — which, I believe, contains the secret.

Man of La Mancha is not, as most people believe, an adaptation of *Don Quixote* but a play about a few hours in the life of a playwright, Miguel de Cervantes. It invokes certain characters and situations of his creation, but emphatically it is not a version of the novel, nor is meant to be. It's a drama written originally for television and later musicalized for a broader range of expression. My man of La Mancha is *not* Don Quixote; he is Miguel de Cervantes.

I *believed* this play. It was written from the gut. Initially I didn't, believe it, that is. Initially I had challenged myself to solve a problem of adaptation at which a legion of writers had failed, on the

9

unlikely assumption that I might succeed. Somewhere en route that motive changed. What replaced it was a quest burning no less hotly than the Don's, a quest to discover personal values through a defined and clearly articulated credo. Whatever motive commenced the process, quite another completed it.

Life magazine's headline has always amused me; more, it has impressed me as being of all labels the most apt. To quote further from that review, written by their theatre critic, Tom Prideaux:

> It is easy to dismiss this play as sentimental. But the audience's tears are shed not so much for Quixote's death as for his undying valor — his bravery in still being, in the end, his own dream-ridden self. In a time when men complain about losing their identity, of being mere cogs and numbers in a computerized world, the spectacle of a rampantly individual Don Quixote is welcome. His constant homage to spiritual ideals touches a chord, especially among the young today who are so earnestly and vociferously trying to find ideals among political realities.
>
> The audience's tears testify to the achingly human ambivalence of Quixote, who is both a criticism and a defense of man's idealism. In making us love him and recognize parts of him in ourselves, this absurd but magnificent dreamer has revealed deep truths. He has shown to what an important extent all men can, and must, create their own reality — and how inspiring and dangerous it can be.

True, then and now.

Allow me to identify myself. Though I work in the fishbowl of show business, I am a private person, reclusive even, and more than a bit antisocial. As to my public self, here are biographical notes from a recent theatrical program:

> DALE WASSERMAN (Author) says: "I was born. That seems fairly certain, but where or when less so, since I could not boast a birth certificate. By profession I'd describe myself as a Showbiz Hobo, having made the jump from riding the rails to theatre pro at the age of 19. I've been a stage manager, lighting designer, producer

and director. At the age of 33, in the midst of directing an unspeak-
able Broadway musical, I walked, feeling that I couldn't possibly
write worse than the stuff I was directing. Writing was difficult due
to an almost total lack of education. In my years of jumping
freights, though, I did a heap of reading, 'borrowing' two books at
a time from small town libraries, returning them to another library
in a town further down the line, and hooking two more. (It's
possible that single-handed I brought the Dewey Decimal System
to its knees.)

"I succeeded as a writer by lucking into the Golden Age of television, and thereafter segued into stage plays and movies. I have
written around fifty works for TV, some two dozen stage plays and
musicals and fifteen feature films. For a time I occupied an executive suite at MGM as a producer-writer. Upon being sprung I wrote
the stage adaptation of *One Flew Over the Cuckoo's Nest* which flies
lustily to this very day...

"As to awards, I have received the usual quota of Emmys,
Tonys, Ellys and Robbys and, for all I know, Kaspars and Hausers.
I'm unsure of the number because I don't attend awards ceremonies and so receive the knick-knacks by mail if at all. Ah, yes,
one exception: when the University of Wisconsin offered an
Honorary Doctorate I did appear in cap and gown to address the
audience in the football stadium at Madison, because a scant
quarter-mile from where I was being Doctored I had hopped my
first freight at the age of 12. Irony should not be wasted."

There you are. There's more of course, but perhaps it can be
absorbed by osmosis. Now, in order to enjoy the *La Mancha* saga, it
will be useful to enroll for a short course in Showbiz Mendacity.

Figures lie. Figures in show business lie even more shamelessly
than elsewhere. Never believe what you read in *Variety*. Never believe
producers' trumpetings in their advertising or, for that matter, anywhere else. It is not only difficult, it is literally impossible to obtain
reasonable statistics on a show's actual box-office gross, its number
of performances, or anything else that may be distorted, inflated,
massaged, or otherwise warped for advantage or just for the joy of it.

Nevertheless, and confining comment to the musical theatre, the people who license the production of shows are required to keep accounts, less for the beneficiaries of the business than to stave off assaults by the IRS as well as by lawyers waving blue-backed Orders to Show Cause. With input from experts, it is possible to form estimates of how many productions a given show has enjoyed and may be projected to enjoy over a given span of time.

I'll pause to apologize for my reliance on such input. I plead incompetence. I have a poor head for figures, but I have been advised that this account must include such statistics to demonstrate, presumably, why readers owe it attention.

When it has all been done—research, accountancy, and projections, through agents, attorneys, publishers and licensors of musical plays, one show, *Man of La Mancha*, seems to lap the field. There is evidence, I'm told, that *Man of La Mancha* may be the most popular musical play of the last half-century. Some take it further: figures affirm that it may be the most popular play of the century. Further still, based on a creeping increase in the number of productions yearly, it may be eligible to become the most popular musical of all time.

"Popular" doesn't refer to seats warmed by ticket buyers' bottoms or to laudation by the press, but to the number of productions worldwide. Musicals successful on Broadway, including *Man of La Mancha*, may go on to play in German, Swedish, Hebrew, or Japanese. Not many also play in Urdu, Icelandic, Gujarati, Uzbekistani, Siamese, Magyar, Slovenian, Swahili, Polish, Finnish, Ukrainian, or nine distinctly different dialects of Spanish. *Man of La Mancha* has played or is playing in all of these.

People make claims. Who's to stop them? Hyperbole is the native language of press agents. In advertisements *Les Misérables* trumpets, THE WORLD'S MOST POPULAR MUSICAL. (In any given month *Les Misérables* may have perhaps five productions, compared to *La Mancha*'s twenty or thirty.) *Miss Saigon* more modestly blazons, THE SHOW WHICH IS ALREADY A LEGEND! (A legend? Where? In whose opinion?)

Another, which out of delicacy I decline to name, says simply, GREATEST MUSICAL OF ALL TIME!

Cats, of course, can legitimately claim LONGEST RUN IN

BROADWAY HISTORY, though it doesn't quite meet its own measure of NOW AND FOREVER, since it's already gone. Also, there enters a question of civic geography, for *The Fantasticks*, a mile or two south ran far longer, though in a pocket-sized theatre.

Superlatives in show business are a penny a gross, including those claimed for *Man of La Mancha*. But there are oddities about *La Mancha* that set it apart. It has no office. No press agent. No producer. There is no management minding the store. It just fumbles and bumbles its way about the Earth, an object lesson in how a successful *oeuvre de theatre* should not be handled.

As to the number of productions of *Man of La Mancha* per annum, a fair count places it between 300 and 400. I make no claim to competence in this field, but by invoking some primitive mathematics: productions per annum multiplied by thirty-five years in which rights have been available, bring one to the figure of some 10,000 licenses issued for productions of the play. Let us discount ten percent for inflated reporting and add ten percent for pirated productions, and still we have an improbable horde of Dons dreaming Impossible Dreams.

The financial side of *Man of La Mancha* may be dreamier than its philosophy, since it is possible to state the philosophy, but impossible to capture true statements of profit. I can personally testify to the following: the play was budgeted at $200,000 for New York and went $20,000 over budget due to losses in previews and its first weeks. The investors have realized several thousand percent on their investments. The other beneficiaries continue to receive largesse for the life of the copyright.

Who are those beneficiaries?

Well, there are the authors, of whom I am the principal. (By force of necessity I was also an investor.) Then there's the director, who, by some legal legerdemain, also had himself declared "collaborating author." The music publishers. The licensors of stock and amateur rights: in the United States the Tams-Witmark Music Library; MusicScope in the United Kingdom; Stage Musicals in Canada; The Marton Agency for foreign languages; MCA Records for the Original Cast Album; various music publishers in foreign lands; various publishers of the text in various languages; and

Random House as the publisher of the play in English. When last I glanced at a copy, it read: "Thirtieth printing."

And there are more.

There are cast albums in French (starring and translated by the ineffable Jacques Brel), in Hebrew, in Czech, in Japanese, and also in Dutch, Mexican Spanish, Spanish-Spanish, several other Spanishes, and also in Polish, Czech, German, and other languages. How many, no one knows, for most are illegal or unauthorized. Star performers on cast albums have run the gamut from Placido Domingo as Quixote (surprisingly pallid) to Jim Nabors (surprisingly effective.) The making of videotapes of the production in any language is strictly prohibited, but there are at least twenty in existence. So much for the big stick of copyright protection.

Dealing with the financial side of *La Mancha* is baffling. Accuracy is impossible; show business is conducted largely in cash. Its legal structure is baroque to the point of incomprehensibility, a source of joy to a legion of lawyers. Income passes through many hands with sticky fingers. What is indisputable, however, is that a smash musical is Big Business.

Authors in general are passionately focused on their art. Matters of contract and accountancy take time and attention they are reluctant, or simply incompetent, to give, although this order of precedence may cost them heavily. I say this in wonder, not bitterness; after all, once the deductions and misappropriations are accounted for, there is still plenty left. About 65 percent of authors' royalties goes to tax collectors and to agents, domestic and foreign; still with a musical as popular as *La Mancha* there is plenty left.

Further, a successful musical spawns ancillary rights like crabgrass on the velvety lawns of Art. All of these rights generate income, some minor, some eye-popping. Consider a few:

> Movie sales, rights and participations
> Television uses
> Stock and amateur licensing
> Foreign language licensing
> Cast albums
> Music publication and licensing

Print publications
Foreign language publications
First-class productions, including Broadway
First-class tours
Non-union tours
Foreign tours
Small rights
Miscellaneous

Surprising what can pop up under "miscellaneous." Book authors wish to quote from the play. A TV series (e.g., *Quantum Leap*) wishes to build an episode about a rehearsal of *Man of La Mancha*. A movie (*Moon Over Parador*) asks to have Richard Dreyfuss, its leading character, in an impersonation of a dictator make a speech to the masses that is a paraphrase of "The Impossible Dream." The Royal Philharmonic of London asks permission to present a concert version with opera stars in the leading roles. A famous German singer requests permission to perform a cabaret version. There seems to be no end to the permutations of "permissions."

Return for a moment, to music rights. This is a cocktail-tree bearing multiple kinds of fruit. One sort is called "Mechanicals," which is recording for the ear. Cast albums, CDs, and tapes fall in this category. Another is "Synchronization," which is setting music to pictures, whether the pictures are moving or still. Then, of course, there's the use (often the abuse) of individual songs as played by lounge pianists, sung by singers, Muzacked, in elevators or set to march-tempo by college bands at football half-time shows. These uses are licensed by ASCAP or BMI in behalf of the composer/lyricists, modes of licensing so arcane as to be incomprehensible to normal human intelligence. I will not even attempt an explanation; it dazes the brain.

As to "small rights," this is a misnomer. They aren't small; actually, they include the licensing of lyrics and music and the income therefrom. Here we collide with an archaic usage that gives those rights (*and* the income) exclusively to the composer and lyricist, excluding the so-called "bookwriter." This arrangement dates from the mid twenties, when the "bookwriter" for musicals was a hack who wrote jokey dialogue between musical numbers, allowing dancers to catch their breath and singers to sip whatever liquids their tonsils craved. What this adds up to is that the composer and lyricist are thus able to operate a lucrative business that is theirs alone.

We have come to that invidious term, "Bookwriter." In the case of *Man of La Mancha*, one may note that it isn't used: the billing reads, "Written by," or simply "By." That's because I am irritable about the term and forbid its use, on this or any other musical I am connected with. I am a playwright. The plays I write may be musical or non. I write the plot, the people, the ideas, and the philosophy, and many of the words and phrases incorporated into the lyrics. In short, the armature on which is hung the work as a whole.

It works like this: I, the "bookwriter" wrote, "To dream the impossible dream, to fight the unbeatable foe..." The lyricist then wrote:

> To dream the impossible dream,
> to fight the unbeatable foe...

—whereupon, through the alchemy of contractual usage the words became his forever.

I, the "bookwriter," speaking through the character Aldonza, wrote, "I was spawned in a ditch by a mother who left me there..." The lyricist then wrote:

> I was spawned in a ditch
> by a mother who left me there...

Is the ability to type in uppercase letters a talent worthy of great reward? Of course not—in the case of *La Mancha*, lyricist Joe Darion brought wit, humor, and a highly specialized talent to his task. Yet everything he wrote derives from the words, characters, and inventions on exhibit in the original play. This is how it must be. If it's otherwise, we have a musical that has already closed.

I note that I am indulging in the vertical pronoun perhaps overmuch. But, *au fond*, what is more subjective than a play that argues a specific philosophy? More self-revealing, more authentically autobiographical? For years I denied the investment of spirit, claiming only technical dexterity with the dramatic form, especially as applied to television or to the screenplay. But as *Man of La Mancha* took form, I realized that the mask of objectivity had turned transparent.

There was more to that "metaphysical" side. It was evidenced in the flood of mail I began receiving at the opening of the show and that, though diminished, continues to this very day. The wild variety of interpretations of a text I had thought to be simplistically clear astonished me. There were many who identified Quixote with Jesus Christ, which I found puzzling, since neither I nor my play have any interest in religion whatsoever. Others found various spiritual interpretations, most of which represented not interpretations of the play so much as verification of the letter-writers' own beliefs.

But there was one theme that chorused through almost all of the communications. In one way or another, they said, "The play changed my life." By this I understood not so much that the play had actually changed anyone's life but that it had reawakened the ideals of adolescence, ideals that had died of the attrition of living. It was less change than restoration.

There we have it, the curious mating of metaphysics with the facts of smasheroo, still going strong in the 45th year of their marriage.

How, exactly, did all this come about?

CHAPTER TWO

Do not pursue pleasure,
lest thou have the misfortune to overtake it.

Man of La Mancha was conceived in error and grew by reason of curiosity. Unlike most literary projects it had a precise date of conception, the 8th of August, 1958. The location of the event can be fixed just as exactly—an outdoor café in the Plaza de España, Madrid, in a Spain vastly different from the Spain of today. A true account of the epiphany would go like this: I was scanning the International Edition of the *Herald Tribune* over my customary breakfast of espresso and empanadas when an item caught my eye. "Dale Wasserman in Madrid," it said, "while researching Don Quixote for motion picture adaptation. He'll be seeking Yves Montand for the title role."

The item was nonsense. I was in Spain for nothing of the sort. It was likely that Montand's press agent had planted the item to get his client's name in a column devoted to the (mostly mythical) doings of showfolks, a practice smiled upon by those in the know. Like most people on Earth I'd never read *Don Quixote* nor had the faintest interest in adapting it.

But here Fate rapped me on the head. Even while chuckling over the item I had the uneasy sense of someone looking over my shoulder. I turned to investigate, and there, at the top of the Plaza, was the great marble monument to Miguel de Cervantes. At his feet were the equestrian statues of Don Quixote and Sancho Panza, the Don riding up to the sky on his nag, Rocinante, Sancho astride his donkey, Dapple.

They'd been there all the time, of course, though if I'd noticed them before I wasn't aware. Possibly they were too prominent or my disinterest too great. In any case, I hadn't come to Spain to do deep thinking or to consider new projects but for the opposite; this trip was dedicated strictly to pleasure. Having completed a cycle of eight plays for television and two feature films, I'd granted myself a vacation in which do-less-ness was writ large and brain-sweat of any variety, including brooding on new works, was off-limits. In short, I was there to kick back, goof off, pursue pleasure.

Spain had always had a special allure for me. I was fascinated by its history, its multiple cultures, by its exotic racial mix and harsh landscapes, although I'll readily confess that my interest was less scholastic than romantic. I felt comfortable in Spain, something not always true of New York or Hollywood, which was reason enough for this interlude of self-indulgence, and was determined that for this time I'd banish show business from my mind and diligently do nothing at all.

Earlier that same year I'd been asked by San Bon Matsu, my Japanese artist-neighbor in New York, to advise him on where one might go and live cheaply while creating. "Easy," I told him. "The Costa del Sol." And I named a village, Fuengirola, which had caught my fancy on a previous meander along the Coast. San had taken my advice, gone there, fallen in love with it, and reported he was painting at a prodigious rate. Why, he asked, didn't I join him? He listed the inducements: he'd acquired a house with numerous rooms, only steps from the beach. It was innocent of heating, cooling, telephone, or TV. It boasted a primitive kitchen with a charcoal stove and an abundance of fleas. The rent was $8 a month.

Clearly irresistible—and clearly before the Costa del Sol had become scabbed over with "development." I was fond of the Coast because it was old Andalucia, untainted by progress and far more primitive than it was a millennium ago when the Andaluz culture was surpassed by none and its capital, glorious Cordoba, was known as "The Ornament of the World."

I went, and found all as advertised, including the fleas.

Fuengirola was a fishing village. By day the boats were drawn up on the broad beaches, and in the shadow of each slumbered a fisherman. I dreamed in the sun, swam in the sea and observed the ritual of siesta. From 1 to 5 PM, no one— *no one*—was to be disturbed.

Towards evening, if one faced the Mediterranean and looked over his right shoulder, Gibraltar would rise mysteriously out of the mists. On rare occasions one might see the snowy tips of the High Atlas across the water in Africa...there and yet not there, illusive as a mirage.

On certain occasions, by burro or on foot we'd make the arduous climb up a goat track to the ancient village of Mijas, there to see bullfights in a Roman era Plaza de Toros that was shaped exactly like a bathtub. The bulls were culls or had obviously been caped before, which made them unpredictable and doubly dangerous. The matadors were young and desperate to succeed. They wore colorful names such as "Terremoto" (The Earthquake) or "El Terror." There was one in particular of whom it was said, "See him—quick." Popularly known as The Hippie, he not only managed to survive but to gain fame under the sobriquet "El Cordobés."

Idylls end. A producer in Madrid located me and insisted I come talk with him. As it happened, the movie he had to offer was unexciting in subject, poorly paid, and easy to turn down. The throbbing life of Madrid was another matter. For contrast with the rigors of Fuengirola I moved into a suite on the top floor of the Castellana Hilton, where my neighbors to left and right were Ramsay Ames and Ava Gardner, respectively.

Ramsay, despite her name, was a girl. Definitely. When she walked through the hotel lobby, smiling her double-barreled smile, one could hear spoons dropping and hisses of, "Ay, guapa... guapissima!" I'd known Ramsay from Hollywood, where she'd been a minor movie star, more famous for her figure than her thespic ability. She was invariably cast as the girl being carried off by a monster, the barely dressed beauty with the incredible body. Finding monsters monotonous she'd decamped to Spain where, aside from playing occasional roles in movies, she'd made a place for herself with her own celebrity radio show. Ramsay was cheerful, bright in spirit, with a ready laugh and a flair for adventure.

At the Castellana Hilton evenings were spent in a hedonistic haze either on Ramsay's terrace or on Ava's. The ladies seemed almost interchangeable except that Ramsay laughed often, Ava rarely. Both had bullfighter lovers who, in the Spanish fashion, were faithful to their bourgeois wives as well as to their mistresses. Both mixed good martinis, both kept record players going constantly, flamenco or classic guitar, with little variation. I noted that, despite rumor, Ava did not keep Frank Sinatra albums stacked beside her record player. (I don't recall her ever playing a Sinatra record.)

I didn't really know Ava; I had the impression Ava didn't really know herself. She was quiet, moody, and usually, between midnight and dawn, to be found cruising restlessly among the flamenco clubs. She drank steadily without much visible effect and was fond of dancing to gitano guitars in night clubs. She danced well if inauthentically, but the Gypsies were happy to see her. She shed luster where she walked.

Madrid seemed to be Hollywood East. In those years Spain was a favorite location for moviemaking. It was cheap and it desperately needed the Yanqui dollar. One could rent the Spanish army from El Caudillo for a pittance, at least in terms of movie budgets, and so Spain's army stood in (or marched in) for Huns, Visigoths, Carthaginians, Greeks, Romans, and Chinese. Or, for that matter, any other historical fighting force. Customarily it stood in for both opposing armies with no more than a reversal of direction and a change of uniforms.

My Spanish sojourn continued in a hedonistic haze until, one memorable evening, Ramsay and I had dinner at the home of Joaquin Rodrigo, composer of the haunting "Concierto de Aranjuez," which had become famous in America through Miles Davis's rendition in "Sketches of Spain." Rodrigo was a charming man and a vivacious host, serving drinks, exhibiting original manuscripts, demonstrating flashes of melody on guitar or piano. So sure were his movements that only gradually did I come to the realization he was blind. Later I learned he'd been blind from birth. Post-dinner, he played piano for us, excerpts from works in progress. Adjectives cannot quite cope with the profound pleasure I felt both in his presence and in his music. This was truly *una noche encantadora*, an enchanted evening. But something in that evening worked profound unease in me.

Spain, after all, was not the Castellana Hilton nor the sipping of martinis in the company of beauties of high style and limited discourse. The city resonated with names and places associated with men of genius. There were streets and plazas named for them—for Lope de Vega, darling of the court, who claimed to have written 1,500 plays. For the playwright-monk who called himself Tirso de Molina, and for Juan Ruiz de Alarcon, who was born in Mexico but made his name in Spain, and for Pedro Calderon, author of the disturbing *Life Is a Dream*...the writers of Cervantes' time, Spain's Age of Gold. Artists like Diego de Velazquez had walked these streets, and Zurburan and Murillo and Francisco Goya and, in nearby Toledo, the mysterious El Greco. The place names drew me like pheromones. Their aura was a golden haze overlying the Old City.

I checked out of the Castellana Hilton and moved, anonymously, to a seedy hotel off the Plaza de España, at the junction of the old city and the new.

Madrid by day was cheerless, poor, and hot. By night it came alive. Business was conducted. Serious drinking was done. Offices opened, and the cinemas unspooled their Spanish-dubbed American movies. The streets swarmed with currency-spivs and con men as in postwar London, each with his pathetically obvious scam. The prostitutes were numerous but soft-spoken and unfailingly polite. Though offices were open, business seemed to be transacted chiefly in the tavernas, the bars that started filling at about seven in the evening with men in cheap suits chattering at high volume while packing away *tapas,* which were free provided one ordered at least one glass of wine. In those days Spain was very poor. Francisco Franco reigned; all was wrong with the world. Political discussion was taboo. Spain was totally El Caudillo's turf. His spies were everywhere, and the miasma of his presence very nearly palpable.

Mornings I strolled in the park and breakfasted at a pleasantly shaded outdoor table over the *International Herald Tribune,* through which I caught up with the uncensored world. There, one sunny morning, I read that item that lit the fire: "Dale Wasserman in Madrid while researching 'Don Quixote' for motion picture adaptation..."

Willy-nilly—or, more accurately, contrary to will—my mind began chewing on it. Why had there never been a successful movie of *Don Quixote?* I recalled four such attempts, all quite different.

The Russians had done one, in 1957, directed by Grigorio Kozintsev, starring a fine actor, Nicolai Cherkasov, as the Don. It was visually beautiful, somber in tone, doggedly Marxist in philosophy—and profoundly dull.

Even earlier—1933—the great Russian basso, Chaliapin, had filmed a non-singing version. On the 400th anniversary of Cervantes' birth, 1947, Azteca Films of Mexico had released "A Motion Picture Based on Cervantes Immortal Book, and to Use the Author's Own Words" as a foreword to the film:

> Reader, thou wilt believe me, I trust, without an oath, when I tell thee it was my earnest desire that this offspring of my brain should be as beautiful, ingenious, and sprightly, as it is possible to imagine.

Lovely and ambitious. It would be pleasant to report that the movie lived up to these ambitions. But it didn't. It was lively but shallow, interesting but uninvolving and, eventually, a failure.

Spain had done a *Don Quixote* movie. It was surprisingly bland considering they were dealing with their own literary heritage, and, unsurprisingly, it failed.

At the moment (1958) in what had become an in-joke of sorts, Orson Welles was engaged in shooting a *Don Quixote*, suspending production in a series of hiccups as money ran out, actors died, and film had to be re-shot. It was denied an opportunity to fail, for it was never completed. Despite Orson's obsession with the project his script was a patchwork, signifying no clear design at all.

It seemed each moviemaker was working with a different story or intention.

I found also—though I wasn't looking for them—more than a hundred musical settings of Cervantes' works, the great majority of them versions of *Don Quixote* (Appendix C). There have been many more since this list was compiled; indeed, the list of adaptations in all the permutations of theatre is staggering, and the compilation of a masterlist all but impossible.

What is remarkable is the record of failure. It is very nearly 100 percent. Possibly the four-act ballet by Minkus (1869) is an exception, though in truth it has little to do with the character or story of *Don Quixote*. Jacques Offenbach's opera, *Don Quichotte*, with a libretto by Sardou, had a brief life as a pantomime (1874) at the Paris Opera. There were versions by Massenet, de Falla, Telemann, Johann Strauss and Richard Strauss, a song cycle by Maurice Ravel . . . and countless more by those of less illustrious name. Some lived briefly, but time, that ultimate critic, has dealt cruelly with them all.

Digging further, I learned that adaptations of *Don Quixote* were almost literally without number. They covered all the theatrical fields — puppets, plays, movies, musicals, operas, ballets, and entertainments of every stripe. At one time I compiled a list of 400 or so, but there seemed no end.

They had one thing in common. They failed. To me the reason did not seem obscure. In one way or another they tell the tale of a delusionary oldster who sees one thing and thinks it's something else. The first time this happens, it's funny. And perhaps the second time, upon which the law of diminishing returns sets in.

My curiosity was piqued. More than that, challenged. The question: if *Don Quixote*, "the world's greatest novel," was so famously seminal, so rich in character and idea, why should it be so difficult to dramatize? Why had no one been able to capture its essence? Why had it been the source of a multitude of failures and of no clear-cut success at all?

What better place to investigate than Spain itself? I'd never read *Don Quixote*, but certainly the place was right, and the time, too. After all, I didn't have to *do* anything about it, merely occupy some lazy days in reading.

Accordingly, I bought a copy of the Putnam translation, which also included the *Entremeses*, and dove in, not realizing that this version was itself an abridgement. In later years when lecturing or conducting seminars, with malicious intent I'd ask my audience, "How many of you have read *Don Quixote*?" A forest of hands would spring up. Then I'd spring the trap: "The full unabridged, thousand-page, fine-print *Don Quixote*?" Ninety percent of the hands would sink like periscopes retracting. Clearly, this was the book that everyone knew and few actually read.

A confession: I belong with the majority. I have never, to this very day, read all of *Don Quixote*. I have read *in* it, finding that the writing ranges from the sublime to the scatological, and at times sinks to the simply nauseating. In truth, I don't like *Don Quixote*, with the exception of portions of Volume II.

I found that everyone can find what he seeks in *Don Quixote*, even to the choice of a dozen or so movies luring the unwary. What he cannot find is a unifying philosophy, a firm intention, a dramatically coherent story.

I found an astonishing difference between Volume I and Volume II. It was so drastic that one might suspect they were written by different authors. In a sense perhaps they were—ten years had intervened between publication of the two, during which Cervantes had been hammered by fate and was failing in health. Volume I is frequently base in humor, repetitive, studded with interpolations of unrelated novellas, and occasionally downright vulgar. Volume II, one the other hand, reaches sublimity, in observation of behavior, in the study of illusion as a transcendent force, in implications and ideas more adumbrated than specific. It sets forth social and political commentaries, which were dangerous in Cervantes' time but so delicately balanced that it seems the author must consciously have been walking a tightrope to escape the attention of both the Court and the Inquisition. Volume I left me indifferent. Volume II captured my attention and my admiration.

On the other hand, trying to encompass the entire novel would be like emptying a lake with a bucket—ambitious but impractical.

I came to a firm conclusion. The novel *could not be dramatized*. Anyone attempting it would simply be adding to the catalogue of failures. Whereupon I put it out of my mind.

But something other than the novel had caught my interest. What sort of man was this Miguel de Cervantes—poet, soldier, slave, and jailbird—who could suffer a parade of misfortunes and yet, in his declining years, produce the staggering testament that is *Don Quixote*? I set aside the novel and decided to investigate its author.

Almost immediately I discovered one fact that any student of Spain's Golden Age might have told me: the author of "the world's greatest novel" was not a novelist at all. *Don Quixote* was written in

Cervantes' declining years in a desperate attempt to make some money he could leave to his debt-ridden family. The novel, in fact, was an aberration. Miguel de Cervantes actually was a man of the theatre, an actor, director, and playwright, passionately devoted to the making and production of plays.

A bell rang, a curtain rose. No longer was I in alien territory, the province of scholars better educated than I. His was a vocation I understood very well, since I shared it. I'd discovered a bridge across the centuries, one I might conceivably cross to establish rapport with the man behind the legend.

Miguel de Cervantes y Saavedra...who was he?

CHAPTER THREE

I can no more avoid bad fortune
than I can strike the sky with my fist!

He was almost precisely contemporary with Shakespeare—though there's no evidence that either was aware of the other—and much of his life is equally shrouded in shadow. Miguel de Cervantes was born to a down-at-the-heels Hidalgo family in the year 1547, the exact date unknown. He lived a life of danger and of adventure on the physical level, and of even greater adventures in the wilds of literature. His maverick years were punctuated by terms in prisons, but they were equally illuminated by lightning strokes of genius. Had he been fictional instead of real, his escapades would have justified a picaresque novel, perhaps one written by Rafael Sabatini, with Cervantes playing the pícaro, a charming rascal surviving endless hairsbreadth escapes. He lived a life of deprivation and of danger, and struggled endlessly for a place in the sun. But he never lost hope nor his underlying optimism, a fundamental faith that tomorrow would be better. The author of "the world's greatest novel" was often angry, but he never surrendered to despair.

We know something of his appearance from his own description of himself as expressed in the introduction to his *Exemplary Novels*:

> The person you see here, with aquiline countenance, chestnut hair, smooth and unruffled forehead, merry eyes, a nose hooked but well-proportioned, a silvery beard that less than twenty years ago was golden. Large moustache, small mouth, teeth not much to speak of…his figure midway between two extremes, a heightened complexion, rather fair than dark, somewhat stooped in the shoulders, and not very nimble on his feet…

He goes on to tell more of himself, past and future, describing adventures with emphasis on his record as a soldier in Christian forces fighting against Moslems bent on conquest of Europe. Oddly enough, in *Don Quixote* he mentions himself by name, describing actions of the slave known as "Saavedra" during servitude in Algiers.

His father was a barber-surgeon who lacked a diploma and scratched out a bare living for his household of seven children, of whom Miguel was the fourth. The rootless family moved from town to town, locating finally in Madrid where Miguel was able to study under a humanist philosopher, Juan Lopez de Hoyos, the first to discern the gleam of talent in "my beloved pupil," and who published Cervantes' first poems. However auspicious this debut might be, the pattern of a lifetime was established when Cervantes, at the age of 19, wounded an upper-class gentleman named Antonio de Segura in a fight. The circumstances remain mysterious but seem to have involved a woman. The consequences were less mysterious. A trial was held, and Cervantes, who'd judiciously fled to Italy, was condemned *in absentia* to ten years' exile from his native land, in addition to which his right hand was to be severed.

The irony is that while retaining his right hand, he was to lose the left.

In Italy, the intelligence and talent of the young man was soon noted by prominent Churchmen. Through their interposition he was engaged as a secretary to Cardinal Giulio Acquaviva, promising a life of ease and security...which, typically, he abandoned to enlist as a soldier of lowest rank in the army opposing the advance of Islam.

It was a time of crisis and confrontation, the inevitable collision between the growing power of the Ottoman Empire and the forces of Christendom. Cervantes found himself one of 80,000 men in a vast fleet of ships under the command of Don Juan of Austria.

The climax came in the Battle of Lepanto, a naval encounter in the Gulf of Corinth. It was a savage clash lasting four hours, in which 300 Italian and Spanish galleys faced a Turkish fleet and decisively routed them. "Nothing was left undamaged that day but human hatred," wrote Cervantes.

Actually he wasn't supposed to have fought at all. He'd been felled not by the enemy but by malaria, and lay in sick bay aboard the sloop *Marquesa*. But it would have been unthinkable for a hot-headed soldier to miss so great an adventure, so when the fleets engaged he summoned up all his strength and joined the battle. He fought gallantly, recklessly even, sustaining two wounds to the chest as well as a musket ball through his left hand, which would permanently cripple it.

As he noted, wryly, "I gave my left hand for the greater glory of the right."

The experience gave him the heady taste of victory, and a sense of nostalgic euphoria that would last him a lifetime. During his months of recovery he encountered his brother, Rodrigo, also a soldier, and together they re-enlisted to fight the fragmented Moslem forces wherever they reared their heads. In November of 1574, his army service came to an end, and for "extraordinary courage" he was rewarded with letters of commendation that normally would have secured his future.

But the pattern of misfortune was to repeat itself, as those same letters brought about the most painful humiliation of his life.

With his brother Rodrigo he'd sailed for Spain on the frigate *El Sol*. On September 26, 1575, *El Sol* was attacked by Turkish galleys and, after a brave but futile fight, the vessel was seized and all on board captured, to be sold into slavery. Now the irony of those letters became clear: they convinced the Turks that Miguel was a person of importance who'd bring a bonanza of a ransom.

For the next five years he'd be a slave to the Bey of Algiers, in Africa.

His charm, wit, and in particular his facility with pen and language also served him ironically, for his owner esteemed him so highly that he set the ransom terms formidably high in the hope no one would pay it. Cervantes escaped or led escapes no less than seven times, and was seven times recaptured. In the usual course this would have led to a flogging or, even more likely, a beheading, but such was the Bey's affection for his talented captive that he incurred no punishment at all. Others were less lucky. In sadness Cervantes wrote, "I wept for those who were killed or tortured in place of myself, and longed for my own death in place of theirs."

His family begged, borrowed, sold all they owned, and mortgaged its future in order to raise the ransom. Eventually it was paid, and the Bey, weeping at his loss, personally escorted his slave to the ship that would return him to Spain.

The ransom bankrupted Cervantes' family. His two sisters took to the streets to keep bread on the table. Miguel, having escaped death more times than a man should expect in one lifetime, resolved to devote himself to the profession he loved beyond all others: the theatre and the writing of plays.

He'd lucked into Spain's theatrical Golden Age, and yet luck remained elusive. Playwrights were the darlings of nobility without whose sponsorship they had small opportunity for success, or none at all. There was Tirso de Molina, the Mercedarian monk whose real name was Gabriel Tellez. By far the most famous of his works was *El Burlador de Sevilla* (*The Trickster of Seville*), the archetype for all the Don Juan plays to follow. Another was Juan Ruiz de Alarcon, born in Mexico but who made his way to Spain at the age of 20 to write comedies with so critical an eye for behavior that his works have been compared with those of Moliere. Pedro Calderone de la Barca was perhaps the most significant of the "big four" dramatists of the time. His most famous play, *La Vida es Sueno* (*Life Is a Dream*), bears startling similarities to *Don Quixote* in its questioning of reality, in suggesting that what we see as evident fact may be something quite otherwise. His plays have been compared to Shakespeare's, not unfavorably, in their beauty of verse as well as for their trenchant explorations of the human mind and spirit.

And there were others. But by far the most successful was Lope Felix de Vega y Carpio, known simply as Lope de Vega, who boasted of having written over 1,500 plays. He was a true darling of the court, petted and praised, powerful in his ability to help (or to hinder) others. In his ability, specifically, to be of possible help to the aspiring playwright Miguel de Cervantes, who desperately needed a nod from a notable in order to gain access to a theatre in Madrid—in order, simply, to make a living.

But here again the template of misfortune undercut Cervantes. Vega had studied at Miguel's feet, and originally there was affection between the two and, certainly, respect. Yet somewhere the worm of jealousy had crawled in, and now Vega displayed malice, expressed in needle-witted criticism of Cervantes' work. The effect was to block his mentor's access to the court or to any sort of sponsorship.

It was not in Cervantes' nature to strike back. Good-humoredly, he termed Vega "that monster of comedy," because of the younger man's prodigious output.

Cervantes wrote plays and he directed them and performed in them, becoming familiar with the villages that were to figure in his masterwork. In a comparatively short space he wrote some forty plays, only two of which have survived: *Numancia* and *Pictures of Algiers*. They have color but are undistinguished as drama.

My search for Cervantes, no longer fueled merely by curiosity, was becoming obsessive. I decided to retrace his travels, to follow in his footsteps, hoping, in some vague fashion, to encounter an illumination. One by one, I'd visit the places that he—and his Don Quixote—had visited.

First to La Mancha, "The Channel," a wide bleak plain stretching from Cordoba on the south to Toledo on the north. In La Mancha, the songs of the people wail and cry. Its climate? "Nine months of winter and three months of hell." Its sky is a hard and unforgiving blue, its horizons too wide; they stupefy the eye. It's easy to invent fantasies in La Mancha, to believe that here men might go mad and invent worlds not yet made.

The road led me to Argamasilla, the village from which Don Quixote had set forth on his sallies. The country was flat, blank as a canvas awaiting the artist. Then on to Tomelloso, and to the Cave of the Montesinos where Quixote had experienced astonishing visions. To Alcazar de San Juan, hot and dusty, where women in black sat outside doorways facing always inward. To Esquivias, where Cervantes had sworn to give up the artist's life, married a prosperous farmer's daughter, and tried to settle into a bourgeois existence. There I climbed a flight of stairs and sat at the desk where Cervantes had worked. But he'd not sat there for long.

He renounced his wife and returned to his mistress, the theatre.

I continued in his footsteps. To Toboso, home of the imaginary Lady Dulcinea. To Campo de Criptana, where there are windmills with great, swinging arms that in the hard and angry light do indeed resemble giants.

Finally to Seville, that crossways of cultures with its treasure house of documents. Here I learned something of interest: Cervantes had made application to emigrate to the Americas. His heart was in the desire, but his application was denied. Spain had little use for crippled poets in the New World.

The Spanish passion for record-keeping revealed something even more interesting. Cervantes had been hauled before the Inquisition and tried under the *Limpieza de Sangre*—Purity of Blood—statute, whereby employment by the government was barred to anyone with even a drop of Jewish blood. Were the Cervantes or Saavedra families Jewish? Or were they, perhaps, among the thousands of *conversos*, those who accepted nominal conversion to Catholicism while secretly maintaining their religion? He was excommunicated on this and on a similar occasion, escaping more drastic punishment. How did he manage? Through the eloquence of his tongue? The record fails to inform.

In Seville, I crossed the Triana Bridge over the fabled Guadalquivir, where treasure ships from the New World had discharged their golden cargos. To one's right, at the far end of the bridge, was the Plaza de la Inquisicion and, squatting there, the prison itself. The now-abandoned building was half-sunken into the earth...or was the earth rising up to enfold it? I entered and remained there in its mordant chill a long time, meditating on the Inquisition and the horrors it had visited upon Jews in the name of a Judaic religion. Something between oppression and rage at last drove me out. But Cervantes had stayed longer and, of course, with less choice.

It was illuminating to verify that first and foremost Cervantes considered himself a man of the theatre. It made no difference that this was true only at a level of semi-starvation. He'd have preferred it otherwise—a sponsored engagement in Madrid, a subsidy from some noble drone from the ranks of whom, always unsuccessfully, he was seeking sponsorship.

Partially out of lighting up these "lost" years of Cervantes, but equally out of my own experience of a lifetime in the theatre, I felt an affinity. I myself had "graduated" into the profession after spending my entire adolescence as a hobo riding the rails in America and thereafter embracing the Gypsy existence by traveling with road shows. It was a life in which one learned to live *sans* home, attachments, or family, accepting alienation from society as a norm. Consequently I had no problem in empathizing with Cervantes' career in the same profession.

My imagination conjured up a painted Players' wagon, magically unfolding its splintery boards to become a stage. The audience, largely illiterate bumpkins but possibly including a local poet or a grandee or two, applauding, whistling, and, one hopes, tossing coins into hats passed about by the actors. Cervantes as actor-in-chief, declaiming versions of his own adventures. The days of hunger when it rained, or when audiences whistled the players out of town. Nights under the stars when the little band of players drank and roistered, enjoying the insular society of strolling players down the ages. And lovemaking, for it was in this period that Cervantes expressed his passion for Ana de Franca, the actress who gave birth to the natural daughter he acknowledged, Isabel de Saavedra.

To one of my profession, Cervantes is recognizable as a playwright, no matter in what form he's writing. *Don Quixote*, the novel, is inherently theatrical. Psychological motivations drive the plot. His characters change, they aren't static, they grow. His stories show the dynamism of the stage. His scenes are pictorial. Depictions of costumes and setting are meticulous. Dialogue shows acute observation of behavior; it's terse, muscular, direct.

Most of all Cervantes deals with the matter fundamental to all theatre—the collision of reality and illusion. It was a single line in the novel, however, that unveiled the clue as to how a coup de theatre might be accomplished. Its prelude lies in an encounter between Don Quixote and a neighbor, the farmer Pedro Alonso, to whom Quixote has spun out a tale of capture by the governor of Antequera and imprisonment in his castle. The farmer is astonished, for he knows Quixote perfectly well as his lifelong neighbor. Says the farmer, "Cannot your Grace see that I am not Don Rodrigo de Narvaez, nor the Marquis of Mantua, but merely Pedro Alonso, your neighbor? And that you are my friend, the good Alonso Quijana?"

Don Quixote replies, "I know who I am and who I may be if I choose."

I know who I am and who I may be if I choose.

This is not the statement of a madman. Nor of a man obsessed, nor of one with empty rooms in his head. To one whose profession is theatre, it's instantly recognizable as a statement of an actor. An actor perfectly aware of the role he's playing and quite properly annoyed by any who refuse to honor his chosen persona.

From this point on, I felt quite comfortable with Quixote. I understood him: an actor. That's what he was first and last, writing his own role, holding center stage. "In my childhood," he tells Sancho, "I loved plays, and I have always been an admirer of the drama." He adds: "Plays are the semblance of reality, and deserve to be loved because they set before our eyes looking-glasses that reflect human life. Nothing tells us better what we are or ought to be than comedians and comedy."

Of course there's a Shakespearean echo in these words. They recall the ruminations of another actor, Hamlet, who spoke of a mirror held up to nature, who had a love of theatricals, and who may or may not have been mad. It seems no coincidence that Shakespeare and Cervantes were contemporaries. Or that *Hamlet* and *Don Quixote*, by a fascinating coincidence, were published on the same day.

Now I knew what had long been known but largely overlooked: Miguel de Cervantes was passionately and preeminently a playwright. Quite logically, his literary creation was an actor fully aware of the role he was playing. Here I found both an affinity with the author and a possible solution to placing the essence of the novel within a coherent dramatic form. If there was a play lurking in the material, it would be found not in the novel but in the man who created it.

For the moment I was finished with Spain. But not with Cervantes.

CHAPTER FOUR

I create in here. I invent other lives. I live them all.

The rain in Spain is dank and chill, reminding one that it's time to travel. I returned to New York where in good order I fulfilled commitments for television and, further, learned that a movie I'd written, *The Vikings*, was enjoying considerable success, triggering further offers to write screenplays. But — not unusual a situation for writers — some compartment of my mind was reserved for the problem of dramatizing the epiphany of Miguel de Cervantes, nagging for a solution. Since there was no turning away, it seemed healthier to confront it head-on.

I read everything I could on the subject. Bruno Frank, Mark van Doren, Miguel de Unamuno, Salvador de Mariaga, and many others, an input of eloquent but wildy divergent theories on the meanings of the novel *Don Quixote*, but little illumination of its author. Also, of course, there were the many other works by Cervantes himself. My Spanish was unequal to coping with them in the original, but in translation I read brilliant short works by the Master, works more illuminating for my purpose than *Don Quixote*. *The Exemplary Novels* in particular, a wonderful canvas of Madrid's underworld equal to the best of London's Hogarth. "Rinconete and Cortadillo," portraying Madrid's criminals, their specialties and their crook-lingo in crackling detail, was fascinating. These were portrayals that could only have been gained firsthand by Cervantes in the deepest of depths. It was to serve me well in the invention of the prison population of *Man of La Mancha*, though in that version the strictures of drama forced the lumping of all of them together simply as "The Prisoners." I felt affection for them all, and originally had entertained myself by defining them individually, as they are expressed in the television play.

There was, for instance, Judas Macabeo, by profession a professional slanderer. "Engage my services and I will spread stories about your enemy that will ruin his business, his reputation, and the good name of his wife." Or Mother Bane, poisoner. "Five drops of my potion will send one straight to hell." Lobillo, "The Little Wolf," who calls himself a "Broker," proudly displaying his merchandise, which consists of two nubile prostitutes. There is El Médico, The Doctor, who cuts throats by way of a wicked little spring-blade in a ring he wears. And The Scorpion — "Here is my sting," he explains, and presents the steel hook that has replaced his right hand. And also the girl, Escalante, called "The Ladder," because she's so frequently climbed; and the boss-criminal, Monipodio, "One Foot," who claims great judicial expertise because, "I have spent more time in court than most lawyers."

"There you have it," says Monipodio to Cervantes. "A jury to hang the whole human race!"

Clearly, Cervantes had known each and every one in person.

The Dialogue of the Dogs by Cervantes made an impression, as did other short works, but the most useful book was a compilation by Angel Flores, *Cervantes Across the Centuries,* a collection of commentaries by noted scholars.

Any writer will confirm that the hardest work on Earth is thinking, which undoubtedly is why it's so rarely done. But for me, having come this far, there was no longer a choice. At my apartment on 56th Street at Sixth Avenue, with the never-ceasing cacophony of traffic in my ears, I'd lie on my backside for hours, mentally chewing on the problem. The solution, when it came, was a unique experience in my professional life, a classic frisson, the chill up one's spine, the "eureka" of the imagination.

In theory the answer seemed simple. I'd write a play about Miguel de Cervantes in which his creation, Don Quixote, would be played by Cervantes himself. The two would progressively blend in spirit until the creator and his creation would be understood as one and the same.

Here's the one-page outline of the story as I wrote it down that day. I was able, even, to give it a title:

MAN OF LA MANCHA

Miguel de Cervantes, aging and a lifetime failure, is thrown into prison for levying against a church in his job of gathering supplies for the Grand Armada. His fellow prisoners, dregs of the underworld, convene a kangaroo-court for the purpose of seizing all of Cervantes' possessions. These possessions include a manuscript which we may surmise to be the history of a certain eccentric who calls himself Don Quixote.

Cervantes cleverly persuades the "court" to allow him to present a defense in the form of an entertainment. Given permission, he assumes the character of his Mad Knight and involves the other prisoners in playing roles in the seemingly ridiculous story. There are interludes of return to reality when the presence of the Inquisition, before which Cervantes will be tried in reality, makes its ominous presence known.

As the entertainment proceeds we will detect the character of Cervantes blending with that of his creation until we come to understand that in spirit and philosophy the two are essentially the same.

In the process the prisoners are entertained, then involved, by emotions long since chilled, in particular one upper-level criminal called, "The Duke." The story of Don Quixote is interwoven with the life of Cervantes; actually we don't know how either one will end.

After the climax of the play improvised by Cervantes, the prisoners give him back his precious manuscript. He and The Duke are summoned by the Inquisition at the same time. Cervantes lends courage to the terrified Duke as they go.

I was pleased, feeling I'd achieved something. But that was the sort of happy delusion writers feel in having made one decisive step. The steps ahead would be more difficult. Assuming I could write so ambitious a play, who would commission or produce it?

Even more puzzling, to which medium should it belong? As a dramatist I was somewhat unusual in that interchangeably I wrote dramas, comedies, and musicals for movies, television and, stage. Always, in my mind, came the preliminary debate—which medium? Often the answer was self-evident. In this case, not so. Yet, in analysis it presented itself. The concept was abstract, which was anti-movie—abstraction in film simply doesn't work. Film is aggressively "real"—the audience sees what it sees, no more, no less—and abstraction is lost on moviegoers. Stage...well, possibly, but I shuddered at the prospect of persuading investors that a period play about a failed playwright and a self-deluded oldster who dies onstage could be profitable.

Never, at this point, did I consider the notion of a musical.

Which left that illegitimate spawn of both movie and stage: television. But what producer or network would undertake so esoteric a piece, one calling not for passive viewing but for a certain investment of brain sweat? Not to mention the financial risk—this play would be expensive, both by reason of the large cast, the period settings, and costumes, and the physical demands. It would have to be a live production. Tape was in its primitive stage in those days, and film far too costly. All of which added up to the need for an adventurous producer who was also a spellbinding salesman, for against all good sense he'd have to persuade a network and a sponsor that they must undertake this project.

The combination added up to David Susskind. David was the bravest producer I knew. I'd written other "controversial" plays for him, including *Engineer of Death*, the first account of the career and the capture of Adolf Eichmann to reach the American public, for which I did an extended investigative job on three continents. It shocked the audience and evoked headlines like, TOO STRONG FOR TELEVISION, from critics not yet attuned to the horrors of the Holocaust. But against network pressure David had stood by me and by the documentary, and had allowed no softening.

I called David and said, "I've an idea for a play."

"What's it about?"

"Miguel de Cervantes."

"Don Quixote, eh? Good, I'm interested in doing a Don Quixote."

It wasn't expedient to correct David. Instead, I went by the office of his company, Talent Associates, and dropped the single-page outline on his desk. He took a full two minutes to read it, and said, "This isn't *Don Quixote*."

"No."

He read it again.

"Interesting."

I waited. David liked a little think-time.

He said, "D'you know how tough this would be to sell?"

"Yup."

"You've left big spaces. Know how you're going to fill them?"

"Not exactly."

"What do you need to write it?"

"An advance. Big enough so I can back off someplace where there's nothing in my life but writing this play."

"How much?"

I had him.

Ronco Sopra Ascona is a village clinging vertiginously to the side of a mountain overlooking Lake Maggiore. It's in Switzerland, but to the right, as I face the lake, a mile or so away is the Italian border. This is the place Hemingway set *A Farewell to Arms*. This is the Ticino, Switzerland's most southerly, subtropical tip, a place of fabled beauty and tranquility.

To my left, out of view, the city of Locarno. Straight down the mountain, at the lakeshore, is Ascona, home of distinguished refugees in the arts, whose houses have their feet in the water. The lake is breathtakingly lovely, changing colors by the hour. The Isles of Brissago, afloat in its middle, are evocations of fabled Avalon.

My house lies down-mountain from the village. It has no telephone, no TV, no neighbors. What it does have is a shelf of good books, a working fireplace, and stunning views from all windows. One can climb the 110 stone steps up to the bar/bistro in the village

where one may take a glass of wine—Valpolicella is my favorite—
and sample the excellent cheeses of the Ticino.

My typewriter is a Lettera Venti-Due Olivetti, a lightweight but
tough little typewriter that has traveled the world with me. I keep
my shades down when I'm working. The view is a distraction; it's
simply too entrancing. The month is April, still quite cold at this
altitude, so I must keep a fire going when working at night. To
my surprise, small brown scorpions come scampering from the fire-
wood, escaping the heat. What are they doing in Switzerland? I
catch some and put them in jars for company against the extreme
loneliness of the place, but they're disconsolate and won't eat anything I try to feed them. I'm ignorant on the subject of scorpion
diets, so I set them free.

My routine is quite rigid. I'm at work by 6 AM, quit by noon, eat
an impromptu lunch and then read books having nothing to do
with Cervantes, Spain, or *Don Quixote*. The point in this is to
switch off, to not think about the play or its problems until evening,
when I read the day's output and revise it. The scheme isn't totally
successful, but I do manage to finish reading Lawrence's *The
Plumed Serpent* (what hubris the man has, to invent another religion
when such a multitude have already failed!) as well as *Salammbô* and
Under the Volcano on this schedule.

Tiny owls flutter against my windows at night, catching moths
attracted by the lamplight. Once a week a housekeeper, retained by
the house's owner (a friend known by the single name of Treviranus),
brings supplies, cleans the place, and builds a formidable soup that,
kept on the simmer, lasts for days. I can't converse with her. She
speaks neither Italian nor German but a language I've never heard
before. It's called Romansch, I'm told, and sounds like an extreme
dialect of Italian. In fact it's very close to what the Romans spoke a
thousand years ago, the more wealthy of whom had summer homes
here on the lake.

This is where I wrestle with the problems of the play. I stumble
along, working more from instinct than from plan. The play is
becoming increasingly subjective. I'm surprised, again and again, by
what emerges from the typewriter. What surprises me is that I'm not

aware of deepest feelings until they appear on paper. On the day I write—

> To dream the impossible dream,
> To fight the unbeatable foe,
> This is man's privilege,
> And the only life worth living.

—I stop abruptly, troubled by such lofty philosophizing. I strike it out. Put it back. Twice.

But my real surprise comes with the climax, the death of Quixote and his affirmation through his one disciple, Aldonza. I hadn't planned that ending. Had something more sophisticated in mind. My eyes, surprised by the words on paper, produced tears... but I never cry, and this angers me. Then I'm resigned, accepting that this may be what I truly believe, as distinct from what I profess.

Writing this play is becoming an exercise in self-examination, and I'm increasingly disturbed at the discoveries.

But I'm pleased in my invention of the character Aldonza, whom I describe as: "A savage alley-cat, veteran if not always victor of many back-fence tussles." She's the catalyst who may make the play "work." It's she who'll make possible the climax and the catharsis. Without her there can be no play.

Weekends, to escape my self-imposed monkhood, I climb those 110 steps to the village and catch the bus to Locarno. There I unwind so far as that proper city permits, and converse with Locarno's meager troupe of castoffs, druggies, and prostitutes—but compared to Cervantes' population of rascals they're pathetically decorous—and by dawn Monday am back at the typewriter.

One day, two months after beginning, I'm astonished to find that the script is finished. No, not finished; in my experience a script is never "finished," but there's a complete draft, and to prove it there are those most beautiful words in the language, "The End."

I mail the script to New York. Take the train to Florence, Italy, where I will unwind at the Torre del Diavolo, a small 14th-century castle belonging to my friend Trudy Goth and her imperious mother, Gisella. For the moment I'm through with Cervantes, though I leave his company reluctantly.

I enjoy tooling around Tuscany with Trudy in her white Fiat convertible. It's June, a fine travel season in northern Italy. Trudy has famous friends; we visit Berenson at I Tatti, and go on to Siena, Pisa, check in with Giancarlo Menotti at Spoleto, and then my favorite Italian town, San Gimignano, with its skyline of fourteen improbable towers. Here a cable catches up to me:

> Script very exciting. Production CBS show of the month. Rehearsal October fifteenth or thereabouts. Some revision in order. Where are you and when do you return? Susskind.

I am astonished it should be accomplished so swiftly. And with such formidable sponsorship... David is amazing.

Then dismay sets it. I'll send a message: Wait! It's not ready! It's only a first draft! Hold everything!

Instead I cable Susskind: *On my way*, and in short order am in Milan boarding a plane for New York.

CHAPTER FIVE

Hunger drives talent to do things
which are not on the map.

New art forms are always open to experimentation, and television was no different. Before the standardization of programming, before genres such as situation comedies, talk shows, or dramatic series had been formulated, the landscape of TV was filled with exotic blooms: vaudevillians like Red Skelton or Ernie Kovacs; plain-speaking avatars such as Jack Paar and Dave Garroway; and buffoons like Milton Berle and Jackie Gleason. But most of all the earliest years of television were filled with serious dramatic writing—remarkable in a medium with endless hours to fill.

Still, it must be admitted that the so-called Golden Age of television was principally brass. The flood of dramas on the air was, without question, mostly mediocre. What had happened, however, was that a door of opportunity had been opened to a legion of writers who otherwise wouldn't have survived as professional drama-tists. The better playwrights of the New York gang formed a coterie in which all knew each other, at least via telephone or through meetings of their union, the Writers Guild of America East. (Writers Guild West was the disdained contingent of work-for-hire hacks in Hollywood.) The legion of writers engaged to feed the insatiable maw of network television originating in New York included talents such as Horton Foote, Paddy Chayefsky, Rod Serling, Gore Vidal, Neil Simon, and Woody Allen, all of whom began their careers as writers for television. In the fifties there was minimal conflict with advertisers, who gladly associated their product with quality writing, though even then there were occasional, ominous clashes over the content of the plays. Further, the East Coast contract, negotiated by a tough and smartly run Writers Guild, had a tremendous advantage over the West—the New York writers owned all rights in their plays after a single broadcast on television, whereas in Hollywood they "worked for hire," which meant the producers of their works became the authors, and the actual authors were forced to sign over their copyrights. The result? In the East, authors of such works as *Marty, Requiem for a Heavyweight, Days of Wine and Roses,* and—yes—*I, Don Quixote,* retained ownership of their work and could later convert them into stage plays or movies.

Between 1950 and 1960 you could watch the Philco Playhouse, the U.S. Steel Hour, General Electric Theatre, Lux Video Theatre, the Kraft Television Theatre (for which I wrote or adapted my first half-dozen plays), the Hallmark Hall of Fame, the Chrysler Corporation's Climax, and many others.

In general, the material these shows presented was uncontroversial and benign. At that time most households owned no television set at all; viewing was principally in bars or in gatherings at the homes of neighbors who did own a set. Because of this, serious subjects had a way of creeping in under the radar of the censors. The audience, attracted by this free entertainment, was non-censorious, and if they were inclined to disputation had few tools to do anything about it. Nor had the corporate sponsors yet learned how to throttle the writers. Few themes were untouchable—war, racism, mental disorders, alcoholism, and other "difficult" subjects all received serious treatment and sometimes quality productions on television.

The New York writers in general were born to family nurture and to formal education, whereas my life was an improvisation that allowed no schooling whatsoever. My entire adolescence was spent on the road. Of that career I have written elsewhere—

> ...I'd ridden the high iron: crack passenger trains and every place possible on rocketing, racketing freights. I loved the wail of steam whistles and knew the language of their signals...I learned to sleep riding the bumpers between cars, stood atop runways rolling through the High Sierras, yelling myself hoarse with jubilation,

drunk on the wine of life. I worked the harvests and the lumber
camps, did time at a couple of detention camps, in fact, did a bit
of everything one does to stay alive on the road...

Not exactly the usual MFA qualifying folks in the arts. And
later—

> I drifted into theatre at the age of nineteen and proceeded to
> become a stage manager, lighting designer, director and producer...
> It was in the midst of directing a Broadway musical (which out of
> revulsion I decline to name) that I quit and decided to become a
> writer. I was tired of interpreting the work of the creators, but I
> had great respect for the principle of creation and yearned to join
> its fraternity...I gave myself a year in which to learn to write and
> to sell my work, and made it—barely—though with drastic loss
> of weight and an empty bank account—when stories and scripts
> I'd written began to sell.

I'd lucked into television's Golden Age.

The Dupont Show of the Month was a 90-minute program that
aired on CBS irregularly from the fall of 1957 to the spring of 1961,
producing only as they found plays "of exceptional merit." It was
they who had accepted and scheduled my *Man of La Mancha*, under
the aegis of David Susskind.

Upon my return to New York I found casting already under way.
Lee J. Cobb, the unforgettable Willie Loman of *Death of a
Salesman*, had been signed as Cervantes/Quixote. Eli Wallach would
play Sancho Panza; Hurd Hatfield, of *The Picture of Dorian Gray*,
would portray The Duke; and Viveca Lindfors would be Aldonza.
The prisoners were being cast from an impressive array of Broadway
actors. I was impressed.

Audrey Gellen would be our producer. She was surprisingly
young, something of a prodigy, married to Peter Maas. Audrey
dressed like a hippie, and with feet up on her desk seemed the
embodiment of Greenwich Village avant garde. But she was smart,
extremely, and highlighted my own lapses in language. In chatting

with me, Audrey used the phrase *cave canem*. I asked what it meant. She thought I was fooling until I explained that there were few Latin instructors on freight trains.

Karl Genus, who'd directed an earlier work of mine, *American Primitive*, was engaged to direct. Karl was a transplanted Swede of enormous enthusiasm, in action something of a human typhoon, but a fine director.

To Karl I expressed concern about Viveca Lindfors. She seemed sullen in her readings, depressed rather than feisty. Said Karl, "Don't worry, I'll holler at her in Swedish, I'll use a big whip! She'll come through."

The production, as I'd feared, would be live, exposing us to all the horrors that can happen to a show playing its first and only performance in the presence of a multi-million-strong audience.

From a diary on the production process of the TV version of *Man of La Mancha*:

> ...The revisions which Susskind mentioned in his cable are not extensive but they are significant. I'd intended the prisoners to "improvise" the roles in the story Cervantes is telling, but it's considered potentially confusing to an audience whose brow is considered lower than that of the theatre's. A bigger problem: I am asked by network Standards and Practices to delete the Inquisition and make my prison secular. I demand to know why, and am told that my portrayal of the Inquisition might offend Catholics. I wonder, "Are Catholics still defending the Inquisition?" I suppose it's possible...after all, many Germans are still defending Hitler. But inevitably I lose the argument...

Rehearsals are held over Ratner's Delicatessen on lower Second Avenue. Our stage manager is an argumentative fellow named Papirofsky who doesn't hesitate to take me to task over what he considers deficiencies in the script. I'm astonished—it's not usual for stage managers to argue with authors. But this isn't your standard stage manager, I learn; he's won his job by taking CBS to court over political discrimination. He'll pop up again in my life after shortening his name to Joe Papp and founding the New York Public Theatre, with its Shakespeare in the Park.

Viveca Lindfors is not "coming through." She's playing Aldonza with darkling angst. Her Aldonza is not Spanish; she'd be at home in an Ingmar Bergman movie. Karl Genus, confessing that hollering in Swedish has gained little, asks me to talk with her. I do, and get nowhere; we end up in harsh words and a definite failure to communicate. Viveca is determined to play it her way. I talk to her husband, George Tabori, himself a playwright of quality, but even he can't persuade her otherwise. For the first time I ask that an actress be replaced, and overnight Viveca is gone.

With just three days of rehearsal remaining, we search frantically for a replacement. Audrey proposes an actress by the name of Colleen Dewhurst, who's unknown to me. It turns out a brilliant proposal. Colleen will be a smash in the role, launching a distinguished career in the theatre.

I have one more problem, this time with the Dupont Corporation. They object to the title, *Man of La Mancha*. David Susskind sides with them, and I must agree their reasons are sound: the greater part of the audience will not be familiar with La Mancha, either on the geographical or the symbolic level. A substitute title, *I, Don Quixote*, is hastily chosen. I disliked it then and I dislike it to this very day, but such are the exigencies of live television.

The performance of *I, Don Quixote* suffered no catastrophes. Almost all of its troubles came during dress rehearsal at our cavernous studio on Manhattan's East Side. Lee Cobb fell off his horse—a real horse—and suffered bruises but no broken bones. The windmill, consisting of two vanes standing in for four, refused to function as intended, spinning Cobb into bewilderment. Lines were butchered as actors were pushed to handle an elegance of speech for which The Method served them not at all.

The play ran too long by at least eight minutes. Had we been in England, it wouldn't have mattered—in England time was not sacrosanct, a play ran as long as it ran. But in TV-America we slice and dice down to the second. Said director Genus, "Want to make the cuts?"

I did so, rather haphazardly as, dazed with fatigue, I'd lost perspective. Among the words I chose to cut was the bulk of Don Quixote's answer to Aldonza's question, "What does it mean — quest?"

From the control booth I watched as the script cuts were handed to Cobb—and from the glowering look he turned on us in the booth, knew we were in trouble. Cobb left the set and broke a rule by charging up the stairs and into the booth. He loomed over me, a big, *big* man, and a furious one.

"Put it back," he growled.

I was genuinely bewildered. "Put what back?"

"That fucking speech."

"Which fucking speech?"

"That fucking impossible dream speech."

I turned helplessly to the director, who came to my rescue.

"Put it back," said Karl. "I know a spot in Act One where we can pick up the time without cutting."

And so the speech beginning, "To dream the impossible dream...to fight the unbeatable foe...and never to stop dreaming or fighting—this is man's privilege, and the only life worth living..." came back into the script. It was the same speech that, in Switzerland during the writing, I'd twice cut from the play and twice restored.

Dress rehearsal wrapped at around midnight, at which point we'd failed even to accomplish a complete run-through. At the studio's exit door, to my surprise, I found Cobb waiting for me. He asked, "Care to get something to eat?"

His tone was friendly, apologetic even, so I agreed. We went to Reuben's on Fifty-eighth Street; a New York institution, it was central and open all night, popular with performers who came there after doing their gigs on Broadway or in the clubs. The sandwiches were superb (yes, the Reuben was invented there) and the coffee excellent and free-flowing.

As Cobb eased himself into a chair I realized how tired the man was. His face was gray, his shoulders hunched. He hadn't said a word on the way over, nor did he now until we'd placed our orders, gotten our coffee, and drunk deep.

Finally he said, "I'm sorry I spoke to you like that." Before I could answer, he corrected himself, somewhat belligerently. "No, actually I'm not. You should never do that again."

"Do what?"

"Damage your own work. You wrote a play, it's got intentions, it's got something to say. Why in God's name would you change it?"

I had answers on the tip of my tongue. Perfectly reasonable answers, to do with the nature of television, the tyranny of the clock, and also with the wisdom of yielding a peninsula to save a continent. He didn't allow me to get them out. Something was troubling him, and it went beyond this rather trivial argument.

"In this profession everybody claws at you," he said. "Everybody's got an opinion and a mandate direct from God to lay it on you."

"Sometimes they're right."

"Yeah... but right or wrong, if you listen too much they'll destroy the best in you." And he added, earnestly, "This is an important play. It flies in the face of the news, the mood... of all the crud that's a blight on living here and now. It could have a life."

"It's got a life."

"I mean a *life*."

"I know it's got flaws..."

"Damn right it's got flaws. So? Try to understand what I'm telling you. It's got an opinion. A point of view. An approach. It aims to go somewhere, to say something. So be sure the flaws are *your* flaws, not the notions of some cockamamie committee."

There was more of this, unremembered now, deep into the night as Reuben's slowly emptied out. Something very odd, however, had caught my interest. The customers, snacking, chatting, table-hopping, were almost entirely performers. Most of them knew each other by sight or reputation. All of them, surely, knew the famous Lee J. Cobb, but with no more than a couple of exceptions no one greeted or spoke to him. Until Lee, sensing my puzzlement, answered an unspoken question.

"I'm a pariah," he said. "I gave evidence."

"The blacklist?"

"You didn't know? The House Un-American Activities Committee. That son of a bitch, J. Parnell Thomas. Who is now doing time in a Federal pen. Helluva lot of good that does me."

"A lot of people gave evidence."

"I named names," said Cobb, bleakly.

"Oh."

"Larry Parks ratted on me, first under my real name, Leo Jacoby. That was in 1951. I fought 'em off for two years...hell, I was ignorant, knew from zilch about politics. But I'd been a member of the Group Theatre, so I was dirty by association."

"Maybe you'd rather not talk about it."

"I'm surprised you didn't know."

"I guess I did, actually. Lee, you've got to give a performance tomorrow. You should get some sleep."

Silence for a bit. Then, Cobb: "You've no idea how they work on you. All I ever wanted was to act. So that's the first thing they took away from me. My profession. Finally, I was just worn down. I had no income, no credit, no way to make a living. I had the expenses of taking care of my wife, my family, my kids. I was going crazy, figuring why am I subjecting my loved ones to this? Is it something worth dying for? Because I was dying and taking my family down with me. Integrity? Is that what it was? I've got news for you, integrity is worth shit when your family is hungry. So I decided it wasn't worth dying for. If naming names would give me back my profession..."

He fell silent for a while. Then he said, fiercely, "So don't let anybody fuck up your play."

"I'm not sure there's a connection."

I'm not sure he heard me.

"Twenty names," he said. "I gave them twenty names of people who'd been members of the Communist Party. They gave me back my profession. I could be an actor again. Only when I come to a place like this...well, you saw...I'm the invisible man."

I, Don Quixote was performed on November 9th, 1959, to an estimated audience of 20 million people. Cobb gave a sterling performance in the dual role of Cervantes and Don Quixote.

Colleen Dewhurst was heartbreaking, particularly in the final scene where she pleads with the dying Alonso Quijana to recognize her once more as Dulcinea.

The performance over, the fallout began. It would go on for a long, long time. It's going on still.

CHAPTER SIX

Love not what thou art
but only what thou may become.

In a peculiar, now-long-gone phenomenon, the truly important reviews on television plays came not from critics but from anonymous members of the audience throughout the country. It was necessary only that they be enterprising enough to check out New York Information and, surprisingly, many did. In those days it wasn't unusual for folks in Oregon or Iowa to telephone immediately upon the conclusion of a play and unload into the author's ear exactly what they thought of it. I was certainly not unique in receiving such response. Some of my colleagues, notably Reginald Rose, Robert Alan Arthur, and Rod Serling, regularly had the same experience. Original television plays were events in those days; the audience responded not only viscerally but vocally to let one know how they'd received it.

Don Quixote's deathbed scene wrapped up at about 10:30 PM Eastern Time, and less than five minutes later the telephone rang.

Texas calling. An irascible male voice: "You the guy wrote that play?"

Modestly, I acknowledged authorship.

"Listen, why don't you get your facts straight? Didn't you know that Cervantes had only one hand?"

"Well, that's not exactly true—"

"He got his left hand shot off fighting the Turks. So how come your actor had two perfectly good hands?"

"Actually his hand wasn't shot off, it was only—"

"Next time try to get it right." Click.

Ohio calling. Female voice.

"Mr. Wasserman?"

Cautiously: "Yes?"

"Thank you for that perfectly beautiful play. I haven't been so moved since...excuse me, I'm still in tears..."

Alabama calling. A male voice, soft southern accent: "You know, sir, you took me straight back to my adolescence...I mean when all things were possible and we knew exactly how we were going to live..."

"And since then?"

"Things happen."

"What things?"

"Living."

Montana calling. A male voice, deep, hesitant: "I've never been so moved by a play, sir, as I was tonight. I've got to tell you, sir, I laughed a lot and then I cried, real tears I didn't know I had in me. And then I felt, you know, revived, I guess I mean renewed, you know, in spirit. Thank you...well, actually that's all I wanted to say, thank you."

Michigan calling. Female. "I can't believe that you were allowed to express those perfectly poisonous opinions on television. Obviously you are anti-Catholic, one of those dedicated to smearing a magnificent institution. From your name I would assume that you are of the Hebrew persuasion, which might explain it. But when you descend to outright lies and libel to express your propaganda..."

"Wait a minute—"

"What have you got against God?"

"I've got nothing against God. Nothing for him, either. I happen to be an atheist."

"Well, now, there's a confession. I'm writing to the network. I hope they bar you from broadcasting forever." Bang.

New York calling. "Dale? That was a bitch of a play, old boy, maybe a touch highbrow but a bitch," said my fellow-writer, Reginald Rose. I hadn't met Reggie in person, nor had I met other colleagues, Rod Serling or Lee Pogostin, both of whom also called. Their generosity meant more to me than opinions by the critics.

The calls kept coming until 3 AM.

The twenty million people CBS told me had seen the play was an abstraction; of greater meaning to me were the couple dozen who had called on the telephone. They were live! Caring! Argumentative! Some praised, some questioned, but nearly all thanked me for provoking thought, for reawakening ideals once deeply felt but more lately forgotten. They were affirmations of the equation for which a writer lives.

Then came the print critics. John Crosby of *The New York Times* waffled uncertainly over judging this oddity, never noting, apparently, that *I, Don Quixote* was not, nor had pretended to be, an adaptation of the novel *Don Quixote*. However, he was kind to the actors:

> Colleen Dewhurst, in the part of the kitchen wench who finds beauty and liberation in the imagination of Don Quixote, imparted both spirit and poignancy to Dale Wasserman's endeavor last night to find a drama in the life and works of Miguel de Cervantes.
>
> In the all too brief scene in which Miss Dewhurst so artfully made the wench seem a noble figure the work came alive, and Lee J. Cobb portraying the dual parts of Don Quixote and Cervantes seemed a touching human whose illusions were credible.
>
> Unfortunately, in other respects, Mr. Wasserman did not succeed in conquering the traditional difficulties in mounting *Don Quixote* to the stage (sic)...here again his approach proved a rather small and unwieldy device...once again the task of translating the dreams of Quixote into believable theatre was beyond the capabilities of TV.

I'd have bet a bundle Crosby never read the novel.

Crosby also opined that, "This was a notable effort and frequently it was stunningly successful. But frequently it wasn't. I must confess that I am unable to keep from squirming at any play wherein a bunch of $250 actors pound their tankards on a picturesque tavern table and roar: 'Hola, there, wench, bringest me a firkin of mead and what dost say to a kiss?'"

It led me to wonder, *What play wast thee looking at?*

Tough-skinned *Variety* was more analytical: "The beauty of the presentation is that it reached such a significant number of people at one time—the audience that television ordinarily so disdainfully neglects. For the medium, it was a refreshing change of pace and a moment to shine. If the rating numbers betray the effort, the very nobility of this attempt at dramatic artistry should silence for a while those who claim it is a medium of ceaseless mediocrity." And further, "Wasserman's teleplay was an important dramatic achievement, rekindling the flame of Cervantes' words and the spirit of his characters without losing the basic substance of this inspiring story...most people have read only bits and snatches of the novel. Here was a clear, concise picture of the overall work. Probably as difficult a transition as has ever been attempted by television, this Susskind production of a distinguished Wasserman teleplay should serve as the inspiring model for future tries at 'Don Quixote.'"

Time magazine, uncharacteristically, gave its review major space. After a précis of the play it went on to say, "In humanism's world of reason, Don Quixote's crime was not his madness but his faith. So is it in today's world of analytic couches. 'It is my reason that laughs at my faith,' wrote Spain's top philosopher, Miguel de Unamuno. 'And it is here that I must betake me to my lord Don Quixote in order that I may learn of him how to confront ridicule and overcome it.'

"Don Quixote overcame it by letting the world overcome him. 'The divine tragedy is the tragedy of the Cross,' said Unamuno. 'The human tragedy is the tragedy of Don Quixote.'"

The review continued: "TV writer Dale Wasserman caught the tragic essence of Don Quixote's comic role. In a tricky but effective device he fused author and hero into one character, and let both proclaim, 'To dream the impossible dream, to fight the unbeatable foe, and never to stop dreaming or fighting—this is man's privilege and the only life worth living.' Viewers and critics inclined to snicker at such idealism missed the point of a fine TV drama whose central theme was man's eternal search for truth."

In January of 1960, a month or so after the showing, Cecil Smith, a noted commentator on the dramatic scene for the *Los Angeles Times* wrote his summation of the year in an extensive article headlined, How Original is Originality?, saying:

The point that at the moment is disturbing my beleaguered belly is the word "original" as applied to a television play. My own choice as the best "original" play of the year was Dale Wasserman's lush and imaginative script, "I, Don Quixote." But for some reason the gods of awards have chosen to relegate this to the category of "Best Adaptation." I can't imagine why. True, Wasserman took from Miguel Cervantes' monumental novel several of the more familiar scenes and dramatized them — the tilting against the windmills, for example; the battle with the sheep and the knighting of Quixote by an innkeeper. Yet fundamentally the Wasserman play was a study of the writer Cervantes as contrasted with the immortal foolish knight he concocted — the author and his creation.

This, to me, is an absolutely original conception and should be so regarded. Plus the fact that Wasserman found at the time that the sprawling novel "Don Quixote" has never been successfully dramatized because it is "un-adaptable." How original is originality anyway? Can we pinpoint it? Can we say that this is completely original because it had no antecedents anywhere? Does such a work exist?

In a year when television more than ever lacked originality, a year in which fortunes were spent in presenting new versions of old movies or mediocre plays, it seems to me that any sort of truly original dramatic conception should be hailed and huzzaed, trumpets should sound and red carpets should be rolled out for an author.

Producers in New York, interested in the potential of the play, got in touch with me or with my agent, inquiring as to my interest in converting the television play to the stage; one or two even mentioned the potential for adding music.

There was no surprise for me in this. I'd specified music quite elaborately in the television script, not in terms of a "musical" in which peak moments are expressed in song, but as an underscore to punctuate and broaden the play's expression. I insisted even that a bona fide composer be engaged to create this underscore. David Susskind had obliged by commissioning the score from well-known composer, Rafaello Busoni.

The very first lines in my script read, *There is music. It sweeps and rolls with the bombast and blind arrogance of Spain at the end of the sixteenth century…a confident march to nowhere.* A bit later: *The music has given way to the muffled drums and chanting of the Men of the Inquisition. The sound is inimical, chilling.* And as the prison is revealed, *The* GYPSY *is dancing a 'seguiriya gitana' with epicene sensuality.* LOBILLO *sings and beats the rhythm on a 'sanbomba.'* GRACIOSA *wields a palm-broom in dry, shuffling accompaniment.* JUDAS MACABEO *tinkles with a spoon on an iron bar, nodding his head in a dignified, approving manner.*

Clearly, I had music in mind. But then I always do. Though not a musician (if I could swing it, I'd be reborn a composer) I think and feel some form of music underlying every play I write. Again, referring to the television script, Don Quixote makes his first entrance, singing:

> *Never was knight so served*
> *By any noble dame*
> *As Don Quixote was*
> *When down the road he came*
> *With queens to wait on his every need*
> *While princesses cared for his steed…*

—clearly not up to a Joe Darion standard of lyric writing, but still musical.

The musical motifs keep reoccurring in the playscript. The Barber comes capering along, *singing a lively seguidilla.* The Inquisition has its own leit-motif…*the slow-march rolls of drums and a chanting which echoes from distant corridors.* As The Muleteers are introduced, they…*strike up a song of Rabelaisian flavor.* Aldonza is discovered in the kitchen *bawling out a ditty as she works:*

> *For a red-headed lad of old Seville*
> *My heart is all aflame*
> *For a little brown lad I know*
> *Any girl would part with her good name…*

As Don Quixote enters upon his vigil the script prescribes, *An atmosphere of serenity. Of mystery. The guitar and singing are heard softly.* It is this scene that culminates in "The Impossible Dream" speech; the words are set down in poetic scansion, very nearly a song-lyric already.

Another song appears as Quixote and Sancho take to the road after their sojourn at the inn, with Sancho singing ... *merrily but not beautifully*—

> *I have danced at all the dances,*
> *Many serenades I've sung,*
> *But I always was unwelcome,*
> *Spurned by maidens old and young.*
>
> *One I loved was named Teresa,*
> *She lived up there on the hill,*
> *Said I kissed her like an angel*
> *But I was a monkey still.*

At Quixote's death scene, *Music establishes a somber mood, a ticking of time,* and then continues. At the final moments of the play, *The drums strike into their slow-march roll, and the chanting resumes ...* THE DUKE *walks stiff-legged.* CERVANTES *keeps an arm about him, lending him strength as they go. The arrogant Spanish march-music swells as* THE PLAY ENDS.

Certainly I didn't have a musical in mind as I was writing. Just as certainly, the demands for music were emphatic. The end result was that show people seeing the play also saw its potential for expansion into a full-blown musical before I did, nor did some of them hesitate in calling it to my attention.

I examined the script and did indeed see the possibility. The ornate language ... the "aria" speeches that could comfortably become lyrics ... the flamboyant style ... all these invited musical form. In addition, it was evident that from inception I'd been pushing, even if unconsciously, toward the use of music.

For the moment I put it aside. Much as I enjoyed the company of Cervantes, I felt it time to join my contemporaries and deal with someone more contemporary. At that time, ironically enough, came a call from Hollywood inviting me to move not forward in period, but back—sixteen hundred years further back, to be exact.

The call came from director Rouben Mamoulian, who said he'd seen and admired *I, Don Quixote,* and did I think I could cope with a fabulous subject, the greatest since *Gone With the Wind*?

Who could resist such a challenge? Certainly not I, and even less my agents. My previous brush with screenwriting had occurred some five years earlier when I'd undertaken *The Vikings,* another complex historical story. The "fabulous subject" Mamoulian had in mind was called *Cleopatra.* When I agreed to undertake it, two conditions were laid down: first, that the budget must not exceed six and a half million dollars, and second, that the script must be written for Elizabeth Taylor.

When *Cleopatra* was eventually produced, the budget had swelled in excess of $50 million, though Taylor did indeed play the role. All other circumstances had changed. Mamoulian, after beginning shooting from the script I'd written, abandoned the project when Taylor became desperately ill, in London, and eventually it passed to the writing/directing hands of Joseph Mankiewicz...and into movie legend, as well.

But how had I disposed meanwhile of Cervantes? In haste, prior to leaving New York, I granted a Broadway option to producer Philip Rose, who proposed to present *Man of La Mancha* as a straight play. There was an oddity here. Mr. Rose was known as a presenter of plays-turned-into-musicals. There was his *Purlie!* for instance, based on the play *Purlie Victorious.* Or *Raisin!* based on *A Raisin in the Sun.* I felt sure that if Philip Rose actually got my play on the boards it would have an exclamation point in the title: *Quixote!* probably, since that exclamation point seemed for Mr. Rose a juju guaranteeing success.

I felt guilty about abandoning the play. But it was only for the moment, with a sworn promise to return when I'd refreshed my thinking.

That, at any rate, was my excuse. It turned out to be a refreshment of long duration, during which radical changes would come to bear on my so-called career.

CHAPTER SEVEN

When they offer you a heifer,
come running with a halter.

In my first meeting with Rouben Mamoulian I was able to question
him on a matter that had long puzzled me: how does an Armenian
intellectual with a European education qualify to direct a piece of
quintessential Americana such as *Oklahoma!*? His reply was curt and
lacked warmth: "Ask Agnes DeMille."

What he was saying, I inferred, was that it was her sensibilities
rather than his that informed the production. But clearly I was in
touchy territory. Showing good judgment in this instance, I
retreated two millennia to a discussion of the culture of Egypt in the
time of Cleopatra.

Mamoulian wanted a love story, he insisted, the greatest love
story ever put on film. As to historical context, well, that was up to
me. In that respect, he asked many questions about my Cervantes
play. How had I arrived at the concept? Why had I made certain
choices? Why did I choose to deal with the death of Quixote rather
than his return to sanity?

I answered as best I could, but my answers were not adequate,
falling back on a simple truth: that many writers' choices aren't
conscious but intuitive. He listened attentively but, I felt, without
complete understanding. Mamoulian's mind, brilliant in its own
ways, was analytical and pragmatic but not necessarily intuitive
or creative. Between us there'd always remain a certain barrier to
understanding.

I had a question I'd long been waiting to ask. Knowing he'd been
offered the direction of Meredith Willson's *The Music Man* for
Broadway, why had he turned it down?

"Because," he said, "there was a cancer at the very heart of it. The leading man was a crook, a con man."

I thought it an odd answer considering the extravagant success of the show, but it seemed wiser not to press the point.

Eventually, after harrowing events including the starting and then the suspension of production in England, Mamoulian left the project and Joseph Mankiewicz took over, moving the entire menagerie to Rome and swelling the budget to over 50 million dollars in a saga too well known to repeat here.

I declined screen credit on *Cleopatra* even though it might have been awarded through the usual Writers Guild arbitration. Too little of my script remained, too many other cooks had stirred this broth. Considering the minefields Joe Mankiewicz had danced his way through, he deserved all the honors his back might bear.

Upon return to New York in March of 1960, my first question to Philip Rose was, "Where do we stand on *Man of La Mancha?*" The reply was not encouraging. "It's a tough play," he said. "Expensive." And he added, gloomily, "It's very hard to raise money for a period play."

Flush with Twentieth-Century Fox earnings from *Cleopatra*, I made an offer. "Look," I said, "I'll give you back the option money, you give me back my play."

"No, no," said Philip. "I absolutely intend to get it on."

Frustrated once again, I decided to divert myself with other projects until *Man of la Mancha* should go into production or return to my hands. It turned out to be a three-year cavalcade of diversions, during which some of the more provocative were as follows:

The Citadel, written for television, was the story of idealistic young doctors who risked their own careers to perform pro bono service for the public, which seemed a quaint notion even then, but today would probably be regarded as comedy. I wince in reporting that it won awards.

The Lincoln Murder Case, also for television, demanded in-depth research into the terrorist group that planned the assassination not only of Abraham Lincoln but also of his cabinet officers and

Vice President Andrew Johnson. Unraveling precisely what was planned and what had come to pass was like peeling a very large onion in search of a nugget of fact. The more I peeled away the layers of conspiracy the deeper it reached, until it was clear that the eight conspirators who were eventually hanged were the tools of people more clever, and certainly more ambitious, than these rather pathetic instruments.

In a live TV production, anything can and probably will go wrong while you're on the air. We "Golden Age" writers learned to suffer this and to survive. *The Lincoln Murder Case* was no exception; indeed, it boasted a particularly nerve-wracking incident. The play, which dealt with the conspiracy surrounding the assassination of Abraham Lincoln and the intended extermination of his cabinet, was proceeding swimmingly until the intermission between the second and third acts, when the actor playing John Wilkes Booth bent double in apparent agony, claiming he couldn't continue — in which event we were faced with no third act and an outraged audience. Our director, Alec Segal, affectionately known as The Screamer, concluded that the actor wasn't really sick but suffering a panic attack, whereupon he applied an ingenious remedy — he hit him. Hard. With this encouragement our miserable little assassin found the strength to stumble back onto the set and continue. I found this an interesting directorial ploy, possibly not endorsed by Stanislavsky but highly effective, and have wistfully considered using it a number of times since. I was pleased when *The Lincoln Murder Case* was nominated for both the Emmy and the Writers Guild awards that year. As usual I didn't attend the ceremonies, though the plaques were mailed to me.

The most ambitious project in the field of television during this interruption in the progress of *Man of La Mancha* was *The Power and the Glory,* produced by David Susskind, who was determined to present the most impressive cast ever assembled. Laurence Olivier played the "whiskey priest," with George C. Scott as his pursuing nemesis. Cyril Cusack was the crusty dentist exiled in a remote Mexican town in the period of Marxist domination of Mexico, and Roddy McDowell was cast as the Judas to the priest. Julie Harris was the priest's woman, mother of his illegitimate daughter, and there were stellar names such as Keenan Wynn and Thomas Gomez in other roles. The role of a child of American parents in Mexico was played by Patty Duke, who was simply brilliant. The production required the biggest studio in the New York area in order to accommodate the physical demands. Nothing was spared. David Susskind and his delegated producer, Renée Valente, were determined to make this production the absolute apex of live television originating in New York.

Unfortunately, it wasn't very good.

To this day, I don't know why. Overkill, possibly. Or expectations impossibly high. But a certain episode connected with this project remains vivid in memory. During the rehearsal of a scene — Patty Duke's only scene — being played out between herself and Laurence Olivier, Patty's acting was seemingly simple — no tricks — but somehow she broke one's heart.

A bit later, "Larry" strolled over to me. "Did you watch that scene?" he asked. I answered yes, and he inquired, "What did you think of the little girl?"

"I thought she was bloody marvelous."

"So did I," mused the great Olivier. And he added, "Let's kill the little darling, shall we?"

I proceeded to kill the little darling by judiciously cutting lines. When working with a star of the magnitude of Olivier, one must pay attention to which side of his bread is buttered, and to hell with absolutes of integrity.

In performance Patty was still a standout. I received no awards, nor did I deserve any.

A telephone call from an old friend, agent Hope Taylor, turned out profoundly important to my next "diversion."

"I've just read the galleys of a new book," she said. "It's going to be important, and if there's a play in it, it should be written by you."

"I'm waiting on the production of *Man of La Mancha*," I told her.

Hope said, firmly, "You'd better read this."

"What's the book?"

"It's called *One Flew Over the Cuckoo's Nest*. I'm sending it over."

CHAPTER EIGHT

Why are you poets so fascinated by madmen?

The novel, *One Flew Over the Cuckoo's Nest,* was impressive, a mix of gutbucket realism, nightmarish fantasy, and surrealism, evocative of the primal fear of loss of reason and control of one's body and emotionally effective on a raw, primitive level. It was also over-the-top, wildly exaggerated, and seemingly written with the glee of a small boy running and throwing stones, cheerfully offensive on a number of touchy matters. It was blatantly misogynistic, for instance, and also indulged in some gratuitous anti-Semitism.

When I challenged Ken Kesey on this latter point, he was genuinely shocked. "My God, no," he protested. "Nothing like that intended. My wife would kill me."

"Why would your wife kill you?"

"My wife is Jewish."

But with everything that could be criticized—and there was much—without question the book had imagination, power, and, most potent of all, a theme that was exquisitely timely.

One must remember that in the early sixties the cancer of the war in Vietnam was beginning to sicken the land. There was a growing spirit of rebellion, diffuse but seeking focus. In the wings, awaiting only an entrance cue, there was a brewing revolution of the young. It was leveled against hypocrisy and against governmental authority, which was being unveiled as corrupt and mendacious. The time was ripe for a book that would speak passionately to these matters and *One Flew Over the Cuckoo's Nest* was that book, a parable using the inmates of an insane asylum as the cowed populace into whose midst comes a rebel who may be Jesus Christ, or possibly a con man, or both.

It's been said that in writing fiction there are two basic themes. In the first, someone sets out on a journey and the author then portrays the vicissitudes of that journey. In the second, a stranger enters, and one deals with his effect upon others. *One Flew Over the Cuckoo's Nest* clearly was an example of the second.

But then so is *Man of La Mancha*.

Only later did I realize that my passionate response to *The Cuckoo's Nest* was born of its similarity to *Man of La Mancha*. Or take a giant step further—thematically they might be considered the same play.

Initially this notion seemed nonsensical, but upon looking deeper I was surprised to find there was truth. In *Man of La Mancha*, Don Quixote, a rebel against society, sets out to right wrongs. In *The Cuckoo's Nest* Randle McMurphy, a rebel against society, sets out to right wrongs. Both protagonists are stubborn individualists who won't conform. Both are punished and eventually crushed by the society against which they rebelled. Both leave behind one convert who may keep the rebellion alive.

The settings may be centuries removed but the parallels are clear.

It has also been said that each writer has only one theme, upon which he plays variations. Recently I looked into the rear view mirror of my 60-some plays, and observed that in truth they are thematically consistent: the rebel versus the society in which he finds himself. Luckily it seems broad enough to embrace variety.

I made an immediate inquiry as to theatrical rights to the novel, only to be told that "somebody else" was interested, with the implication that the somebody else had more money to offer than I did. But the agent said he'd tell the other applicant of my interest, and possibly, "Someone will get back to you."

I was saddened; the book had genuinely thrilled and excited me. Now it seemed out of reach.

The next telephone call was from an old acquaintance, movie star Kirk Douglas. While not exactly dear friends, we were mutually respectful. After all, I'd solved the adaptation problems of *The Vikings*, which Kirk had then made into a bloody but profitable epic.

Kirk started the conversation:

"I understand that you're interested in this book."

"Right, but it looks like I've been beat out by someone."

"Tough," said Kirk, sympathetically. "Know who it was?"

"Nope."

"It was me."

"Well. Congratulations. But I was interested in it for the stage."

"So am I."

"What?"

"So why don't we get together on it?"

I was incredulous. "You want to play this piece on stage?"

"Listen," said Kirk. "I came from Broadway. I've always looked forward to coming back. In the right vehicle, of course."

The use of that word "vehicle" sounded an alarm, but it was heard only remotely. Kirk Douglas had indeed come from Broadway. He'd made his mark in Sidney Kingsley's *Detective Story*, had replicated the role on the screen, and with his craggy features and superhuman energy had taken the quantum stride to stardom. Was he ready to become an updated Don Quixote?

There was no doubt Kirk had earned his status the hard way. He was not born to the name of Kirk Douglas; his birth name was Issur Danielovitch, the son of a poor family in a decaying town upriver from New York City. In his youth he'd known poverty and anti-Jewish prejudice. In spite of, or possibly because of, these handicaps, he'd clawed his way into the theatre and, spurred by ferocious ambition, had moved to the top.

Kirk and I shared similar backgrounds, similar struggles toward establishing identities of our own shaping. There was an affinity between us in this degree, but our fundamental natures were decidedly different.

A pragmatic difference between us was money. Kirk had a lot. I didn't. Without doubt he could outbid me for the rights to *The Cuckoo's Nest*. But the main consideration, as I considered his offer, was that he might indeed be exciting in the Quixotic character of Randle McMurphy, that possibly there was a lucky concurrence here.

We agreed. I'd write it, initially for the stage and later for the movie, and he'd star in both.

A contract was negotiated, an awesome document, an authentic masterpiece of Hollywood legalese due to become as famous, in its own territory, as the play or the movie that it presumably governed.

There were two preparations I assigned myself prior to beginning the writing of the play. The first was a conference with the book's author, Ken Kesey. This was easily arranged. Kesey flew south from his home in Pleasant Hill, Oregon, and we met in my cottage at the Chateau Marmont, in Hollywood.

At the outset of our get-together there was tension in the room. Kesey, who was built like a wrestler (which in fact he was), clearly was carrying a very large chip on his shoulder. He was sullen, truculent, and mistrustful. The principal reason, I discovered, was that he considered himself best qualified to write the play. He'd taken courses in playwriting in college, nursed theatrical ambitions, and was wounded that he hadn't been asked. But I discerned that his principal unease was over an assumption he'd made, that he'd be meeting a New York esthete with whom he couldn't, or didn't want to, communicate.

To disabuse him I said, "I'm not a New Yorker. I come from the north woods of Wisconsin and have bummed all over the lot. I don't really live anywhere at all. And I sure as hell am not an intellectual. You've got degrees from Stanford, right? By profession I'm a hobo with not a fraction of your education. So let's get over that stuff."

Kesey was intrigued. "What do you mean, you're a hobo?"

Exactly that, I told him, and explained that for years I'd ridden the freights and worked at whatever. That I'd followed the harvests, bucked barley, worked lumber camps, anything that might earn a buck or a meal. Small-town jails were not unknown to me, nor detention camps. "A *real* hobo," I said. "Not one of your Jack Kerouacs or your middle-class hippies in fashionable poor-people's clothing."

Kesey came back with a challenge. "You worked lumber. Where?"

"Redding, California," I told him. "I swung a peavey and worked the pond. Fell in pretty often, too."

Kesey, who knew lumbering very well, said, "Well, I'll be damned."

After that we got along. His truculence faded. We talked for three hours, in fact, Kesey discoursing at length about his experimentation with "psychoto-mimetic drugs." (The phrase was his; I'd never heard it before.) I'd done my own experimenting with grass and LSD, but drugs weren't my scene.

The conversation was lively and enjoyable to us both, but there was one topic we never got around to — how to make a play out of his novel.

That was my first and last meeting with Ken Kesey. We were to stay in touch, to correspond, and, rarely, to speak on the phone. We maintained cordial relations, but were never in person to meet again.

The second demand I'd set myself was to learn as much as possible about the insane and the asylums that housed them. I'd met a considerable population of schizophrenics on the road. They were mostly harmless, except for those who heard command voices or were too quiet. I'd learned to be wary of them, especially the very quiet ones. I'd learned they were capable of explosive violence without notice. Now, I investigated the mental hospitals, starting with a posh clinic in New York City and sliding down-scale to the abysmal asylum at Milledgeville, Georgia, a classic snake pit where patients spent their days chained to radiators.

I'd learned enough to write the play. Following a customary routine, I picked a place on the map — Jamaica this time — and under an alias holed up at a small, slightly disreputable hotel and started writing. In six weeks I had a complete draft.

In the spring of 1963 I returned to New York, where promptly the gears shifted into the production process. The nominal producer would be David Merrick, also known as The Abominable Showman. The production authority in actuality was a corporation headed by Kirk Douglas and his Hollywood partner, Edward Lewis.

In movies, Kirk was known to be a handful. In his return to stage he'd sworn to become putty in the director's hands. But old habits don't just die hard, they don't die at all. Strong directors shied away from confrontations with this bright but headstrong movie star. Finally, we engaged Alec Siegel, my old friend "The Screamer," who'd endeared himself to me by punching out that live-television actor —

an act that boded well for anyone aspiring to be ringmaster on *The Cuckoo's Nest*, where prodigious strength might be needed to take and hold control.

Rehearsals went well, if only because Kirk was impressed by the evident talent of the cast. Gene Wilder was Billy, the stammering mother-fixated boy. William Daniels, an extraordinary performer latterly known to television audiences as Dr. Mark Craig, chief of surgery on the medical series *St. Elsewhere*, was the effete Dale Harding. Joan Tetzel, star of *I Remember Mama*, was the Big Nurse and Ed Ames was Chief Bromden.

We opened in New Haven. Those are fateful words for any show, but for *The Cuckoo's Nest* they were memorable for the shock of critical outrage. A pattern was established wherein a few critics trumpeted that a brave new breed of theatre had been born, and the majority condemned the play as offensive, tasteless, and scatological, never sparing the invective.

There was a phrase I was to see tiresomely often: "How dare you make fun of the insane?"

But the most memorable scene occurred not on stage but in a suite of the Taft Hotel, that weary old inn adjoining the Shubert Theatre where so many showfolk had suffered the horrors of out-of-town openings.

The first preview had been, as expected, ragged in performance, rich in miscues, and generally disastrous—in short, par for the course on any complex play. The production staff, eight of us including two women, had gathered in Kirk Douglas's suite for post-opening conference, waiting for him while cheerily chatting among ourselves. We were astounded when Kirk, just after his shower, exploded into the room and launched a nonstop tirade very like an erupting volcano, which continued for fifteen minutes. We'd betrayed him, it seemed, not merely by incompetence but possibly by some malign design. By far I came in for the worst of it. As I listened in astonishment, he roared accusations of incompetence. He included a warning against my trying to use The Dramatists Guild to defend and maintain my ineptitude, a notion that had never occurred to me. In colorful and profane language he gave notice that now he, and only he, would be in charge and that he fully intended to take whatever measures he might find necessary to "save his ass."

The amazing thing about the scene, however, was Kirk's costume. He was nude. Totally.

Among the measures Kirk adopted was the classic Hollywood solution: more writers. When the show moved to Boston I observed two "submarines" and listened in dismay to lines I never wrote.

As David Merrick and I stood at the rear of the theatre during a performance, he indignantly demanded to know what I was going to do about it. In turnabout I said, "You're the producer, David. What are *you* going to do about it?"

Nothing, of course. One could no more stop Kirk Douglas than one could halt a charging bull.

The play opened at the Cort Theatre in New York on November 13th, 1963. It was not my play. It was a dramatic goulash cooked by Hollywood chefs. A very few critics praised, wildly; the others condemned. One review in particular hit me hard, notable because it was by Walter Kerr, Broadway's dean of critics. Kerr was normally the most temperate of men, but it was evident that the play infuriated him. He lashed out:

> "One Flew Over the Cuckoo's Nest" is so preposterous a proposition for the theater that it could be dismissed very briefly if it weren't for the extraordinary tastelessness with which it has been conceived... I'd like to make it plain at once that when I speak of the evening's essential cheapness I am not thinking of its deep and abiding fondness for the scatological: of its interest in whores who are therapeutic for male virgins, of the whooping and hollering that goes on over a toilet flush, of the vodka that is served out of enema bags, of the "Frig 'em all" that is intoned like a litany...
>
> The coarseness of Dale Wasserman's play is more nearly a quality of mind, and it expresses itself in two ways. To begin with (and to go on endlessly thereafter) the author makes a vast, greedy joke of mindlessness, of all the fun and games that are possible when one looks at lunatics long enough. Catatonics are funny, a fellow who stands immobile forever can be made to serve as the hoop in a basketball game, a night in the loony-bin with liquor on

hand, cabinets to crawl into, and doors to slam wildly can be the gayest thing of its kind since "Brother Rat" was a mouse...

There's much more, but one gets the idea. In any case, I never saw the Kirk Douglas production of *One Flew Over the Cuckoo's Nest* in New York; I'd chosen to save my own sanity by decamping to California, where I'd been offered a producer/writer position at MGM, before it opened.

There's an interesting postscript to the Kerr review. Some years later Kerr, now critic for *The New York Times*, was assigned to review a production of the play once more, the production that starred William Devane in the leading role and Danny de Vito as Martini the Hallucinator. The play—now *my* play—was in the midst of a five-year run in New York simultaneously with productions in most of the world's capitals. Kerr's re-review was a marvel of confusion, of embarrassed retraction, of reaching toward comprehension of what he'd failed to comprehend initially. Like a gentleman, he conceded that the play had virtues that he'd missed the first time around.

But by then he was simply irrelevant. The play had become a thundering success, not only in New York but worldwide.

CHAPTER NINE

Look always forward;
there are no birds in last year's nest this year.

A few days after having fled *The Cuckoo's Nest* debacle in New York I reported to the office of Robert O'Brien, the boss of production at MGM Studios. By way of greeting he said, "I've always wondered how a playwright feels after being beaten up by the critics. If you don't mind talking about it."

"I do mind. But what the hell. I feel humiliated. Ashamed. I feel like apologizing to the world for having committed a nuisance. I feel like I've been exposed as a con man. I feel like I should be jailed for impersonating a writer." I plumbed my vocabulary further, trying for the *mot juste*. "I feel like...pigshit. That explain it?"

"Well, it does give me a hint," said O'Brien.

My last conference before leaving New York concerned the status of *Man of La Mancha*, whose option had expired. Philip Rose had asked to keep it in effect, but upon my learning that actually there was little progress toward production I declined to renew it. The play was near and dear to me, and in light of the fiasco on *The Cuckoo's Nest* I was determined never again to abandon it to others.

I'd come to MGM not as an employee but as a partner in the firm of Trident Productions whose three tines were composed of director Delbert Mann, producer Douglas Laurence, and myself. It was my delegated responsibility to ferret out "properties" eligible for production and to write or perform repairs on those I'd chosen. It would give me grief to list the fascinating projects I submitted and which thereupon didn't happen, so I won't. On the other hand, a list of movies that we *did* get made shows a distinct lack of distinction.

There was, for instance, *Stay Away, Joe*, which starred Elvis Presley and was shot among the rattlesnakes and the fabulous red rocks of Sedona, Arizona. It did little for the arts of cinema, but did instill in me an abiding love for the dream landscapes of Arizona.

We made another called *Quick, Before It Melts,* a tale of two *New York Times* reporters (in actuality Gay Talese and Philip Benjamin) who are sent to check out Naval operations in the Antarctic. It still shows on television in the hours when no one is watching, with its best scenes deleted by the dead hand of the censor.

Still another was called *Doctor, You've Got to Be Kidding.* It starred those Hollywood waxworks, Sandra Dee and George Hamilton.

We made a movie called *Mr. Buddwing* in which I built suspense for two hours and then, in a sudden attack of perversity, thumbed my nose at the audience and declined to tell them what happened. It was little comfort years later to hear that eminent professor of cinema, Dr. Nicholas Salerno, say: "If that movie had come from France it would have been a big winner."

I took refuge from these films by renting a house off-season in Palm Springs and moved down there in order to write still another movie with which to redeem myself. Its title was *A Walk With Love and Death,* and I'd barely started on the screenplay when I was interrupted by a call from New York.

The interruption was to last four years.

The call was from a director, Albert Marre. I knew of him only vaguely...academic theatre, I recalled, plus one Broadway musical, *Kismet,* a war-horse based on a movie that had starred Alfred Drake and featured a pleasant singing actor named Richard Kiley. After introducing himself, Marre asked: "Have you thought of converting *I, Don Quixote* into a stage musical?"

"Often," I said.

"Would you consider it now?"

Marre went on to explain he had a composer (whom initially he declined to name) and a backer with the front-money necessary to finance the work. Could we discuss it?

"Come out to Palm Springs," I said. "You can stay at my house and we'll talk it over."

He arrived within a few days and as a bonus brought his wife, Joan Diener, whom I remembered seeing in *Kismet* as the incendiary Lalume...Joan of the forty-inch bust and eighteen-inch waist, of the spectacular figure and the four-octave singing voice. Joan improved the desert scenery immensely by lounging at the pool as Albie and I talked shop.

Albie explained. "I saw it on television," he explained. "The last twenty minutes of your play cry out for music."

This was not a gambit which enraptured me. "They cry out for music because the play puts a platform under those climactic twenty minutes."

"Agreed," he said. "But in a musical, because of time given to musical numbers one must use words very sparingly."

True. But I wasn't really interested in taking lessons. I'd cut my teeth on musical theatre in various capacities. Indeed, after a long indoctrination in staging dance and concert spectaculars, my first production for Broadway was the Duke Ellington–John Latouche *Beggar's Holiday*, the highest budgeted musical ever seen on the Street to that time, when I was still in my twenties. It was an enterprise that had given me the priceless experience of sitting on a piano bench night after night with Ellington after he'd finished the evening's gig, as we labored on fitting lyrics to music rather than, as was normal, the other way around. I had co-written a musical, *Livin' the Life*, for a substantial run at the Eden Theatre, Off-Broadway, and had been making my living at writing, staging, and producing musical forms in a range from folk dance to grand opera for most of my years. In actuality, I was more at home with musical theatre than I was with straight plays.

I asked who'd be the producer. We'll find one, Marre replied. In the meantime he had a gentleman who'd be putting up the seed money. He also had a composer, by the name of Mitch Leigh.

I asked the obvious, "Has he ever done a show?"

Well, not exactly, explained Marre, but he'd written the incidental music for a play called *Never Live Over a Pretzel Factory*.

Since I'd never heard of Leigh or the play, this information was not reassuring. I asked about further credits. Albie (everyone called him Albie) explained: this composer ran a company known as Music Makers, which turned out advertising jingles for use on radio and television, his principal success to date being, "Nobody Doesn't Like Sara Lee."

These credits struck me as underwhelming, but Marre insisted that Leigh was a good composer who'd studied with Hindemith and with Nadia Boulanger. (I've always wondered how Nadia Boulanger managed to accommodate the thousands of musicians who claim to have studied with her. Possibly she held her classes at Madison Square Garden?)

However, Leigh's talents were enhanced by Marre's next revelation: the man who was going to put up the financing and the tyro composer were one and the same. Mitch Leigh, Marre informed me, was independently wealthy.

Being at least a little confused by this information, I suggested that we go to dinner.

I had two purposes in adjourning to dinner. We'd go to a tiny one-woman restaurant in Palm Desert known as "El Besame Mucho," or, translated into English, "Kiss Me Plenty." Only friends of the proprietor went there, not because it was exclusive or expensive but because with only four small tables there simply wasn't room for strangers. There was no menu because only one dish was served. But what a dish! A blend of Mexican and Yugoslav cuisine, it was unique, delicious, and certainly it simplified ordering.

The food was wonderful and the clientele distinguished—I'd regularly run across such fellow-habitués as Hal Wallis and Marlon Brando. But the real attraction of "El Besame Mucho" was its proprietor, Olga. No last name, just Olga. Olga was a smiling exotic, rather Gypsy-like in appearance. She was not only a brilliant (if limited) cook, but a psychic of formidable gifts. She was, in fact, one of two authentic soothsayers among the many I've encountered in my lifetime.

Her gifts were not for sale but were available to people she liked. Luckily I was included in that category, so when opportunity presented itself I spoke to Olga privately, explained I was conferring with New Yorkers about writing a show, and asked, "Should I work with these people?"

To my surprise, Olga, who was not at all unsophisticated, answered with an immediate, "Yes."

"Would such a show be successful?"

"It will be extremely successful," said Olga, firmly. "In fact, it will overwhelm your life."

I was staggered. One seldom got answers as loud and clear as this, especially on occasions when Olga had unpleasant news to deliver—not that she ever flinched from delivering it, but she did contrive to phrase it gently.

"I don't think I want my life overwhelmed," I ventured.

"You don't have a choice," said Olga.

Marre and I, in the course of one high-intensity week, laid out the text that would become *Man of La Mancha* and noted which words would become songs and which scenes would convert to musical sequences.

It went this atypically fast because it was, in fact, quite easy. The text of the television play offered every single character and situation the musical would require, plus 90 percent of the dialogue. The chief job would be stripping away redundant words, as well as deleting scenes to make room for songs and musical development. That most important and difficult element required for any play, musical or otherwise—construction—was already in place.

Our notes included a preliminary list of songs to be:

"Highway to Glory"
"The Golden Age"
"The Windmill's Song"
"All a Man Wants"
"Dulcinea"
"The Quest (The Impossible Dream)"
"The Inquisition Chant"
"The Players' Song"
"The Enchanter's Theme"

Most of these songs would change title, if not content, during the development ahead. In any case, I realized, with trepidation, that I'd committed myself to a project in company with a director I didn't know, a composer without credits, a money man who also happened to be the composer without credits, and no lyricist at all.

Still, according to Olga, things were looking good.

CHAPTER TEN

Have patience and shuffle the cards.

One of the weariest questions authors of musicals are subjected to is that oldie, "Which comes first, the lyrics or the music?" The answer has been supplied once and for all by His Majesty, Oscar the Second, who answered with Hammersteinian finality, "The book."

Think about it. Before the music there's the lyric. Before the lyric there's...what? If we're regarding the theatre musical, there's the Book. It's the Book from which all else flows. It's the Book that supplies characters, plot, theme, mode of speech, level of reality, quality and nature of emotion, the choice of approach, and a dozen other matters germane to final intentions.

Ah, yes, and style—are we dealing with the giddiness of *Crazy For You* or with the gritty emotion of *Carousel*? With the folk-fantasy of *Brigadoon* or the gut-wrenching social realism of *Les Misérables*? With the camp burlesque of *Hairspray* or the fragile fantasy of *The Secret Garden*? The folkloric naturalism of *Porgy and Bess* or the calculated fake-reality of *The Sound of Music*?

In each case someone decided upon an objective and made a calculated run at it. That someone can invariably be identified as the author of the Book, whether the Book is derived from an under-lying work (which most often it is) or is original (which rarely it may be). In either case the Book inscribes the map of intention. The lyricist and the composer and the director and the designers and the sound and lighting people and all the other so-called creative staff obediently follow. If they don't, we have a costly embarrassment on our hands.

The Book makes all basic decisions. Contradict any of them at your peril. Mix fantasy and naturalism and you'll close out of town. Let your burlesque go serious even briefly, and you'll close on Saturday night. Make a musical of something that's already a musical, such as, say, the play *Cyrano*, and you'll be inscribed in Broadway's Black Book. There are thousands of literary and cinematic works that should not become musicals, but do. Their ghostly wreckage fills Shubert Alley.

Audiences will accept nearly any convention or intention or conceit, provided one stays true to it thereafter. "Staying true" is the First Commandment to be obeyed in all modes of expression in your musical, and it's first and foremost a function of the Book. So Oscar Hammerstein, a superb lyricist, couldn't have been more bluntly honest when asked that cliché question about the primacy of lyrics or music, and having answered, "Neither. The Book."

As to which comes first during the working process of writing the musical, the question is simpleminded: in the modern musical of course the lyrics come first. The lyrics are alternate expressions of key moments in the play and must be obedient to the same demands made of the Book...move the story, reveal character, hit emotional high peaks. It's this latter that is the unique tool of the musical. Nothing can transcend music in twanging the heartstrings of an audience.

It's a frequent source of sadness to the playwright that during the sea-change of play into musical a play's most eloquent passages are generally preempted by the lyricist, and thus are lost to the play-wright forever. Fair or unfair, so it goes, according to usage and The Dramatists Guild. So it was natural that in the case of *Man of La Mancha*, where I'd written such deeply felt passages, I was passionately interested in which lyricist would be acquiring title to the "aria speeches" that were the emotional heart of my play.

When Marre put forward the name of W. H. Auden, my heart leapt—and then went into a holding pattern while I considered. Would my play be illuminated? Or would it become, possibly, a new and recondite work by a collaborator who wasn't merely a librettist himself but, by general consensus, the greatest poet of our time? In short, should I be awed or apprehensive? I reviewed what I knew of him.

Wystan Hugh Auden—a name that echoes thunder. Early on, a rebel curiously parallel to Bertolt Brecht—one a convert to Catholicism, the other to Communism. Auden could fairly be called the Poet Laureate of the mid-Atlantic, English but not aggressively British. In 1939 he first came to America in flight from the war and thereafter maintained a pied-à-terre in New York. He was a homosexual who considered homosexuality a sin. A proud man who publicly warned against the sin of pride. No English poet since Byron had become famous so swiftly.

His libretti for opera were famous among the cognoscenti if not the general public. With Isherwood, *The Dog Beneath the Skin;* with Kallman, *The Ascent of F6;* for Igor Stravinsky, *The Rake's Progress...* and other works, of distinction if also of an esoteric bent.

With some trepidation I moved my home base once again to New York to work with him.

When we meet, Auden calls me Vah-serman, and I call him nothing at all, unsure how to pronounce Wystan. Until I have the answer from Auden himself:

> *My first name is Wystan,*
> *Rhymes with Tristan,*
> *But—oh dear!—I hope*
> *I'm not quite such a dope.*

In 1964 when we meet he's a rumpled wreck of a man, his clothes shabby and perpetually sprinkled with cigarette ash. A chain smoker and a consumer—on a curiously rigid schedule—of prodigious amounts of vodka, he lives among litter in a tiny walkup on St. Mark's Place in the East Village. The ashtrays are perpetually overflowing. Discarded clothing, dregs in bottles, a cleaning woman's nightmare. Stacks of manuscripts on a heavily burdened desk. Books, books, books, in precarious stacks. The stink of cat urine, though I don't recall ever seeing a cat...possibly lurking among the books?

I had enormous respect for him. But a worry gnawed at me—

if there were to be differences, which would prevail—my respect for his talent, or respect for my own work? Although it inkled about in my mind it was a contingency I sincerely hoped wouldn't occur.

Auden informed me that Chester Kallman would be co-lyricist. They had a permanent arrangement to that effect.

"Fine. Where is Kallman?"

"In Kirchstetten."

"Where is Kirchstetten?"

"Austria. He lives at our house."

"How," I inquired, "will Kallman collaborate on the lyrics if he lives in Austria?"

"By mail, of course."

Years later I was to read an excerpt from a letter by Auden to a friend: "Naughty Chester has not written nor sent me any lyrics for the Don Quixote musical, the director of which is breathing down my neck."

But the problem with "Naughty Chester" was to prove the lesser of those that began troubling the waters of our collaboration. Auden was a quasi-expert on the novel *Don Quixote*, having written and lectured on its more arcane aspects. I was no scholar, but this was my play, my own willful invention, and it was not an adaptation of the novel. Almost immediately we clashed, politely but with fervor. As the work continued, the fervor grew.

Auden wrote at incredible speed, and I marveled at his ability to do so, though later I was to discover much of his work was actually the reworking of material from the past. Nevertheless, his "lyrics" were stunning, rich in imagery, eloquent in language.

But they were not lyrics. Some were poems. Some were diatribes, not against the world of Cervantes but the world of today. They made free use of anachronism, which tore the fabric of the play to shreds. They were gall-and-wormwood attacks on the vulgarity of an inimical society—not the society that Don Quixote railed against, but our own. Some possessed inspired language—eloquent on the page but unsingable on stage.

Here is Auden's declaration of mission when, in the script, Don Quixote and Sancho first declare their crusade:

DON QUIXOTE

Out of a dream of ease and indolence
Woken at last, I hear the call
Of the road to adventure, awaiting me, beckoning
Beyond the gate in my garden wall.
See, how it runs, now straight, now sinuous,
Uphill and down! The world is wide.
Onward it leads to noble deeds:
Saddle our steeds, and forth let us ride.

DON QUIXOTE AND SANCHO

Forth we'll ride together,
A knight and his esquire,
To the world's end if need be
To find our heart's desire,
To raise the weak and fallen up
To knock the tyrant down:
On, on, on to glory, valor and renown.

SANCHO

I, too, could do with a change of scenery:
There comes a day in a married man's life
When he needs a break, to take a long holiday
From the noise of his kids and the voice of his wife.
When my master comes to an inn at sundown,
Having done his noble deed for the day,
After we've dined, I shall not mind
If the maid looks kind and ready for play...

The words are lovely, the rhyming ingenious, the narrative elements artful. But the demand of this moment is for passion — passion of purpose, expressed in the driving rhythm of hoofbeats and the exultancy of commitment. (In the eventual production, Joe Darion's lyric became "Man of La Mancha," beginning:

Hear me now, oh thou bleak and unbearable world!
Thou art base and debauched as can be...

—and a chorus—

I am I, Don Quixote,
The lord of La Mancha,
My destiny calls and I go;
And the wild winds of fortune will carry me onward,
Oh Whithersoever they blow.

Whithersoever they blow,
Onward to glory I go!

In my original play I'd written a response by Don Quixote to
Aldonza's demand, "What does it mean—quest?" Don Quixote
answers, "The mission of each true knight. His duty—nay, his
privilege. To dream the impossible dream. To fight the unbeatable
foe..." I felt sure that "the impossible dream" phrase would be
seized upon by a lyricist as an impassioned if somewhat highfalutin'
proclamation of the Don's credo.

Auden chose to ignore it, offering instead his own "Song of the
Quest":

DON QUIXOTE

Once the voice has quietly spoken, every knight
Must ride alone
On the quest appointed him into the unknown
One to seek the healing waters, one the dark
Tower to assail,
One to find the lost princess, one to find the grail.
Through the wood of evil counsel, through the
Desert of dismay,
Past the pools of pestilence he must find the way.
Hemmed between the haunted marshes and the
Mountains of the dead,
To the valley of regret and the bridge of dread...

The lines are exquisite, but they are also narrative and didactic.
They read well, but they're passive...a meditation lacking energy or

the simple statement of mission that would answer the challenge of Aldonza's question.

Auden's "Song of Dejection," on the other hand, scans beautifully and might sing well:

DON QUIXOTE

> *There's a buzz in my ears crying: "Is there*
> *A point in these*
> *Romantic antics of yours at all?*
> *Is it quite sane to attempt in this century*
> *To act like Gawain or Amadis of Gaul?*
> *You a knight errant? Don't be ridiculous!*
> *You're much too poor and too old for a start."*
> *Sancho, my squire, am I a lunatic?*
> *Should I retire? I'm sick at heart.*

SANCHO (Aside)

> *Truth would require that I say he's a lunatic,*
> *But I'd rather turn liar than break his heart.*

DON QUIXOTE

> *The world is so much vaster,*
> *More indifferent than I thought;*
> *It has no use for glory*
> *Or knights of any sort.*
> *The road is endless and the hills*
> *Are waterless and brown;*
> *Why, why, why, they ask me,*
> *Seek valor and renown?*

Yet these words troubled me. They were alarmingly self-conscious. And would the Don Quixote of *Man of La Mancha* indulge in such self-doubt? An essence of Don Quixote's madness is the *absence* of self-doubt.

I felt that Auden's treatment of "The Knight of the Mirrors" was condescending, with indulgence once more in anachronistic language. My doubts began to find a focus: was Auden showing resentment for his lack of control over all the play? Further, I felt that in this lyric he was more the poetaster than the poet:

The Knight of the Mirrors

Look! Unlearn your bookish lore.
Look! And learn the motives for
Your acts.
Look again! Don't shut your eyes!
Look! It's time to recognize
Some facts.

Look! Those noble knights of old
Were, when the whole truth is told,
All crooks.
Look at Dulcinea! Mutt!
She's the common kitchen slut
She looks.

(after their duel)

Look! Have I not laid you low?
Look! Confess that you are no
True knight,
Only crazy in the head.
Look! Admit that all I've said
Is right.

For the scene I'd written wherein Quixote encounters a troupe of masked players who may or may not be what they seem, Auden wrote a truly amazing speech-song sequence, which deserves reproduction here. I enjoyed it greatly. I also rejected it out of hand as a shockingly cynical vendetta against the play's philosophy. In this song-speech diatribe Auden takes aim at technology...at psychobabble...at religion...sociology...even at the theatre itself.

Voice Of Sin (*Shouting*) One moment! Hold everything! I have an announcement to make! Lights please!

(*The house lights come on.* SIN, DEATH *and* FOLLY *are standing on stage with their masks off, that is to say, wearing fresh masks of a modern kind.* SIN *steps forward and addresses the audience.*)

SIN Ladies and Gentlemen: I and my two friends here are most grateful to Mr. Cervantes for having given us this opportunity to meet you all, and we hope he won't mind if we interrupt his story for a few minutes. You see, we aren't really a bit interested in imaginary characters like his silly old Don Quixote, we only care about real people, like yourselves. Oddly enough, our real names are the same as those in your programme. I am Sin, and my colleagues are, on my left, Folly, on my right, Death. As soon as we heard we were to have the pleasure of meeting you, each of us composed something special for the occasion without telling the others, so that what you will hear will be as much a surprise to us as to you.

Well, Folly, you're always the impatient one. Suppose you start the ball rolling.

FOLLY

Let's get together, folks,
Let's hear a laugh from you,
Swallow a benzedrine,
Put on a party smile,
And join the gang.
To be reserved is gauche, all
Privacy anti-social:
Make life a bang.

Take off your silencers,
Turn up your radios,
Pile on the decibels,
Drown the unbearable
Voice within.
Who knows our why or wherefore?
Don't ask what we are here for,
But make a din.

Let's have some action, folks,
Swing from the chandeliers,
Smash up the furniture,
Crazy as particles
In a cyclotron.
What is all the fun for?
Don't ask or you'll be done for.
Don't stop. Smash on.

SIN Bravo, Folly. Now, Death, let's hear from you. What have you got for us?

DEATH (*reciting against music*)
The progress you have made is very remarkable,
And progress, I grant you, is always a boon:
You have built more automobiles than are parkable,
Crashed the sound-barrier, and may very soon
Be setting up juke-boxes on the silent moon.
Let me remind you, however, despite all that,
I, Death, am still and will always be a cosmocrat.

Still I sport with the young and the daring; at my whim
The climber steps upon the rotten boulder,
The undertow catches boys as they swim,
The speeder swerves onto the slippery shoulder;
With others I wait until they get older
Before assigning, according to my humor,
To one a coronary, to one a tumor.

SIN Thank you, Death. I'm sure we've all been most edified. (*To audience*) I'm sorry ladies and gentlemen, but he's always been like this, and you can't teach an old dog new tricks, you know. And now it's my turn. I hope you'll enjoy my little song; at least it's cheerful.

SONG OF SIN

RECITATIVE
In my game of winning

Mankind to sinning,
To vice and to crime,
From the very beginning,
When men murdered each other with stone axes
And paid no income taxes,
Down to the present time
When any taxpayer can see
Live murders on TV,
In every age,
At every stage,
In spinning my fiction,
I've always tried
To adapt my diction
To the contemporary-ism of pride.
At this point, I should like to remark
How grateful I am for your help.
In leading you all by the nose
Down the path which gradually goes
From the light to the yelping dark,
Having no, thanks to you, existence,
Has been of enormous assistance.

SONG

Since social psychology replaced theology,
The process is twice as quick.
When a conscience is tender and loth to
Surrender,
I have only to whisper: "You're sick!"
Puritanical morality
Is old-fogey, non-u:
Enhance your personality
With a romance, with two.

If you pass up a dame, you've yourself to blame,
Shame is neurotic, so snatch:
All rules are too formal, in fact, they're abnormal
For every desire is natch.

So take your proper share, man, of
Dope, or drink:
Aren't you the chairman of
Ego, Inc.?

Truth is a mystical myth as statistical
Methods have objectively shown,
A fad of the churches: since the latest researches
Into motivation, it's known
That virtue is hypocrisy,
Honesty a joke.
You live in a democracy:
Lie like other folk . . .

So believe while you may that you're more o.k.,
More important than anyone else,
Till you find that you're hooked, your goose is
Cooked,
And you're only a cypher of hell's.
Till then, imagine that I'm proud of you:
Enjoy your dream.
I'm so bored with the whole fucking crowd
Of you
I could scream.

Sin Thank you. You've been a wonderful audience. But it's time for us
to say good-bye now and let you get back to Don Quixote. So off
we'll go with a farewell chorus. (*To* Death) If you can't sing, croak.

Trio
We must go now,
On with the show now,
Ever so nice to have met you all,
Look forward to meeting again,
For, in the end, we shall get you all
And won't that be jolly!
Till then, we beg to remain

Yours sincerely
(or very nearly)
Death, Sin and Folly.

Wonderful! This piece of work I thought truly brilliant. Also, I thought, if allowed through the gates it would absolutely destroy *Man of La Mancha.* Could Auden possibly have been unaware?

In these song-scenes, Auden abandoned the play to express his loathing for bourgeois values. Their burden was disillusion, despair, and, curiously, the dominant trait I invariably felt in my personal relations with him: loneliness.

On the more pragmatic level, what on earth was he up to? Something so simple as "take the money and run?" That's what he did, of course—a substantial settlement was made and he vanished. But I felt something else at work—a profound disagreement with the play's philosophy and the consequent impulse, conscious or otherwise, to sabotage it. It wasn't a matter of missing the mark in the words he wrote, it was a case of selecting another mark entirely. In which case—bull's-eye.

I found, to my horror, that Mitch Leigh was obediently setting music to some of these words, that in fact with Marre's approval he'd already composed Auden's "Song of the Quest"; I have a copy of that peculiar essay in my files. It was quashed, promptly.

In any case, Auden and "Naughty Chester" were gone. Nor had any lesson been learned other than one I already knew: that a play can flourish despite flaws provided that the flaws fall within a single intention: one unswerving point-of-view. The imposition of disparate or conflicting intentions invariably will be the death of it.

I'd written a play about Miguel de Cervantes, invoking his fictional creation as an alter ego. Auden insisted upon viewing it as an adaptation of the novel, *Don Quixote,* which it emphatically was not. I recall saying to him, "Frankly, I have never even read the complete *Don Quixote.*" Auden astonished me by replying, "Frankly, neither have I." Affectation or confession? To this day, I'm not sure.

But I do recall precisely when the final nail was driven into the coffin of collaboration. It came in a discussion concerning the ending of the piece. "Don Quixote must repudiate his quest as he dies," Auden maintained.

"Oh, no. In his final moments he reaffirms it."

"Quite impossible," said Auden. And went on to recite a lyric he'd already written:

> *Humor me no longer, Sancho; faithful squire,*
> *All that is past;*
> *Do not look for this year's bird in the nest*
> *Of last.*

> *Don Quixote de La Mancha was a phantom of*
> *My brain;*
> *I, Quijano, your Alonso, am myself again . . .*

"Lovely," I said.

"So you see, old boy, he does recant."

"Only in your play," I said.

Our collaboration was at an end.

It's possible that in those declining years Auden was too bitter, too barren of hope to cope with Cervantine optimism. Nor could I be so presumptuous as to estimate his state of mind. But I do believe that his mind and spirit were only too eloquently expressed in the lyrics he wrote for *Man of La Mancha*, lyrics that had their own brilliancy but were utterly *mal à propos* to the project at hand.

I admired almost everything that Auden wrote, even while noting that he was engaged in a philosophic vendetta against the spirit of the play I'd written and that he'd undertaken to serve. Curiosity led me to examination of other of his libretti, in which I noted his felicity in phrasing, together with an ingenuity in rhyming unmatched even by Sondheim. He was so admirably a master of both meter and word-music!

And yet, aside from differences in intention, I saw in them the same flaw that infected his lyrics for *Man of La Mancha*.

Auden's words sing on the page. The addition of music creates a fatal redundancy.

In any case we had wasted valuable time and were now in urgent need of a lyricist, one who'd understand my play and faithfully fulfill its needs.

"We routed them, did we?" Joan Diener, Richard Kiley, and Irving Jacobson celebrate victory over the muleteers as Ray Middleton deplores.

OPPOSITE PAGE: **Top** Our rickety-rackety theatre on East 4th Street in the Village—bless its shabby heart. **Bottom** "My armor! My sword!" Don Quixote re-dedicates himself to The Quest. Irving Jacobson, Richard Kiley, Joan Diener, Mimi Turque.

THIS PAGE: **Top Left** "Only wait and thou shalt see amazing sights." Richard Kiley, Irving Jacobson, and their entranced steeds. **Top Right** "Sweet maiden, what wilt thou?" Don Quixote (Richard Kiley) encounters a Gypsy trollop (Gerianne Raphael). Sancho (Irving Jacobson) remains unconvinced of her sweetness. **Right** "You spoke of a trial. By your own word I must be given a trial!" When Cervantes protests, the Governor (Ray Middleton) convenes a kangaroo court.

THIS PAGE: **Top** "I shall impersonate a man…" Richard Kiley, as Miguel de Cervantes, begins his transformation into Don Quixote. **Middle** "From so much reading his brains dry up!" Richard Kiley in the process of becoming Don Quixote. **Lower Left** "I hereby dub thee knight." The Innkeeper (Ray Middleton) does the dubbing, Don Quixote (Richard Kiley) is the dubbee as Sancho (Irving Jacobson) stands witness. **Below** "Thou golden helmet of Mambrino, there can be no hat like thee…" Irving Jacobson, Gino Conforti, as the bemused Barber, and Richard Kiley.

OPPOSITE PAGE: **Top** Theatre de La Zarzuela, Madrid. Opening night at the first foreign production of *Man of La Mancha*. It proved to be a shocker. **Bottom** The stage setting in Prague, Czechoslovakia, a production shut down by the Soviet authorities.

TOP Movie version. Sophia Loren is hassled by the Muleteers, who show good taste but poor manners. **BOTTOM** Movie version: "We routed them, did we?" James Coco, Peter O'Toole, and Sophia Loren celebrate victory in their battle with the Muleteers.

Top Movie version: "I demand a trial." Peter O'Toole demands justice of The Governor, Harry Andrews. **Bottom** Movie version: "He is dead … my master is dead." In foreground: James Coco, Peter O'Toole, Sophia Loren.

TOP Movie version: "Don Miguel de Cervantes—I accuse you of being an idealist, a bad poet, and an honest man." **BOTTOM** Movie version: Common room of the prison.

CHAPTER ELEVEN

We know the sickness, now to find the cure.

Joe Darion was a compass point one hundred eighty degrees opposite W. H. Auden. Joe had written popular songs like "Ricochet
Romance," "Changing Partners," and "Midnight Train." His path
to pop songwriting was wildly offbeat; he had a hit record before he
learned how to write lyrics. He'd developed musical material for
comedian Red Buttons, and out of that material came "The Ho-Ho
Song," which became one of the biggest hits of 1948. As Joe himself
explained:

"I kind of backed into Tin Pan Alley. Then I stubbed my toe. I
couldn't sell anything. I wrote and wrote and wrote, and the boys in
the Alley said I couldn't hit water if I fell off a bridge. It got so I
couldn't get past the secretaries in the front office of the Brill
Building."

One day Darion went into a music store and bought the lyric
sheets for the top 50 songs on the *Billboard* charts for that week—
in those days they were typewritten and mimeographed sheets of
paper crudely stapled together and sold for a quarter.

"I went home and unstapled the sheets," said Darion. "I laid all
these sheets down on the floor in our living room in long rows, and
in the spaces in between I laid my own lyrics. I walked back and
forth, back and forth, studying them...and I saw what I was doing
wrong. I would write, 'the wind cried...' Nonsense! Wind doesn't
cry—people do. The successful songs all had concrete images—
pictures you could see. Not only that, they had plots. In sixteen lines
they had as much plot as you'd find in a two-hour movie."

A lyricist was born.

But I knew something more about Joe, something that brought

97

him to mind for *La Mancha*. He'd written an offbeat musical that played Broadway (briefly) under the title *Shinbone Alley*. It was based on the popular "Archy and Mehitabel" stories, and it struck me as both foolhardy and daring—a musical about a cockroach and a cat? Mel Brooks had collaborated with Joe on the book, which never quite pulled itself together but tried to hold the audience with a series of Brooksian one-liners. The show had starred Eartha Kitt and Eddie Bracken, and inevitably failed. But there was wit in its lyrics, and courage in its concept. Joe Darion just might be our man.

As Joe told me later, he'd read the play and felt immediately he'd kill to be able to work on it. "I'd have done it for nothing," he said, "but of course I couldn't let anybody know that." As it was, his path to commitment was devious. Marre and Leigh, acting as surrogate producers and without my knowledge, initially asked him just to doctor Auden's lyrics. As Darion recalled:

"...they sat me down and told me the problem. The showed me Auden's lyrics—gorgeous poems, of course, but they were not lyrics. They wanted me to fix Auden's work, and I looked at them and said, 'Do you think I'm going to touch that man's stuff? I'm not crazy.' So they said, what do you think should be done? I said, 'Throw it away. You've got to get rid of all of it.' Whereupon Mitch Leigh wanted to kill me because he had already done music to some of them. So they threw me out.

"I went home. It was the most miserable I have ever been in my life. I wanted it so bad. I said to my wife, 'I just big-mouthed myself out of the best thing I'll ever be offered in my life.' For a couple weeks I couldn't do anything. Then they called me back!"

The first draft of the script to include Joe Darion's lyrics is dated June 15, 1964. Several songs in this script are held over from previous efforts, including "Highway to Glory," now with Darion's lyrics:

> *I am off on the Highway to Glory,*
> *And with the world of dull mundanity, I'll part.*
> *With my sword I will carve me a story*
> *Of bravery and purity of heart.*

For Aldonza's opening number he first tried something called, "The Cat That Walks Alone."

> *I am a cat who walks alone;*
> *A prowling cat with yawning jaws,*
> *And if you want to play with me*
> *Beware my teeth, beware my claws.*
>
> *If any man should come my way*
> *Who thinks he's hard, who thinks he's male,*
> *He'll find the night he spends with me*
> *Will singe the fur right off his tail!*

This was cut and replaced with a nearly complete song called "What Kind of Animal Am I?"

> *What kind of animal am I*
> *A tiger wild with knotted jaws,*
> *And if you wander near my cage*
> *Beware my teeth, beware my claws!*
>
> *The cage is narrow as a tomb.*
> *I cannot run or see the sky,*
> *But in my heart the jungle slumbers,*
> *And I'll be savage 'til I die.*

Finally the menagerie was abandoned and the problem solved when Darion came in with the words to "It's All the Same." Nearly a half dozen of his lyrics were cut before they ever made it into any version of the script: a song, presumably for Aldonza, called "The Courtship Is Over," another called "Give a Little, Take a Little," one for Quixote called "Mask of Evil," one for the Gypsies called, "Innocent and Pure." Another possibly delightful song that ended up on the cutting-room floor, so to speak, was Sancho's paean to "The Sweet Simple Joys of Home."

Take the simple joys of married life,
The quiet talks that keep a marriage young,
I would sit every evening and enjoy the pleasant breeze
She made with the wagging of her tongue.

Oh, the sweet simple joys of home,
The sweet simple joys of home,
How I long for the homely, humble,
Lowly, common, ordinary
Sweet simple joys of home!

In general this early draft of the script resembles the final version. The changes to be made were largely cuts; nearly every song ran too long. There were lines cut from Don Quixote's love ballad, "Dulcinea":

I have longed for thee so,
Raptly whispered thy name in the night and received no reply.
All bewitched and aglow,
I have whispered thy name, and the echo refuses to die.

"The Quest (The Impossible Dream)" included these lines, now gone:

This is the quest to which I am sworn
To follow a banner, all tattered and torn,
With my feet in the mud, but my head in the sky,
I will reach for unreachable stars 'till I die.

My impossible dreams will come true,
I'll be loved by my love though I'm far,
No matter how worn and how weary,
I will reach that unreachable star!

The sound of the words and their elevated language are present, but the final version is clearly better:

This is my quest, to follow that star,
No matter how hopeless, no matter how far,
To fight for the right without question or pause,
To be willing to march into hell for heavenly cause!

And I know, if I'll only be true to this glorious quest.
That my heart will lie peaceful and calm when I'm laid
to my rest . . .

And the world will be better for this,
That one man, scorned and covered with scars,
Still strove, with his last ounce of courage,
To reach the unreachable stars!

Not only do the sentences flow more logically one into the next, but the internal rhymes ("how hopeless," "scorned," and "scars") make it entirely more musical. The script also includes fragments of lyrics for songs called "Purity" and "Shame On Thee" for which there was apparently no music.

Darion recognized that my "Impossible Dream" lines were the heart of the play as he expanded them into the lyric to be called "The Quest":

> . . . I knew it was the fulcrum of the whole show. It was the point in the show where the audience would begin to admire him (Quixote) rather than finding him an old fool . . . what happened is, I was sitting at my desk, and I was re-writing the thing, and Hellen [Joe's wife] walked into the room and she looked over my shoulder. She took hold of the paper and pulled it out from under my pencil—I have that sheet of paper, and there's a pencil mark down it—and said, 'You idiot, don't you know when you're finished? Leave it alone.'

Joe Darion was a small man with a big heart. I loved and admired him even when we differed—sometimes *because* we differed. We worked together harmoniously and well, sharing an eccentric sense of humor and mutuality of understanding as to what *Man of La Mancha* was truly about. When we came to temporary impasses in writing, we threw lines back and forth to each other—some of my better lines ended up in lyrics, and some of Joe's funnier ones in dialogue.

Joe's job was made easier in that virtually every song—well, every song but one—drew its idea and its key lines directly from the script. Pure invention was rarely called for. If it was to be "The Impossible Dream" there was the context, fully stated in the script, in addition to the key words themselves. If it was the impassioned "Aldonza," there was the context fully formed, and in addition the words, "I was spawned in a ditch by a mother who left me there... My father? An unknown regiment..." Likewise for, "To Each His Dulcinea."

Indeed, I can think of only one song not cued by lines in the play. That song is "Little Bird," yet even here the script gives explicit clues: "Night lighting...the mood is lyric, sentimental...the singing of the Muleteers lounging about the coping of the well, swells into full harmony to the guitarist's accompaniment."

Incidentally, this is the only song that stands free of the march of narrative. Others are unusually strict in their integration with text. It has been said, in Robert Sennett's analysis, that the play was a near-perfect blueprint for the musical.

The musical aspect of this musical required a large splash of illusion. By the nineties it had become acceptable, if not quite commonplace, to write a musical score that maintained the fiction that the people on stage were singing to each other in a world completely of their own creation. But in 1965 this was a relatively new idea. Tradition held that audiences needed to be coaxed into the show. Songs would stop the action; actors would address the air, and everyone would go home with smiles on their faces. Although, supposedly, the cast would be "acting" as if the audience were invisible, musicals usually included sly bits of "cheating," of playing to both the audience and the rest of the cast, which could have a reassuring effect all round.

There were occasional, brilliant exceptions to this rule before *Man of La Mancha*...shows like *West Side Story* (1958) or *Gypsy*

(1959), where the stars end up distraught or dead. Generally speaking, however, the audiences for musicals expected something more resembling an "entertainment" than a drama.

Man of La Mancha was foremost and firmly a drama. The demand upon Darion's lyrics and Leigh's score was that they support a dramatic narrative further enriched by philosophical argument.

Elsewhere Mitch Leigh has pointed out that the score of *Man of La Mancha*, integrated as it is, only provides the illusion of reality. In 16th-century Spain there was little music anywhere other than in the church. Certainly there was no flamenco music—it would take another two hundred years of Romany immigration before those distinctive sounds and rhythms were heard in Spain. The lay music of Renaissance Spain was written for bagpipes. "I didn't think contemporary audiences would buy that without a lengthy explanation in the program," commented Leigh.

Instead he decided to stick with the anachronistic gypsy style and spread it over the entire score, concluding that if the audience saw the actors accepting the music they'd accept it as well. Before writing a line, Leigh embarked upon an intensive study of the flamenco style in a manner most appropriate to show business— he caught a cab downtown to where flamenco guitarists hung out and gave them money to keep playing until dawn. (One of those guitarists, David Serva, ended up on stage in *Man of La Mancha*, playing the role, not surprisingly, of a guitarist.)

I found Mitch Leigh to be a most peculiar fellow. Initially he embarrassed me by excessive deference. ("You are God!" he said at our first meeting, though later I would be demoted.) After the arrival of success, he would change.

I recall one of my very first meetings with him. We'd made an appointment to meet at the office of Music Makers, a penthouse on Fifty-seventh Street.

I took the elevator to its ultimate and then climbed a short flight of stairs to The Music Makers' aerie, entered, and found myself in a large, shadowy room. Behind a table sat Mitch, his head supported on his two fists, intensely concentrated upon a single object dramatically spotlighted on the table before him. I observed that the object commanding his very considerable brain power was a can of Chungking Chop Suey. I spoke softly, concluded my business expeditiously, and tippy-toed out of his presence.

Constantly in attendance on Mitch was his corps of Music Makers, an assemblage of a half-dozen salaried musical composer/arrangers headed by musical director, Neil Warner, who accompanied him everywhere. I called them the *cuadrilla*, a word remembered from my days in Spain, for they reminded me of nothing so much as a matador's assistants, an ever-present support-staff without which the matador was helpless.

Mitch Leigh, beginning with a name change from Irwin Mitchnick, had traveled the vast divide separating Brooklyn from Manhattan, had attained success in the highly competitive advertising profession, yet in common with innumerable others had yearned for a higher level of recognition, the recognition of those anointed by the word "creative." He wanted passionately to be one of those who create the music to which the public dances...or in the case of Broadway, who create the shows for which the public pays outrageous prices for brief transcendence from a world too much with them.

That Leigh was an independently wealthy man made the continuous presence of his orchestrators possible. On the production of the show they accompanied Mitch everywhere.

Joe Darion and I collaborated. We met almost daily, worked together, and critiqued each other's work, alternately playing audience and critic for the benefit of the other. Mitch Leigh's methods were mysterious. When Joe and I felt we'd done our best with a lyric we sent it to Mitch. Some time later, we'd receive, by messenger, a tape of the song — fully orchestrated — performed by excellent musicians. In general we loved the music we were hearing. It was sinuous in mode, beautifully melodic, exploring the full scale. But had we loved the songs less, there would have been little we could have done about it — they came in such final form.

On one occasion, however, we did take exception. Mitch had sent over his first version of the song "Dulcinea," the song which the besotted Quixote sings to his newly discovered "lady." Independently of each other, Joe and I reacted identically: we felt the song was out of period and out of character, that it had been fashioned less for *Man of La Mancha* than as a bid for a pop single. We told Mitch so by telephone. Agitated, he came to see us.

To say the least, he was unhappy. In fact he seemed resentful, illogically so, we thought, for we were accustomed to criticism every day. Actually, we counted on it as an antidote to complacency.

Joe said, quite reasonably, "Look, let's go over to the piano and work with it a little."

Mitch said, "I don't play piano."

Joe asked, "Well, what do you play?"

"I don't play anything," said Mitch.

That stopped us. A composer who played no musical instrument? Who wouldn't even noodle on a piano?

Perfectly possible, of course, but certainly peculiar. Was he putting us on?

In any event there was nothing we could do but make our comments and trust that something would be done about them. Something was done; in another week or so we received a new version of "Dulcinea," this one perfectly lovely and more properly attuned to the play.

The score was finished. But what score ever is "finished?" The play was finished—but I happen to know that no play ever is "finished."

However, we'd assembled a complete work and were now ready...for what?

For a beginning. The beginning of marketing our efforts in order to secure a producer. To secure financial backing. To secure all of the personnel and the wherewithal needed to mount a production. Now the real struggle could begin.

The search for money was elusive. Leigh had provided enough to commission the authors and get the show written. Financing to get it produced was a different matter, the function of producers, of which we had none. In the autumn of 1964, we organized and undertook a series of auditions that would presumably leap this hurdle.

They were good auditions, directed by Marre and well-cast as to musicians and singers. They were as effective as any I'd ever seen, and were well attended by heavy-monied backers and at least a score of Broadway's leading producers. They couldn't have been more effective capsule presentations of the show.

And they accomplished precisely nothing.

They were applauded politely and suitable compliments were rendered, but checks were not written nor offers of production tendered. The material seemed to fascinate the listeners but also to instill doubts. We were to hear it again and again—a musical about a crazy old man who dies onstage? A musical enfolded within a play that is wrapped within still another play? Isn't that too complex for an audience to comprehend, much less enjoy?

Not even the lovely music seemed to register. I can remember no one who, after hearing a rendition of "The Impossible Dream," saying, "Now, there's a great song." I do remember someone saying, delicately, "Isn't that a bit...pretentious?"

One of the producers who attended our auditions was Kermit Bloomgarden, a man of taste and artistic courage. He was the producer of, among other plays, *Death of a Salesman, The Crucible, Equus,* and *The Diary of Anne Frank.* At this juncture Kermit was only semi-active; he was diabetic, in ill health.

At the conclusion of the audition, he took me aside, into an anteroom. "Look," he said. "I think you've got some kind of a masterpiece here. Don't compromise it. Don't let anyone play tricks. I'm advising you, because they're going to try,"

I said, "Not if you do it."

"I can't," said Kermit. "I would never survive the effort it's going to take to get this one on."

I must not bad-mouth our auditions. Eventually they *did* produce a result. It just happened to be more odd than anything we imagined.

CHAPTER TWELVE

They say that no journey is a bad one
except that which leads to the gallows.

The Goodspeed Opera House is a rambling, 19th-century playhouse high on a bluff overlooking the Connecticut River valley, nearly one hundred miles north of Manhattan. Located in the tiny town of East Haddam, Connecticut, it was built in 1876 by William H. Goodspeed, a prominent local merchant who'd amassed a fortune through shipping and banking investments. Fortunately for posterity, the good Mr. Goodspeed loved music and the theatre almost as much as he loved money. To fully enjoy his retirement, Godspeed built himself a four-story mansion smack alongside one of the most magnificent stretches of the river, and placed a three-hundred-seat theatre inside it. Throughout the Gilded Age, Goodspeed's Opera House regularly featured performances by eminent stars of the day. Every day, steamboats would bring performers and their claques from New York to the East Haddam steamboat landing.

Unfortunately, when Goodspeed died, his dream died with him. The theatre failed. The building was sold to the state of Connecticut, which employed it ignominiously as a warehouse for road-repair equipment. Fifty rough New England winters took their toll. By the late fifties the roof had sprung leaks, the walls were peeling, and the entire building was marked for demolition. Only the intercession of a group of preservation-minded neighbors and a heady influx of cash saved it. On June 18, 1963, it reopened its doors to the public with a performance of *Oh, Lady! Lady!* (whatever *that* might have been).

The restored Goodspeed Opera House is a lovely, small valentine to late Victorian taste. The lobby is barely the size of a closet and is dominated by a sweeping grand staircase. If you make your way behind the stairs, however, you're rewarded with a luxurious sitting-parlor housing a fully equipped bar and featuring a glorious view of the river. The theatre itself is a bandbox, the seats arranged squarely around a nearly wingless stage. Patrons sitting on the sides must twist around to see the performance. It's worth it, for the sound is crystalline and the intimacy inspiring.

The Goodspeed flourishes to this day, presenting at least three musicals every season. Its success is such that it has opened a second theatre, in nearby Chester, Connecticut, dedicated to the development of new musicals. The management also support *Show Music*, a quarterly magazine dedicated entirely to musical theatre.

And all of this success, this fame, stretching nearly 40 years now, is due to a venturesome new musical that opened in the summer of 1965, called *Man of La Mancha*.

Originally it wasn't called that. It was called...I can no longer remember all the titles by which it was called, and in any case I don't want to remember. In my files I have a script marked "Rehearsal—Goodspeed"—and the title on it is *Highway to Glory*, which is one of several titles we went through before reverting to my original.

I've never understood this urge by theatre people to change titles, presumably in the hope of finding a slam-dunk combination of art and commerce in five words or less. Albert Marre kept nagging me to change the title, presumably to something sexier. Mitch Leigh argued for something more marketable—he wanted the play to be called "The Impossible Dream," possibly because there happened to be a promotable song by that title in it.

It was my duty to listen to such suggestions, but not necessarily to agree. *Man of La Mancha* had been the original title of my television play, before David Susskind opted for *I, Don Quixote* as a concession to a presumably dim-witted audience. When it became a play for Broadway, other titles were suggested, but since the production never happened, none of them were perpetuated. In my mind and within the play's intention, the Man of La Mancha was not Don Quixote but Miguel de Cervantes. That's what I wanted the public to infer, and that was the title to which I stubbornly clung in spite of the pressure to change it.

In my experience as well as within the bounds of taste and reason it's the show that makes the title successful, and not the other way around. How, for instance, would you rate *Urinetown* as a title? Or *The Vagina Monologues*? Or *Hairspray*? Before you cast a vote consider that they're all financially successful.

But title aside, the story of how a bunch of hardscrabble Broadway theatre types ended up in an obscure Connecticut river town in the summer of 1965 is an odd one indeed. As a result of our auditions it turned out that the only producer interested in our inspired madman was not interested in being a producer at all. He was Albert Selden, scion of the family owning American Express, and he happened to be chairman of the committee responsible for the museum-restoration of the Goodspeed Opera House. An offer was made by the chairman to present the show at this obscure venue. It was accepted, if only because it was the only offer made.

The plan was to try out the show at Goodspeed at the beginning of summer, go into hiatus while two other musicals were played, then reopen in August to close out the season.

This was only the Goodspeed's third summer, and their first attempt at a world premiere, so they were understandably nervous about it. But the plan had a built-in bonus, for it offered the chance to play, then to revise, then to play again, incorporating the improvements we'd presumably make between runs.

As it turned out, it saved our lives—or at least the life of *Man of La Mancha*. We charged full speed into casting.

For a time we had Rex Harrison as our star, but Harrison's interest chilled when he realized that our songs had to be sung, not spoken. I cannot remember all the others we approached...the list would read like a Who's Who of Actors Equity, but all were unavailable or became so when they read the script. Richard Kiley, proposed by Marre, who'd worked with him in *Kismet,* was perhaps sixth or eighth on our list.

Kiley, arguably, was not a star. He was known as a reliable singer/actor but usually was cast as a second banana. We were running out of time, however, and agreed that under the circumstances he was the best we were able to get.

Metropolitan Opera star Robert Rounseville agreed to play The Padre. His tenor singing voice was pure gold; he was a definite asset.

Ray Middleton, rather surprisingly, accepted the role of The Governor/Innkeeper (in the convention of the play everyone played dual roles). It was a smaller role than Middleton was accustomed to playing, but he'd fallen in love with the play.

We ran into unexpected difficulties in casting Sancho Panza. Seemingly it should have been easy, but suddenly there was a shortage of portly, pragmatic, potato-faced actors. In desperation we settled on an unlikely choice—Irving Jacobson, star of Second Avenue Yiddish Theatre. Irving turned out to be a stroke of serendipity. He was funny, he was agile, he sang well, and despite a trace of lower East Side accent was not only believable but immensely endearing. Irving brought an invaluable asset to the company: his unfailingly optimistic disposition. He'd never been in a flop, he maintained, therefore his mere presence assured success. Irving, utterly lovable, claimed to be 72 years old at the time he entered the cast. He was to continue performing the role of Sancho for the better part of a decade.

Jon Cypher, an excellent singing actor, joined the company, intrigued by the challenge of playing the dual roles of The Duke and Dr. Carrasco. Jon had the profile, the hauteur, the elegance, and the waspish superiority that informed Dr. Carrasco. He had an additional asset, the capability of understudying the Cervantes/Quixote role, which indeed he would play many times for many years.

We ended up with four Broadway leading men. Extraordinary! Few New York productions could boast such an ensemble, much less an obscure theatre in Connecticut.

And now we played out a charade of auditioning singing ladies for the role of Aldonza. It was a cynical activity, for Joe and I and, presumably, Mitch Leigh, knew who was going to play Aldonza. We knew because we'd learned via various informants that Joan Diener, the director's wife, had been taking Spanish dancing lessons for the past six weeks. The charade lay in Marre's gloomy statements that

Joan, wonderful as she might have been in the role, wouldn't possibly be available by reason of demand for her services by others. We went along, expressing our regrets and pressing other candidates on our director, knowing he *must* find them unacceptable until, finally, we'd have to plead with Joan to rescue us by taking the role.

This particular laffer was duly played out. Joan was duly begged to take the role. To no one's astonishment she accepted, and reported for rehearsal wearing Cuban heels and with castanets in hand. Not that Joan was unsuitable—far from it. She had an extraordinary voice with a range of four octaves. She had a spectacular body, a commanding physical presence, and was a hard-working professional. Whatever her initial shortcomings as an actress she worked on them, grew in excellence, and delivered a stellar performance.

The staff we gathered was equally distinguished. Howard Bay, one of Broadway's finest, would be our lighting and scenic designer. Costumes would be by Patton Campbell, and our choreographer would be the tempestuous Jack Cole. The mix of cast and staff was actually quite strange—a figurative crazy quilt of styles—but who knew?—the mix might make an effective brew.

At the beginning of June, 1965, the entire troupe decamped for East Haddam, where it would take up residence for the next three months. Mitch Leigh, of course, was accompanied by his entire *cuadrilla* of orchestrators. As for me, I rented a house on the shores of Lake Bashan, a few miles from the theatre, which became an R&R hangout for the company. The beauteous Ramsay Ames flew in from Spain to join me there and to play hostess for the swimming and barbecue spreads that we held periodically for the ever-hungry actors and crew.

East Haddam was a heavenly place in which to suffer hellish stresses.

Rehearsals began propitiously. The actors, though finding the play an eccentric sort of animal, dove into it with zest and pleasure. In general I avoided rehearsals, both to keep a perspective on progress and also for a more pragmatic reason—I was simultaneously writing a screenplay, which I owed my partners at

MGM. But as I did catch up with rehearsals I noted disturbing deviations from my intentions.

Director Marre evidently didn't trust the concept I considered absolutely basic to the play as written, a concept demanding that all of the action take place within "a prison vault whose furthest reaches are lost in shadow." And that all of the scenes presented by Cervantes be "improvised," using props from Cervantes' theatrical trunk together with whatever trappings might logically be found on the premises. Though this concept was clearly stated in my script, it was initially subverted both by Marre and our designer, Howard Bay. Nor did I have absolute and irrevocable belief in it myself; it was radical and might or might not work. But I did want it tried.

However, I found that Howard Bay was building an elaborate floor through which scenery of all sorts would magically rise up, thus reaching for a theatrical sort of trickery opposed to my concept. When I questioned it, Bay would say only that it was the director's wish. I found other tricks that disturbed me, tricks reaching for a level of convention that indicated a mistrust of the play.

I made no issue of them at the time. We were there, after all, to explore the material, to learn what worked and what didn't, and arguments made prematurely would surely trouble the waters.

This was the situation when we opened at the Goodspeed Opera House on the 28th of June, 1965. Opening night was a benefit for the newly established O'Neill Theatre Center, of nearby Waterford, Connecticut, of which I was a co-founder. The president of the Center was George C. White, an exceptionally enterprising and personable Yale graduate who'd been apprenticed to me at a time I was supervisor of the International Ballet Festival, in Genoa, Italy, years before. George and I had remained close friends, and continue to be up to this very day.

The opening night audience was kind but confused on exactly what it had witnessed. The last half-hour of the play registered strongly, but then, musical or otherwise, it always had. The first act and a half moved erratically. One felt that it beguiled the audience but failed to move them. Without focussed emotion the battle was being lost.

Subsequent audiences were much the same. Clearly we did not have a hit. It was unclear, precisely, what we did have.

The first run at the Goodspeed proved two things: that the play's substance reached the audience with very considerable impact—and that this initial production was seriously flawed. Albert Marre was a good and talented director, but his method of "trying things" was hard on the nerves and used up that most precious of assets—time.

Darion and I fixed gimlet eyes on every performance during that first, three-week run. No longer did we defer politely on matters we felt strongly about. No longer were there abstract discussions of how it might be done this way, or that. For myself, I wrote hard, clear notes taken down on a legal pad at each performance and delivered pre-rehearsal each day to the director. These were typical:

"Kill the scenery and the children"

The magic floor, I felt, destroyed the play's basic premise, aside from the fact that the scenery operated pneumatically, with alarming hisses as it rose or subsided. I wanted to see the play as written, sans any scenery but the basic prison.

There were children in the Gypsy scene. Oddly enough, children were distractingly "real" as contrasted with the stylization of the performance. Added to which they and their parents were a damned nuisance, onstage and off.

"Kill Aldonza's dance"

In her first scene Joan Diener was performing a Spanish dance on a table top, a sort of a *farruca* complete with flashy heelwork and castanets. It was wildly out of character for Aldonza, a kitchen slavey and part-time whore. It did indeed demonstrate Joan's versatility but at the expense of belief.

"Breaches of style"

These were serious. Breaches of style may be one of the most subtle aspects of a musical production and the most difficult to define. But when they happen, the audience knows it instinctually and stops trusting the play. Our style was unusually difficult, beginning as realism and expanding into musical form, but always maintaining believability within that convention. Playing tricks with style could be fatal. This was proved most painfully with our production. It was not a small matter. It could kill us dead. In fact, it was doing so.

"Aldonza's first song is not working"

That first song, as I remember, was "What Kind of Animal Am I?" It was surprisingly sophisticated and self-conscious for "…a kitchen slut reeking of sweat." As far out of character, actually, as her Spanish dance with castanets. It went:

> *What kind of animal am I?*
> *A tiger wild, with knotted jaws,*
> *And if you wander near my cage*
> *Beware my teeth, beware my claws!*

> *The cage is narrow as a tomb.*
> *I cannot run or see the sky,*
> *But in my heart the jungle slumbers,*
> *And I'll be savage 'til I die.*

"The Barber's great—push him further?"

The Barber was played by Gino Conforti, who was also the original Fiddler in *Fiddler On The Roof*. Gino was a talented mime and comedian. I found him delightful, as did the audience. Gino would also improvise lines, some of them so funny that I appropriated them and put them in the script: e.g., spoken to Quixote, "Forgive me, Your Bigness!"

"Stop Disneyfying the horses!"

Animals on stage are treacherous, whether real or human. In our case they were played by two Flamenco dancers. They tend to become "cute." They get easy laughs and there's a temptation to push them further, which is what we were doing.

There were multiple notes such as this—most small, some large, at each performance. But the most contentious, surely, was this:

"Why not eliminate the intermission?"

This was a truly radical notion. No musical had ever done so. Intermissions were considered sacred, for drinks, chats, smokes, and bathroom breaks. But I observed something interesting, as did Marre—as the performance began to work better, it became almost hypnotic. The play depended upon certain fragile inventions for a large part of its impact, none more important than that Cervantes is improvising an entertainment, holding the prisoners in a calculated spell in which the audience, too, must be held. The spell was beginning to work as intended—until shattered by the intermission. I pointed out that my original play had been written without one. Indeed, then or ever since I didn't know a logical place to put one.

The arguments in opposition were surprisingly passionate. "It's never been done," for instance, to which I replied, "Good reason for doing it."

"You can't make an audience sit that long without a break."

"How long does a movie run?" I inquired. "Two hours? Our running time is about the same."

"Yes, but theatregoers *expect* an intermission. To smoke, schmooze, take a bathroom break."

"Okay, warn them in advance. Make an announcement, put a sign in the lobby. The bathrooms aren't crowded before a performance, only after."

The most potent argument of all: "We'll lose the bar business!" To which I had no answer except a flabby, "Okay, so we lose it."

We killed the scenery, and in its place was a simple but strong architectural structure with only one moving piece, a staircase to the outer world. We killed the children. Aldonza was stopped from dancing. "What Kind of Animal Am I?" was replaced by "It's All the Same." Other songs were deleted or revised, and Mitch Leigh's orchestra was split stereophonically and, since there was no orchestra pit, placed in house boxes, left and right. Script alterations were made daily, together with cuts and enrichments of given moments. The Barber was set free and the horses contained. *And we got rid of the intermission!*

The actors had taken hold of the altered ingredients and were rehearsing with pleasure and conviction.

Everybody worked, every day, and the authors on their days off, too, revising, refining, improving.

We opened our improved version of *Man of La Mancha* at the Goodspeed Opera House in mid-August for a run of three weeks. Now it played with power and impact. Audiences were weeping copiously at the death of Quixote, then rising in surge of emotion to applaud the choral finale of "The Impossible Dream." For the first time, we suspected we might have a hit.

Our creative team had spent two years, working very hard, to make this happen. I myself had spent much longer—dating back to 1959, the birth of the original idea, of the television play— writing and rewriting my work, coaxing out the drama while assigning those finest moments that would be transmuted into musical theatre. Joe Darion and Mitch Leigh, through unceasing experimentation, had woven the songs into a musical tapestry. Now Richard Kiley, Joan Diener, and our excellent company of actors were showing the results of their months of work, delving into the material, deepening and constantly improving their characterizations. The costumes had been designed and the set re-designed. All of this plus an audience reacting enthusiastically made *Man of La Mancha* tantalizingly real. All of us were happy with our accomplishment, how far we'd come, how warmly we were now being welcomed.

But East Haddam isn't New York. Three hundred people for twenty nights isn't fifteen hundred people eight times a week. A newborn show is a mighty deed, but mightier still is the potential if, indeed, it has potential at all.

The word had gone out that something extraordinary was happening in an obscure Connecticut town. Tickets started going fast; we were going to be sold out for the remainder of the run. More important, New Yorkers were making reservations. The mavens of show business had become aware of the Miracle in East Haddam and were making the trip to see for themselves.

And the media, as well.

John Chapman of the New York *Daily News* wrote: "I should like to see *Man of La Mancha* in a full-scale Broadway production with about the same cast and with full orchestrations...but this would be the equivalent to wishing that the backers would lose $400,000 or so. This musical has class and character—but it is the story of a crazy, dying old man and it has no young love romance. It would be a sober risk."

Others played variations on the same theme. We had excellence, we had class, we had character, but East Haddam wasn't New York, and we couldn't possibly generate the pizzazz to make it in the Big Time.

Nor were any of the Big Time producers who came to see our production any more optimistic. They were full of praise, to be sure, but it was praise blended with regret. They judged our show was Art, a freak that might succeed in East Haddam but not on the Street. Even in retrospect it was very strange that, despite the evidence of a wildly responsive audience, they could offer us no hope—and certainly no money, of which we had an enormous lack.

Everyone associated with *Man of La Mancha* knew it was a risky venture. None were so bold (openly, at least) as to hold out hope of a life for the show beyond Connecticut, even as the quality and originality of its material became apparent. If there were dreams of fame and fortune, we kept them to ourselves. Still, there's no doubt we were saddened when it looked as though East Haddam might be far as we were going.

But even as our time was running out, the fickle finger of fate lifted to touch us once more.

It happened post-performance one evening, when a genial, smiling fellow wandered backstage and asked if we had the money to move this show to New York. When we told him "No," he said, "I've got thirty thousand dollars that isn't working. Would that help?"

Almost in a chorus we cried out, "You're the producer!"

Albert Selden, who hadn't wanted to produce this or any other show up to this point, sighed and said, "Well, I'm in so deep I might as well go deeper."

Thus the producing team of Selden and James was born. It was to have a long and distinguished life.

We were on our way to New York. But not, as it turned out, to Broadway.

CHAPTER THIRTEEN

Whether the stone hits the pitcher
or the pitcher hits the stone,
it's going to be bad for the pitcher.

The show fulfilled the first of our ambitions by going to New York. But no Broadway theatre would have us. We were considered an undesirable tenant, not disgraceful but scheduled at best to become a *succès d'estime,* which, in New York, is a polite phrase for a loser.

The only theatre we could get was available for a good reason — no one else would have it. It was a long mile from Broadway, a rattletrap building in an awkward location. But the joke was on the evil spirit who'd been assigned to bring us misfortune. At this turn it made a booboo in our favor.

At which point we almost lost our star. In a reminiscence published by the magazine, *In Theater,* Mitch Leigh recalled:

"I remember that, after we did it up at Goodspeed his (Kiley's) agent said, 'Well, Richard, you've done your little summer thing, now let's move on.' Richard wanted to stay with the show, but his agent tried to talk him out of it. When Richard won the Tony Award for *La Mancha,* I was sitting at his table with him and his agent. The agent had this self-satisfied look on his face, which amused me because, if it wasn't for Richard's own persistence, his agent would never have let him continue in the role."

No work of art can exist in a vacuum, nor can success occur without some confluence brought about by the zeitgeist into which it is born. *Man of La Mancha* was no exception. It was lucky to have been written in the sixties and to have played not on Broadway but in Greenwich Village.

The late fifties and early sixties were extraordinarily fervent times to be working in the arts. In painting and sculpture, abstraction was beginning to overtake realism. Artists such as Jackson Pollock and Willem De Kooning were inventing a visual vocabulary of violent blotches of color and angry, almost ugly shapes, in an attempt to try to capture on canvas the excitement and unsettled feeling of living in America in an age of wild prosperity, changing values, and omnipresent nuclear threat. In popular music, the reassuring crooning of the war years was giving way to the angry pulse of rock 'n' roll and the dissonance of modern jazz. All of these separate strands—the novelty, the richness of subject, and the freedom of expression—were equally present in the world of theatre.

The heart of this new theatre in America, from approximately 1950 to 1970, was Greenwich Village in New York City. A new category of stage production, known as Off-Broadway, was born. Off-Broadway actually was not new—there'd been professional productions of experimental plays and musicals in Greenwich Village since the twenties. Eugene O'Neill wrote for the Provincetown Players, who wintered in New York. In the thirties, playwright Clifford Odets and director Harold Clurman taught classes and held readings in the Village. The Village was the focus of forms too adventurous, too experimental, too radical for uptown.

But it wasn't until after the Second World War, when commercial pressures made uptown production too expensive for many companies, that the Village truly began to flourish as a source of new theatrical talent. Theatres and companies sprang up all over lower Manhattan, and to differentiate them from their more established colleagues uptown critics began to refer to them collectively as "Off-Broadway." (This isn't quite the same as the current "Off-Broadway," which is a semi-legal distinction created to fit union rules and has more to do with the size of the house and specific geographic location than with artistic goals.)

A fervent mixture of radical interpretations of classics and startling new shows occurred Off-Broadway. One year, you could see a new production of Bertolt Brecht and Kurt Weill's *The Three Penny Opera*, the next, a new play by Beckett. The simple pleasures of Harvey Schmidt and Tom Jones' *The Fantasticks* thrived alongside the distinctly more difficult *The Balcony* by Jean Genet. New stars lit up the stage by the minute—Colleen Dewhurst, Geraldine Page, Dustin Hoffman, George C. Scott, and James Earl Jones all began their illustrious careers on the Off-Broadway stage. Add to this mix the unprecedented number of talented writers drawn to New York to work in television and journalism, and the stage was set for a creative revolution.

Furthermore, Greenwich Village itself was becoming a home to (and a symbol of) the Age of Aquarius. All the poster-board issues of the day—changes in sexual behavior, experimentation with drugs, involvement with radical politics, and the empowerment of the young and the black—were visible every day on the sidewalks of the Village, an unmistakable advertisement for independence of the mind. One could not walk the length of Bleecker Street without passing a gay bar, a head shop, a used record shop, a cooperative market, a hippie commune, or a bum's dive. New voices of expression erupted from the streets daily—the *Village Voice*, Julian Beck and Judith Molina's Living Theatre, the folk-music mecca, The Bitter End, comedic satirists such as Lenny Bruce and Mort Sahl. In the light of these new forms and landscape, the future seemed bright but highly uncertain.

In November of 1965, *Man of La Mancha* slipped into this whirlpool of social change the way a slightly dotty aunt would behave at a love-in: curious, but reserved. I, personally, had spent too many years of my youth riding the rails and testing the lower depths to find this newfound celebration of bohemia unique or entirely charming. Joe Darion, Mitch Leigh, and Albert Marre were all Jewish boys from Brooklyn, expensively educated professionals dedicated to their craft. None was likely to suggest giving Don Quixote a hit of marijuana to get in tune with the times, nor was I.

Still, the Knight of the Woeful Countenance is a world-class symbol of nonconformity, an idealist, posited against an overly rational, cynical age. He believes in love's power to prevail over all challenges, even death. And he imagines the world not as it is but as it might be.

Don Quixote is a Holy Fool, one of the classic creations of literature, and a radical one for this particular place and time. In this respect, *Man of La Mancha* was a child of the fifties and the sixties, an example of lucky timing that brought resonance to the already timeless import of the play.

Nevertheless, beyond the $100,000 contributed by Selden and James, there was great difficulty in raising the financing. I hurriedly finished my screenplay, collected from MGM, and invested $25,000 of my own money in the production. Darion and Leigh secured an advance against publication of the music and contributed to the kitty. Carter de Haven, of the well-known theatrical family, made a welcome investment as did a few—a very few—friends of Albert Selden, and we were over the top.

Still, on Broadway there was no theatre available for an oddball musical with a production budget of $200,000, which is why, in desperation, we accepted an equally oddball theatre that was available only because no one wanted it. It was the ANTA Washington Square, on West Fourth Street, a temporary structure hastily tossed together to serve Elia Kazan's acting company until Lincoln Square was ready.

There were good reasons no one wanted it. More of a shed than a theatre, it had no proscenium. No curtain. No fly-loft. No provision for scenery and no proper stage. Nor was there an orchestra pit; forced to improvise, we split our orchestra (as we'd done in East Haddam) into two units, stashed in the wings 50 feet apart, an arrangement that drove the conductor dangerously close to a mental breakdown but later garnered praise for the production's "stereophonic effects."

We discovered a further horror. The depth of stage didn't allow for a crossover, meaning that actors would be marooned on whichever side of the stage they began the performance—short of leaving the theatre and running desperately around the block.

This was unacceptable, so we commenced the excavation of a warren of tunnels *beneath* the stage to meet the problem—only to find ourselves encountering un-coffined skeletons wrapped in moldering cerements. Authorities were called in. They ascertained that we had, in fact, collided with a potter's field dating from the Plague of 1798 when our site was marshland north of the city.

We detoured around the burial grounds and resumed our mole-work, only to encounter a further hazard—we struck water. A city

engineer, consulting antique maps, ascertained that we'd rediscov-
ered Minetta Brook, which once flowed merrily through present-day
Greenwich Village. Helpfully, he suggested we might wish to sell
water instead of entertainment, but should that lack appeal, to exca-
vate less deeply. We took heed and our tunnels were completed.

Later, during performances, I dreamed of magically levering up
the stage, as *Sunset Boulevard* was to do years later, whereby the
audience might enjoy the sight of our troglodytic performers
scuttling about like moles underground.

Were we finished with our troubles? Not quite. The first time
it rained we made a discovery: rain falling on our tin roof didn't add
a soothing susurrus to the orchestrations as we'd anticipated; it
resounded like billiard balls cascading onto a tympanum overhead.
So loudly, in fact, that on occasion it was necessary to suspend
performance and ask the audience to sit with folded hands until the
skies permitted us to continue.

Our orchestra at the Goodspeed had consisted of eight musicians.
At the ANTA we doubled it to sixteen. There were no strings other
than "motivated" guitar. The massed brasses made a brave, martial
sound in keeping with Quixote's crusade.

Jack Cole felt slighted for lack of opportunity to show the sort
of choreography of which he was capable. Flamenco rhythms for
horses and belly dances for Gypsies were all very well, but painfully
limited for a choreographer of such talent. I decided to give him
his opening for a major piece in the spot replacing the Gypsy
sequence—itself an improvisation—by a scene in which Quixote
encounters a troupe of players who may or may not be what they
seem. In its implications the scene had a certain darkness about
it, but Cole seized upon it with delight and darkened it much
further than the shade I'd intended. In his interpretation it became,
in fact, a sort of Black Mass, frightening and on the edge of perverse
violence.

Richard Kiley, who was at its center, did something uncharac-
teristic. He stopped in the midst of rehearsal, came forward, and
said, "I can't do it," which he then amended more firmly to, "I won't
do it."

Kiley was a Catholic, lapsed, it's true, and disillusioned by the

Church's hieratical leadership. But he was deeply troubled by the scene's implications, and when he made his protest, I said to Cole, "Cancel it. Now."

The last thing I wanted in *Man of La Mancha* was any invocation of religion. Even though I avoided such references as narrowly as had Cervantes, devout Christians have insisted on seeing a Christ parallel in Quixote. There isn't any, and I object to such interpretation.

Quixote is, if anything, a humanist, denying all but personal responsibility for his thoughts and actions. Over the years I've received numerous letters pointing out the Christ-like qualities in Quixote and praising the "Christian philosophy of the play." Well, one sees what he has need to see, and I deny such philosophy. I deny any religious propensities at all.

On November 14, 1993, Kiley wrote a letter on the subject of Catholicism, of which I received a copy:

> After ten years of Catholic education by Dominicans, Carmelites and Jesuits, I left the church at the age of 18—and 53 years later I am still amazed at the arrogance and hubris of the hierarchy of that institution. Of course I know many lowly priests and nuns who are laboring lovingly at the bottom of its heap—but the "brass" are as rotten—(no, more rotten—because they claim to act in God's name) as any back-room gang in Washington, D.C. And I mean them all, right up to the Vatican. Can you imagine that humble carpenter from Nazareth walking through the obscenely opulent halls in Rome, and being told that all this is done in his name?

Bravo, Richard...for bringing the same conviction to your personal beliefs as you did to the mindset of Don Quixote.

Jack Cole never got his chance to show the range of his talent in *Man of La Mancha*. There was much movement in the play but simply no opening for major choreography. He took his frustration out, in a way, by adding shock to the abduction of Aldonza, an indulgence in violence that has always distressed me. The abduction is not intended to be a rape. Its essence is humiliation, the muleteers working their revenge on Aldonza for siding with Quixote. But

Cole added an entirely subjective ingredient: he had no fondness for women, and his approach to that scene has caused a thousand Aldonzas to suffer insults to their flesh.

Even though theatre is fundamentally collaborative, I've always thought collaboration something like a three-headed snake. Freakish at best. And collaboration on a musical doubly so, except in the case of two halves making a whole. Rodgers and Hammerstein. Kander and Ebb...no, not even the excellent Kander and Ebb, since neither of them is the "bookwriter," and their rare failures happen for that reason. What value has a handsome façade if the architecture won't support it? Hammerstein had spoken hard-edged truth when he answered that question concerning the primacy of music or lyrics with, "Neither. The book."

We, the authors, cast, musicians, and crew, had a couple weeks in which to rehearse and to adapt the show to our eccentric theatre. We went to work at high intensity, refining, adapting the work to our peculiar theatre so that we could "freeze" the performance. It was perhaps the only true collaboration of the whole parade, and it was driven by necessity — so little time, so much to do, so much at stake.

Our relationships otherwise were ego-driven and self-seeking. Albert Marre and Mitch Leigh were tightly allied not only in a financial but in a master-apprentice relationship, with Marre the master. Leigh was to remain Marre's partner until the relationship shattered under stress of failure that, oddly enough, was the product of their initial success.

The actors, as always, bonded with the director, for actors are inherently dependent upon a parental figure to aid, praise, and, in general, to instill the confidence they lack.

Darion and I, not inherently collaborators, worked closely together simply because we were "simpatico" and shared a healthy and humorous skepticism as to life itself.

Albie Marre's birth name was Albert Moshinsky. He was a good director, but would have made a better politician. He had his own agendas. We never quite knew what they were, nor what really went on in his mind.

Marre, educated at Harvard, had taken degrees in an ill-mated pair of subjects — theatre and the law. It was an unhappy confluence for those who had to deal with him in his dual capacity of director and co-producer. It was irrelevant that Marre never wrote a word of *Man of La Mancha;* by demand he became "Collaborating Author" of the play, inheriting a portion of the authors' royalties in addition to his own. But Albie's colliding talents, I think, did him harm.

Misfortune was due to have one more whack at us. On November 9, 1965, on the occasion of our first dress rehearsal, at about 5 o'clock in the evening, all the lights in the theatre went out. We waited. And waited. Everyone was warned to stand still, where they were. Then we learned, via a crew member's transistor radio, that the blackout had targeted not merely our theatre but all of New York. A bit later we learned it was more than merely New York; somewhere in Canada a switch box had failed, plunging the entire Eastern seaboard into darkness. There was no hint as to how long it would last. There was no precedent by which to measure it.

When it became evident we'd have no dress rehearsal, we organized carpools to return the cast and crew to their homes, as all public transportation had come to a halt. I rode shotgun with Mitch Leigh in his green Rolls Royce as we delivered actors without personal transportation to their homes.

It was an eerie experience. New York was a city bewitched... dark, strangely silent, and of course without streetlights or traffic signals. The only illumination came from automobile headlights, of which there were fewer and fewer as evening darkened into night. Pedestrians desperate for transportation stood in the streets, trying to wave us down, to get a ride or commandeer the car. We kept the doors locked against possible attack.

Mitch, after doing yeoman service, dropped me off last of all. I climbed the thirteen flights to my floor, guided by a flashlight wielded by my neighbors from the penthouse adjoining mine. My neighbors were the Hormans, good people who soon were to face a tragic crisis and an unwanted sort of fame when their son became one of the "disappeared" in Chile. A book and a movie, *Missing,* recorded their obsessive search and their maddening frustration by two governments.

The power blackout lasted until 10 o'clock the next morning. Then the horror stories poured in...people trapped in stalled elevators for seventeen hours…subway trains full of rush hour passengers stopped in darkness…the profound dislocation of a giant city paralyzed without power.

No clear reason for the power failure ever was given. It was known that an interrupted power feed from Canada was the source of the trouble, but little else was certain—except that it might happen again.

At the ANTA Washington Square we made do without a dress rehearsal and played our first preview the next evening to an audience of fewer than 50 people. The music and voices echoed cavernously in our barn, which seated some eleven hundred. At the end of the performance our 50 customers rose as one, cheering the cast and the play, but the effect was more wistful than exhilarating.

We had almost no advance sale. The show was simply too offbeat to be explained in advertising capsules. But now began the miracle called "word-of-mouth." At the second preview our audience had doubled, and at succeeding previews there were increases. It seemed evident that the people who'd seen it were phoning others—and probably adding, "See it—quick."

Opening nights are bumps in the road to success. They're big bumps, and inevitably somebody trips over them. In an ideal world of theatre, the opening night is set when the director, producer, and cast feel they're ready to present their work to a discriminating public, and not before. But openings are seldom ideally arranged. Ready or not, a show must open to draw reviews and, hopefully, business. Budgetary and seasonal considerations intrude. Our production had been budgeted at $200,000, and we'd gone $20,000 over.

Our opening night was November 22, 1965, two years to the day from the assassination of President John F. Kennedy. We'd experienced blackouts, empty rows of seats, and sorrow-filled anniversaries—none of them signals for optimism.

All these matters were on our minds on that date. True, the crowds had improved since the first previews. But, as Richard Kiley observed, "There were nights you could have shot deer in that theatre." The money was running out, and with the holiday season approaching, everyone's attention would soon be turning to shopping, parties, and snowstorms.

Ready or not, *Man of La Mancha* had to be submitted to the critics.

Our intrepid producers, Hal James and Albert Selden, had reserved a party room at One Fifth Avenue for post-opening celebration — or obsequies — as it might turn out. With determination equal to the great Manchegan — but considerably less deluded — we assembled there, more or less stoically, post-performance, to await our fate.

CHAPTER FOURTEEN

Fortune's wheel turns faster than that of a mill.

There are countless accounts of opening nights, stage and screen, but nothing exceeds the excitement of a New York opening night. Hearts pound, palms sweat, breath comes short. Actors mumble their lines in terminal panic, directors scream post-last-minute instructions; the theatre is a din of cacophony as musicians play their tune-up riffs. Lighting and sound technicians are in a frenzy of final fixes. Slowly, out of this bewilderment, chaos coalesces into a disciplined sort of splendor.

Don't you believe it.

The emotions one feels are more like fear and loathing. The body feels numb and alienated. There's a desire to self-medicate at the nearest bar, hoping the mind will transport itself to more serene regions in a surge of self-protection. One is seeking indifference, not excitement. Why? Because one's commitment has been made and now is graven in stone. The book of your efforts has been written and printed. You've had your shot at the brass ring. Now the twin beasts known as Audience and Critics will paw over the corpus of your creation, and nothing may interpose or protect you from their mercies.

It is well known that many a musical has both opened and closed on the same night and that the only beneficiaries are tax accountants. Show business requires strong stomachs.

Excitement? Not at all. The recognition that your fate is in the hands of others and that you've given over control isn't a matter for excitement but for resignation.

That's how I felt on the night *Man of La Mancha* opened. That's how I've felt on the nights that any and all of my shows have opened.

That's why I've never seen the opening performance of a show of mine, though I've usually been nearby in some quiet drinkery.

Most creators make the claim that they create for the sake of the work itself, that the rewards of success are secondary. The claim is specious, no more than self-protection talking, the armoring of the ego against verbal and written missiles fired by audience and critics. Still there are the realities attached to the efforts of creation. There may be genuine sincerity, there may be craft and even talent, and there may be — or in the case of *Man of La Mancha,* there definitely was — the conviction among certain of the participants that the worth of the project was at bottom more important than concern for its commercial success.

As it turned out, my co-creators and I didn't have to worry whether our message would be understood. The thunderous applause, the continuing ovation at the conclusion of performance gave evidence that it had been — at least by the audience. The critics were yet to be heard from.

What I didn't dream, at the time, was how this evening was going to change my life, or that there'd be times when I'd wish the whole thing had never happened.

But who could anticipate anything of the sort at this moment? It was time to celebrate — not success, just the achievement of having gotten the damned thing open.

The post-premiere champagne supper at the famous old Fifth Avenue Hotel was also attended by a busload of well-wishers from The Friends of the Goodspeed Opera House, who'd driven down from Connecticut. The admission tickets cost the entrants "Not one doubloon." Miguel de Cervantes himself authorized the entry cards; at least so they read.

Our company party was subdued. Fortified by food and booze, guests began a long vigil awaiting verdicts from the jury of critics. Though the audience had given the cast a standing ovation, standing ovations had become standard practice for opening nights. Critics automatically discounted or even resented them.

At the party we drank sparingly and talked softly of unrelated matters, evading the matter at hand, waiting for the first reviews to come in. About the room TV sets were tuned to the appropriate stations.

The first review, on NBC television, was by Edward Newman. It was condescending, caustic, and mercifully brief. He reviewed the leading lady's bust, which he found admirable. As for the show, he simply dismissed it, suggesting, "Don't bother, after Saturday night it won't be there."

I'd worked too hard, too long, and invested too much emotion to bear with being dismissed in terms of cheap sarcasm. Exhaustion struck, and my heart slumped down into my shoes. I seized a bottle of Scotch by its neck and headed for the exit. Joe Darion, seeing my intention, intercepted me. "Don't do that," said Joe. "We've come all this way...if we're going to sink, let's sink together."

He was right, of course, and I was properly ashamed. I returned to the party so that we could sink together.

The next review was a bit different. "An authentic masterpiece has been born," it began. "Ride, walk or crawl to the ANTA Washington Square where a musical play called *Man of La Mancha* has just opened. Get there any way you can, but *don't miss it!*"

The following air-reviews were equally enthusiastic. In fact, they were ecstatic. But the print reviews counted most, and shortly they began to come in.

The realization of one's worst nightmare was replaced by the giddiness and sense of unreality that followed. The reviews, with few exceptions, were studded with superlatives. Adjectives normally used sparingly were trotted out for this phenomenon. The reviews glowed, they admired, they praised in language rarely employed by critics. They sounded as though our press agent had written them — except he wouldn't have dared go so far.

Howard Taubman, then reviewing for *The New York Times*, clearly was confused by the unconventionality of the play and just as clearly was in a state of wonderment. With relief, he settled upon Dick Kiley's performance as being of inarguable splendor: "He is admirably credible—a mad, gallant, affecting figure who has honestly materialized out of the pages of Cervantes."

Though equivocal, or simply uncomprehending about the play itself, still he came down clearly in its favor and gave our press agent usable quotes: "At its best it is audacious in conception and, tasteful in execution."

Taubman concluded his review by saying, "Whatever concessions *Man of La Mancha* has made to easy popularity, it has not filled the stage with an extraneous chorus line or turned Don Quixote into an oafish clown. One does not expect complete fidelity to Cervantes outside his pages—who reads him these days?—but there are charm, gallantry and a delicacy of spirit in this reincarnation of Quixote."

If I were to make answer—but of course one doesn't make answer to critics, if only because they have the inclination and the means to have the final, crushing, last word—it would be: "I wonder, Mr. Taubman, if your question 'Who reads him these days?' isn't applicable to you yourself? Have you read *Don Quixote*? I'll wager two weeks' royalties you haven't. Otherwise you'd have detected that my play isn't an adaptation of the novel, or ever pretends to be. It's exactly what I intended—a tribute to the tough and tender spirit of Miguel de Cervantes, invoking some of the products of his imagination. How curious that not only you but the great majority of your colleagues didn't catch on. Have none of you read *Don Quixote*?"

I hope that Cervantes, smiling ironically from his cushions on Mount Parnassus, is enjoying the joke.

John Chapman, of the New York *Daily News*, who'd championed the show during its Connecticut tryout, was pleased to point out his prescience: "I was impressed by it then, but expressed a lingering doubt that it could tilt with Broadway. That doubt vanished last night, in one puff." He went on to say, "*Man of La Mancha* is an exquisite musical play—the finest and most original work in our theatre since *Fiddler On The Roof.* As Wasserman magically arranges affairs, *La Mancha* moves enthrallingly from an imaginative beginning to a heart-wrenching end..."

The New York *Post*'s critic, Richard Watts Jr. went quite overboard: "*Man of La Mancha,* Dale Wasserman's new musical adaptation of *Don Quixote,* is a triumph of creative imagination and stagecraft...It is beautiful visually and in its story telling, charming in its score, excellently acted."

There were also the haters. In a pattern that was to repeat itself down the years, those who didn't love the show hated it with an incomprehensible intensity, as though some profound personal insult had been offered. I never quite understood this. I know it had much to do with the philosophy expressed in certain speeches, as in Don Quixote's meditations on the night before he's to be knighted, which state a positive humanist philosophy. Or in his seemingly simplistic answers to challenging questions. Or his presuming to offer answers to such questions at all. May I quote?

ALDONZA (*To* QUIXOTE) Why do you do these things?
DON QUIXOTE What things, my lady?
ALDONZA These ridiculous — the things you do!
DON QUIXOTE I hope to add some measure of grace to the world.
ALDONZA The world's a dung heap and we are maggots that crawl
   upon it!

There's one of the exchanges. We're maggots, or we're hoping to add some measure of grace to the world. We have a choice.

Recently I found out there's an ancient Hebrew phrase, *tikkun olam,* to the same effect — in return for being granted the gift of life we have an obligation to improve the world. Lovely.

I was aware from the beginning that a theatre piece shaped in the form of an entertainment takes dangerous chances in putting forward any clear-cut philosophies at all. If you offer no targets, they'll launch no arrows. This is basic.

Other rules: it's always safe to preach to the choir. Or, one can't miss by setting fire to straw men. Or…but one can go on with these.

Martin Gottfried, writing for *Womens Wear Daily,* was one of those who hated *Man of La Mancha* with puzzling passion. He continued to hate it, not for a day but for years to come. At every opportunity he'd renew his hatred, even when he lacked a forum through which to express it. He wrote with prejudice, with waspish venom, and with considerable inaccuracy.

He'd written in praise of Robert Rounseville's "glorious baritone voice." Well and good — except that Rounseville wasn't a baritone at all; he was a tenor, and quite a famous one at that. Gottfried and I knew each other personally, so I sent him a note calling attention to this. My note was gentle, except that by inference it may have suggested that Gottfried's ear was possibly some alloy of tin. In addition, Gottfried had committed a journalistic sin even more offensive: he'd misquoted a lyric to demonstrate the banality of the show's lyrics in general, specifically a perfectly awful song that begins,

To dream the undreamable dream . . .

The first sin, for a journalist, was merely venial; he'd gotten his facts wrong. The second was mortal — he'd misquoted Darion's lyric to prove his point, which my note pointed out. Humiliating a critic in his own rag is, of course, an injudicious move, so Gottfried lashed out at me again and again, calling the play " . . . a pretty soggy rut . . . with the flimsiest of dramatic structures."

Years later, when *Man of La Mancha* had sailed past its one-thousandth performance, in a book called *Opening Nights*, Gottfried renewed and restated his loathing for the show and, by implication, his certainty that it must fail. In his book he complained once again of "being taken to task in a bitchy letter from Wasserman."

"The thing that kills me," he wrote, "was that while his script remained skimpy and pretentious, there he was, armed with my mistakes, irrelevant though they were. He could (and did) accuse me of having a tin ear, and obviously he was right."

Critics. Well, some of them.

Hoffman, writing in *The Hollywood Reporter*, checked in with, "It's not difficult to butcher Cervantes' *Don Quixote*. But to make it a triumphant success, and as a musical play, is indeed an extraordinary accomplishment. Dale Wasserman has performed this miraculous feat in *Man of La Mancha*."

Norman Nadel, of the New York *World-Telegram*, sang notes even higher. Under the headline, La Mancha: A Dream of a Musical, Nadel wrote, "To reach the unreachable star — what a soaring aspiration for an indestructible dreamer, and what a glorious summation for a bold and beautiful new musical!" Calling the show a feast for the eyes and ears: "*Man of La Mancha* mates theatre and music with excitement and invention…The show is more like Leonard Bernstein's *Candide* than a conventional musical." Considering my respect for *Candide*, this was praise indeed.

Like Gottfried, other critics were less than euphoric. *Playboy*, for instance, took me to task, saying, "A musical based on Cervantes' *Don Quixote* would seem to guarantee a good book but not necessarily a good score. Surprisingly, it turns out the other way around. Playwright Dale Wasserman has been inventive enough to cast the Quixote adventures in a Cervantes framework. Unfortunately, Wasserman has been unable to capture the flavor of the insanely romantic, madly funny nut-errant. Too often he simplifies and sentimentalizes instead of hardening and illuminating." *Playboy* being *Playboy*, however, the nameless critic did enjoy the performance of Joan Diener, "—whose neckline never stops plunging."

Other magazines, having more time, offered more considered opinions. Emory Lewis, of *Cue*, weighed in with: "The best musical of the season! A luminous, touching and melodic double portrait of Cervantes and Don Quixote. Dale Wasserman has magically woven together the life of the author and scenes from his masterwork to create a work of distinction."

The National Review offered comments by Mrs. William F. Buckley, who enjoyed the show in general but deplored, "The major failure of the show, a lapse of taste as sudden as it is offensive, in two dance sequences." She found them "unpardonably gross" and dragged in for shock value, "…wrong artistically since *Don Quixote* is free of garden variety vulgarity." Clearly here's another who hasn't read *Don Quixote*, which I found to be gross at times, and replete with "garden variety vulgarity."

Henry Hewes, writing in *The Saturday Review*, spoke as follows: "In a way this musical is itself an example of attempting the impossible. For although what it has achieved at times comes perilously close to old-fashioned operetta, to children's theatre, to spectacle for its own sake, and even to anachronistic vaudeville humor, we tend to forgive its impurities… *Man of La Mancha* lives gloriously in the theatre, and that is enough."

But one article in particular seemed most accurately to articulate *La Mancha*'s significance in context of its time. The April 8,

1966 edition of *Life* displayed All-American Rhodes Scholar and Army Captain Pete Dawkins in military fatigues and red beret, being honored for mastering the delicate art of "advising" South Vietnamese troops. The duality of the two warriors may have been lost on the public of that time, but under the title "The Unconquerable Quixote," a five-page photo essay began with a full-page picture of Richard Kiley, a wild man's look in his eyes, pointing his out-of-focus sword directly at the reader. The banner trumpets, "Cervantes' addled knight triumphs on stage!"

Tom Prideaux's commentary—perhaps because it was exempt from meeting the time pressure of opening night deadlines and thereby given the luxury of reflection—was rich in insights as to why the play worked, why it was popular, and why relevant to the times.

"The show has tapped a wider kind of audience than Broadway usually attracts," he wrote. "People are taken in by the philosophy of *La Mancha* and by its unabashed sentiment. After a slow start, it has built into an extraordinary, rule-defying hit, that reveals some telling facts not only about popular entertainment but about the temper of our times."

In discussing the tussle between reality and illusion in the musical, he noted, "There's no doubt at all in the new show that illusion and the indomitable Don win out. But what is surprising and, I feel, encouraging is that Illusion wins over the audience. Reality is not precisely in the doghouse. But by the time *Man of La Mancha* is over, the whole theatre is in a happy metaphysical mood, sure that Illusion is part and partner to Reality."

Prideaux declares, "Do they call that entertainment? Yes they do. And it is making *Man of La Mancha* the season's most outstanding musical—a metaphysical smasheroo."

Tom Prideaux accurately captured the basic intentions within the play, intentions that prize truth over facts. All of the critics had some type of insight into the meaning of the play, whether they liked it or not. All found elements of aggressive idealism during an opening night that had, coincidentally, occurred on that second anniversary of the loss of American innocence.

A pattern was established. The show would get brickbats or bouquets, but rarely anything in between. The majority of the critics, however, hailed *Man of La Mancha* as exciting "total theatre" and predicted a successful run. None had the prescience to understand the degree to which this opus, born of a modest television play, would become part of theatre history and its phrases etched into our psyche.

The reviews didn't create an instant hit. The public remained wary of the show and of its theatre's location, except for those being telephoned or told by friends who'd already attended. The box office built steadily, but it was five weeks before we had need of the THIS PERFORMANCE SOLD OUT sign. Thereafter it became a fixture.

Soon $15 tickets to *Man of La Mancha* were being scalped for $50. A bit later they were going at $100 and hard to get at any price.

At the end of a year's run, members of our box office and managerial staff were being indicted by the District Attorney of New York for dealing in ice. "Ice," if you aren't hip to the lingo, is show business slang for premiums paid for tickets in hot demand, and is strictly illegal.

And another year later, sad to tell, our box-office treasurer, Thomas Smith, was being sentenced to prison.

And almost four years later, New York University, which owned the land on which our theatre stood, regretfully informed us we must vacate as they needed to put up an office building in its place.

At last *Man of La Mancha* was forced to move from its beloved rattletrap theatre to a splendid Broadway playhouse, the Martin Beck, where, as I write this in 2003, it is playing again. We proposed to make the move in a parade of our costumed actors and their spavined steeds up Broadway from Fourth to Forty-fifth Street, but the City of New York denied us a permit, claiming we'd disrupt traffic. Which was what we'd fully intended to do.

There are unexpected fringe benefits of and consequences to an over-the-top smasheroo like *Man of La Mancha*. Not all of them pleasant. Which is an understatement. I would learn that they range from the distracting to the disastrous.

CHAPTER FIFTEEN

Manners change when honors come.

Robert S. Sennett isn't a critic but a chronicler of musical theatre. He's blessed by objectivity and scholarship, advantages I lack. According to Sennett's evaluation of *Man of La Mancha*:

> For all of its relevance as a play about the validity, the necessity, of non-conformity, *Man of La Mancha* was in fact a Broadway, not an off-Broadway show. Although it opened in Greenwich Village, at the ANTA Washington Square Theatre on West 4th Street, it was considered a Broadway production. "Broadway," when referring to theatre, is not an address but a legal distinction pertaining to the contract that the producers sign with their employees. Everyone working on *Man of La Mancha* was signed to a standard, Broadway-scale contract. These contracts linked this production to its illustrious (and wealthier) counterparts uptown. But outside of this, and the remarkable professionalism of the cast, creators, designers, and crew, *Man of La Mancha* was a decidedly "downtown" brand of theatrical experience.
>
> *Man of La Mancha* straddled a fault line in the history of the American musical theatre as much as it confused the borders of "Broadway." Uptown, the show was competing for business with much more traditional musical comedies such as *Sweet Charity*, *Mame*, and *It's a Bird, It's a Plane, It's Superman*, and revivals of classics such as *South Pacific*, *The Music Man*, and *Carousel*. Like these other shows, *Man of La Mancha* used an occasional broad joke and sex appeal to relax the audience, and relied upon a fairly even distribution of dramatic scenes and songs to advance the story. Looking at *Man of La Mancha* from this vantage point, it

could easily be called one of the greatest musicals of the Golden Age of American musical theatre.

But this was not all *Man of La Mancha* tried to be. There were many other shows playing in New York at the same time which were clearly not in the Broadway tradition—for example, *Marat Sade*, *The Caucasian Chalk Circle*, and *The Saint of Bleecker Street*. Like *Man of La Mancha*, these shows pointed the way towards a treatment of serious issues in the theatre, which would grow, over the remainder of the decade, from a few isolated weeds into a glorious garden. Within a few years, shows like *Follies* and *A Chorus Line* would allow dark and uncompromising visions of the world to take their rightful place in the canon. *Man of La Mancha* could also be called one of the first great musicals of the Next Age of American musical theatre.

The genius and unique appeal of *Man of La Mancha* is that it managed to be both kinds of shows—a great, Golden Age musical and a great Next Age musical—at the same time. Janus-like, it pointed up the virtues of craft, tradition, and professionalism while it simultaneously celebrated the value of eccentricity, originality, and abandon. Few shows in the history of the American musical theatre have had the opportunity to do so, and fewer still have taken advantage of such an opportunity in so complete and successful a manner.

A short time after the show opened I began to realize, with a sort of horror, all of the potential headaches and distractions that a hit musical implied. My phone rang constantly, lawyers and agents pressing for meetings to discuss diverse offers. Producers with sick shows that, presumably, I might cure. Phonies and charlatans who understood how much money would be pouring in before I quite understood it myself; and most of all, "friends," some authentic but most merely people *claiming* to be friends, pleading for my house seats.

I quickly gave up on handling this breed, turning them over to my secretary, Donna Jones, who thereafter spent most of each day on the telephone granting or denying the requests. Donna was a tall, blonde Texan who kept me laughing with her down-home turns of phrase and an accent that could stretch a one-syllable word to a minimum of three. She was eccentric but also loyal and devoted, and when, one day, having had it with bells ringing, she hollered in exasperation, "Ah'm goin' tuh tuhn yore telephone number intuh unlisted!" I meekly said, "Okay."

"Meekly" wasn't typical of me. I was suffering battle fatigue. Offers poured in for various subsidiary rights to the show, but I was unprepared to discuss them. I did write the program notes for a cast-album, which, recorded hurriedly, was less than excellent (e.g., Kiley sings the opening phrase of "The Impossible Dream" off-key) but the album went gold in no time at all.

Also troubling my mind was my delinquency vis à vis my partners at MGM. I owed them a movie and had fallen behind. On the other hand, during the show's run at the Goodspeed Opera House I'd invited them, separately, to see the show with the notion they might become involved with its production if it struck them as a winner. Delbert Mann had come first to have a look. After he'd seen it, I refrained from asking his opinion, knowing his innate courtesy was such that if he didn't like it he'd say nothing at all. Delbert said nothing at all, not surprising since Del was entirely a movie man.

Later, when the performance had gained more certainty, my primary partner, Douglas Laurence, came to see it accompanied by his wife, Frances. As reported to me later, about a half hour into the performance Fran Laurence pinched her husband and whispered, "Mortgage the house if you have to, but get into this." Douglas declined. Again no surprise; he too was a movie man watching something uniquely of the theatre. Still, I regretted their non-participation. It might have saved me much grief later.

The pressure of success continued. Proposals for this, that, and the other use kept pouring in and had to be handled, if with nothing more than a polite "no interest." Two separate agencies filed lawsuits against me. One I'd never heard of. The second had been my agent for a time but had gone out of business before I'd entered into contracts on *Man of La Mancha* and, although I'd certainly needed an agent, hadn't participated. I was beginning to hear murmurs about movie rights, and I didn't want to hear such murmurs for a long time to come. I was overwhelmed and unprepared. Never anticipating the situation, I lacked the defenses or the legal machinery to cope.

One morning I woke up and couldn't move. I was simply paralyzed. The summoned doctor asked, gravely, "Have you been under some sort of stress recently?" to which I answered a fervent, "Hell, yes!"

After restoring me to mobility and making further examination he pointed out a condition which required, as he put it, "surgical intervention." I'd known about it for some time but had chosen to ignore it as an inconvenience. But now all of the factors put together indicated one recourse — get out. Get out of the pressure, the insane hubbub over this surprise Cinderella of a show.

Get out of New York.

I called friends in Palm Springs, Dorothy and Teddy Hart. Teddy, small and saucer-eyed, was the brother of fabled lyricist Lorenz Hart. Dorothy, also miniature in size, was a darling person of extreme eccentricity who'd been a dancer in the chorus of the original *Forty-Second Street*. Having large income from the Lorenz Hart estate and finding little to do with it, the Harts were house junkies, buying and selling them without much pattern or gain. They always had a few to spare.

"Yes indeed," said Dorothy. "I've got a beautiful furnished place with five bedrooms, a heated pool and a therapeutic spa, so you come right on out."

Almost instantly I was on my way to California.

It seems appropriate to answer a question people frequently put to me. It's a simple question that ought to have a simple answer. The question is, "Where do you live?" The answer isn't simple; the answer is, "Nowhere." It confuses interviewers, who frequently take it as an affectation, but I don't know a more honest answer.

Unlike all those other New York or Southern playwrights who draw upon their geographical or societal origins, I have no roots. I am totally lacking the Brooklyn or the Yoknapatawpha syndrome, a nexus of place and population to call upon for the furniture and characters of one's writings. I have no roots nor any place I might claim as home. Wisconsin claims me, and their great university has awarded me an honorary doctorate, based on the fact that Rhinelander, in Wisconsin's north woods, was my birthplace. Yet I lived there less than a year. I doubt that this qualifies as "roots."

My father was a restless promoter of movie houses, moving on as each was set up, then sold. Born without benefit of a birth certificate, I lived in at least a half dozen towns before I was five, at which time my father died, and my mother followed soon after. My siblings dispersed, and I was sequentially consigned to orphanages and the kindness of elder brothers until I turned hobo at 14, maintaining a peripatetic lifestyle ever since. When money became plentiful from my writings, I bought, built, and sold a dozen houses in several countries, trying, subconsciously perhaps, to put down roots. A psychologist once pointed out that I did so with intent to fail, thus justifying my resistance to conformity. But regardless of reasons, my shots at stability invariably missed their target.

Never did I consider New York my home. New York was a place for effort, accomplishment, risk-taking. I arrived there for the first time in the forties as stage director of Katherine Dunham's *Tropical Revue*. We opened at — of all venues — the Martin Beck Theatre, where I appropriated one of the stage-level dressing rooms and literally lived in the theatre during our fourteen-week run. It was a wonderful place for parties post-performance.

I've always loved theatres when there was no audience to disturb the ambiance, and only a single light bulb fought the caverns of dark. (By the way, in my many years as a stage manager, director, and producer in the theatre, I never heard that bulb referred to as a "ghost light," Frank Rich notwithstanding. To us backstage workers it was known simply as the "pilot light," and its purpose was pragmatic — it was required by law and by the fire department as a safety precaution.)

New York to me was a place of singular attributes and possibilities, but never was it home. Neither was California, where I'd spent much more time.

My partiality has always been for the American West, the primitive West that is the locale of many of my plays and movies. My Mexican-born wife and I have maintained a pied-à-terre in Arizona for many years. It has many amenities, including an orchard and a private wing of the house for a work room that contains the file copies of my scripts—over a hundred of them—as well as "ego walls" covered with posters and trophies.

We maintain several other houses but think of none as "home." We've no home in the familial sense at all, only places to store the detritus of living.

In June of 1966, I went into St. John's Hospital in Santa Monica, California, for my "surgical intervention." There, late on the night of June 13, 1966, two of the nurses entered, bearing bouquets of flowers—probably "borrowed" from other patients. "What's up?" I inquired.

"It's on the radio," my round-the-clock nurse informed me. "You just won some kind of an award in New York. What was it called?"

"Was it the Anthony?" guessed the other. Which is how I learned that *Man of La Mancha* had won the Tony Award for Best Musical. Actually, it had pretty well swept the categories, being awarded... five? Seven? I was never sure. Producer Albert Selden had accepted for me and mailed the silver disc itself it to me several weeks later.

The awards didn't stop there. Actually, they'd barely started; in succession came the New York Drama Critics Award (more prestigious than the politics-clotted Tony); the Outer Critics Circle Award; the Variety Drama Critics Award; The Saturday Review Award; and a host of others following in train over the next year; after which began the awards from foreign countries as productions in other languages began.

Still they keep coming. I do not customarily attend awards ceremonies, but made an exception for Japan Music Award, in New York, in 1997. I accepted in person because it would have been profoundly bad manners to my etiquette-bound Japanese hosts to have done otherwise. They have been notably courteous to me; the Toho Company's biannual production of *La Mancha* is the most meticulously produced and one of the most successful on earth. Previous winners of this award had been Hal Prince and Stephen Sondheim; I was amused to find myself in their company.

By 1968 something unexpected, totally apart from all the activity on *La Mancha* was happening. *One Flew Over the Cuckoo's Nest,* which I assumed had been savaged to death by the Broadway critics, was showing revived signs of life. A production using my original script and starring Warren Oates had opened in Hollywood and was rousing audiences and critics to cheers. Two young men, Rudy Golyn, producer, and Lee Sankowich, a director, had opened a production at the Little Fox Theatre in San Francisco. It turned into a smash that ran for five years, stimulating similar productions in key cities. These very bright young men would further open a production Off-Broadway in New York starring William Devane in his first major role, as McMurphy, and included Danny DeVito as Martini the Hallucinator. In addition to becoming a success on its own, the play was becoming a launching-pad for brilliant young actors.

Productions opened in Boston, Chicago, London, Paris...and then everywhere. They're opening still, at the rate of some two to three hundred a year, including professional and amateur productions. The Tony Award I enjoyed most occurred on the night of June 3rd, 2001, when the Steppenwolf Theatre Company's production of *One Flew Over the Cuckoo's Nest*, starring Gary Sinise, at the Royale Theatre, took the prize for the "Best Revival," and producer Michael Leavitt, accepting the award as I watched on television in Arizona, said into camera, "Thank you, Dale, for your wonderful play."

The growing acclaim for *The Cuckoo's Nest* meant more to me than all the praise-and-blame for *Man of La Mancha*. For the original production—not really my script—I'd been scourged in reviews and articles, even accused of "literary degeneracy." It is not often that a play comes back from the dead, but the wheel had come round, and *One Flew Over the Cuckoo's Nest* was being hailed as "brilliant...powerful...profoundly moving...a play for the ages."

In all fairness, something important had happened between 1963 and 1968. The play hadn't changed, but the audience had. The Vietnam War was assailing the conscience of America, and the rebellion of the young, if incoherent and sometimes mis-aimed, was shocking sensibilities. By 1968 the play had found its time and target. It discovered its audience and acquired a momentum that still is carrying it forward. *The Cuckoo's Nest* flies lustily to this very day, chasing and sometimes exceeding *La Mancha* in number of productions yearly.

As *La Mancha* ran on, the inquiries into film rights became more and more insistent. I'd turned away such inquiries as premature, feeling no one had considered what sort of a movie might be made from the stage musical. I was disturbed by the rumors that Mitch Leigh and Albert Marre were inviting discussion of a movie sale with the implication that they were seeking to be active participants in a production.

Of all the people involved with the play, I was the only one with experience in the writing and production of movies. Even *La Mancha's* producers, Selden and James, had no knowledge of moviemaking, though certainly they had a strong financial interest in a sale of rights. But now, as the play continued its sold-out run in New York and preparations for road companies, I could see the oncoming surge toward disposal of screen rights. It was time to pause and consider.

I considered. Carefully. And came to a conclusion that I knew would cause trouble, but couldn't avoid, regardless. I concluded that *Man of La Mancha* could *not* become a successful movie.

If I were to put the reason in a sentence it would be this: the play was so inherently conceived for the living theatre that there was no way its virtues could be preserved, much less enhanced, on the screen. I considered it comparable, in this respect, to *Our Town*, purely of the theatre and not necessarily adaptable to film at all.

The theatre is abstract. That's its power. Movies are assertively real. That's *their* power. As someone who wrote and produced in both media, I was very aware of the difference. I loved the theatre for its invitation to imagine, to abstract; and I enjoyed movies for their impact of reality. But it seemed clear — at least to me — that these respective powers were worlds apart, and one form didn't necessarily translate into the other.

Man of La Mancha is a work of imagination. It asks the audience to enter into a conspiracy; to believe that they're in a Spanish prison in the 16th century, and that a play — with music yet! — is going to be improvised, for the very first time, before their eyes. And that they'll be required to invest not only their credulity but their emotions in the story and in the actors who will invent the improvisations.

They're asked for much more than the customary suspension of disbelief. There's no attempt even at theatrical "reality," no settings of wood and canvas, for there is no scenery nor properties in the usual sense at all. Nothing to lend the comfort of verisimilitude to the proceedings.

This is the contract to which the audience must agree in order to participate in *Man of La Mancha*. It makes demands of their intelligence. Of their ability to see what isn't there. Of their willingness to set aside the normal perceptions of reality in order to buy into the intellectual and emotional experience the authors are offering.

These are extraordinary demands. They're the reason intelligent and experienced theatrical producers rejected *Man of La Mancha* to begin with. It's too abstract, too demanding even for the theatre, they judged, and though it's a work of my creation I never faulted their judgment. It just wasn't possible to know whether the audience would agree to such demands.

That they did, with such enthusiasm, had no bearing on whether the play would transfer to another medium, specifically to the movie medium, which demands the opposite of abstraction to be convincing.

Which is why I was convinced that *Man of La Mancha* couldn't become a successful motion picture—a conviction destined to make a great deal of trouble for myself and others.

CHAPTER SIXTEEN

Leave the tambourine to one who knows how to play it.

It was time to leave Palm Springs for business in New York and Europe. Prior to departure I went for dinner to "Kiss Me Plenty" and a consultation with soothsayer Olga.

"You hit the nail on the head last time," I told her. "Success and all it would trigger? They happened."

"So I've heard," said Olga, drily.

"So what's next?"

Olga, studied my hand at some length and finally said, "Mmmm."

Not good. Olga, as I said, was by nature a warmhearted and optimistic person averse to the delivery of bad tidings.

I said, "Okay, lay it on me."

"Troubles."

"Plural?"

"Quite."

"How long?"

"Extended."

"Like months?"

"Mmm," said Olga.

In New York it was pleasant to find both *La Mancha* and *The Cuckoo's Nest* going strong. *La Mancha,* in the third year of its run, was still selling out. A road company starring José Ferrer was about to open in New Haven and was booked for two years ahead. Foreign productions were being licensed. Australia was already in rehearsal, and Spain would open the first of the European productions. The team of Selden and James was producing another show, *Hallelujah*

Baby, scheduled to open at the Martin Beck (always the Martin Beck!) and all seemed well.

But it wasn't. I met with my co-authors to find out what was simmering on the griddle. Joe Darion wasn't available; he was in Greece at work with Jules Dassin and Melina Mercouri on the musical version of *Never On Sunday,* which, in its stage incarnation would be called *Ilya Darling.* But Joe and I had stayed in touch, exchanging information and advice by mail and phone.

Albie looked much the same, but Mitch had changed. He wore white Nehru jackets and had grown a beard and a visible aura of self-importance. He seemed bigger, somehow... not a gain in weight, but as though his outer envelope were swelling synchronously with self-regard. What I was seeing, I realized, was a success-syndrome.

"What we've been discussing," said Albie, "is the movie rights." He went on to inform me of what I already knew—the bidding for the rights had a floor of two million dollars and looked to go higher. He informed me of a wish to "keep the team together." What it meant was that Albie proposed to direct the movie and Mitch to produce. I asked Albie, "When did you last direct a movie?"

He explained there was no mystery about it; he felt he was was perfectly capable of directing a movie. Just as Mitch felt capable of producing one.

It seemed we were getting into Alice-in-Wonderland territory, but as the only one in this collection of wannabes who actually worked in movies, I explained that no studio would pay several million dollars for rights and then hire a director and producer who were absolute virgins at the altar of moviemaking.

For the first time we were encountering an invidious provision in our contracts—that in the event of disagreement on any issue such as the awarding of rights, a vote of our gross percentages would decide the issue. My percentage was the largest but I could be out-voted by a combination of Mitch and Joe's. Albie had no vote—I'd had a stroke of wisdom at the time contracts were being negotiated, and insisted that he have none. Since Mitch and I were often opposed to each other, Joe's was frequently the swing vote.

They informed me that they had retained an agent to represent them, and they hoped I'd join in the same representation.

The agent called the next day. He was Irving "Swifty" Lazar, well known to me and to everyone in the profession — for his aggressive salesmanship, which often ignored the fact he didn't represent the properties he sold. But he surely did extract the maximum buck from buyers. Swifty had little or no interest in the artistic side of things; to him the "deal" was all. I liked him, actually, and had been his guest at the splendid parties he threw in Hollywood around Academy Awards time.

"Irving," I said, "you know I'm represented by the William Morris Agency."

"Sure, sure," said Swifty. "I'll make the deal, they'll go along."

"They might," I said. "But I won't."

For the time being I turned my back on the problem and looked to a more urgent one — the pending foreign-language productions of the show.

Elisabeth Marton ran a one-woman agency, which was unique and remarkably without competition. The Marton Agency handled foreign language rights for American playwrights and, in reverse, English-language translations for eminent foreign authors. Elisabeth, known to her friends and clients as "Bözsi" (for reasons beyond me, all Hungarians seem to have alternate names), was an extraordinary woman who'd survived concentration camps and other such horrors yet managed to maintain both her serene good nature and her composure in the face of difficulties. The difficulties typically included dealing in multiple languages (she spoke six, I believe, and "got along" in a few more) as well as currency complications and eccentric-to-insane translators. Her family was also prominent in the profession. Elder brother George Marton ran the largest literary agency in Paris. Younger brother Andrew (known by his Hungarian alternative as "Bundi") was a popular Hollywood director. Bözsi was intelligent, cultured, and rich in that elusive quality known as "class." I grew to admire and to love her dearly.

I was happy when she took charge of the foreign language licensing of *Man of La Mancha*, and she was equally happy to be handling a play that crossed international borders with such ease. We got along well; I enjoyed her company and conversation as greatly as I did her abilities. Further, she handled other plays of mine, including *One Flew Over the Cuckoo's Nest* as it gained world-wide circulation after its success in America. (Actually, it would go into as many languages as *Man of La Mancha*.)

I learned that the first foreign opening would be in Madrid, which seemed poetically right; Madrid was where the play had been born. I arranged to meet Bözsi there for the premiere.

El Hombre de la Mancha opened on September 30, 1966, in Madrid. The script had been translated by José Lopez-Rubio, an eminent litterateur and author in his own right. The production starred José Sagi-Vela as Cervantes/Quixote, and Nati Mistral, a truly major star famous in all the Hispanic countries, as Aldonza.

Trouble struck with the first words spoken in the play. In Spanish, of course, they were: "In a village of La Mancha, the name of which I have no desire to recall, there lived not so long ago one of those gentlemen who always have a lance in the rack, an ancient buckler, a skinny nag, and a greyhound for the chase."

I turned to Elisabeth and whispered in horror, "That's not *Man of La Mancha*, that's the opening of the novel *Don Quixote!*"

Indeed it was, and to our mutual astonishment, that's how the performance continued, an Iberian cocktail that mixed the novel and the play according to some recipe I couldn't fathom. I grew increasingly bewildered, but nearly flipped out when it came to the singing of "The Impossible Dream"—which was sung not by Don Quixote, but by Aldonza.

I had a choice. I could blow up, holler my head off, and possibly accomplish nothing but ill will. Or, with considerable effort I could stay cool and perhaps find out what had happened. Barely, I managed the latter.

The next day I confronted "translator" Lopez-Rubio and said, "You did not translate my play, you adapted it. Why?"

Lopez-Rubio, a man dignified to the point of hauteur, answered, "Look, my friend, every schoolchild in Spain knows the words from the novel. If a play is titled, *El Hombre de la Mancha*, they will expect those words."

"You've had four hundred years in which to do a successful stage version of *Don Quixote*. Now you've got one. Why do you alter it?"

Lopez-Rubio shrugged and said, "This is Spain. We do things our way."

These and other questions were getting me nowhere. Finally I asked, "Why, when 'The Impossible Dream' is Don Quixote's statement of his mission, is it being sung by *Aldonza*?"

"Because," said Lopez-Rubio, "Nati Mistral is a star."

I was struck dumb.

To Elisabeth Marton I said, "We need a contract that bars changes or adaptation of the play, the lyrics, or the music."

"That's what we already have. It didn't stop these people."

I chewed on that a while, and said, "Then we need to make it mandatory that I approve the translations in advance and that there be no deviations."

"Very good," said Bözsi. "That should intimidate them nicely. But I must ask—what will we do when the script comes to you in Polish? Or in Japanese?"

"We will lie," I answered. "You will say I am a master linguist and have read it and approve."

"Ah," said Ms. Marton.

The Spanish treated me with respect. A little too much, actually. I was even invited into one of their "tertulias," intellectual discussion clubs in which the subjects are frequently abstruse or deal with nitpicking points of obscure philosophies. Of course, neither my Spanish nor my education were equal to such demand; still I realized that the invitations were honors rarely offered a foreigner.

Why was it, then, that in actuality I felt less than welcome? That I felt, behind the Castilian punctilio, that their attitude was subtly hostile?

I had lunch one day with James Michener and his wife, Mari. Michener was a dour man, but Mari, a Japanese-Hawaiian, was delightful. She was spirited, witty, and very, very bright. I realized she was fully 50 percent of Michener; his researcher, editor, and idea person, and I envied him such an asset. They were working, at that point, on a book to be called *The Drifters*, dealing with the young hippies and druggies now migrating in numbers to southern Spain. I mentioned to Michener my unease with the Spanish writers whom normally I would have considered colleagues.

"Of course," said Michener. "They hate you. Somebody has accomplished something they've been unable to bring off in all this time. Using their greatest literary treasure, yet. Worse, it's a damned American who did it. So don't be surprised. They'll be very proper to your face, but they will hate you, they will envy you, and they'll kill you if they can."

At the time I thought Michener a little extreme. Later I was less certain.

Elisabeth Marton and I agreed that foreign productions could be protected only by someone with authority from New York attending in person. Her authority wasn't really sufficient. "Would you undertake to do that?" she asked.

"Well...it's a cinch that no one else will."

"Good," said Elisabeth. "Plan to meet me in Prague, Copenhagen, Vienna, and Tokyo."

What had I let myself in for!?

I didn't get to all the productions but did indeed cover the principal ones. Genial Hal James, co-producer of the show, was another who cared enough to travel to these far away premieres. He was always good company, and I was grateful for his caring. But Elisabeth and I took the primary responsibility of guarding the play against bowdlerization or "interpretation." Usually we succeeded, but not always.

The last thing I did in Spain on that particular trip was to arrange the purchase of a particular piece of land on the Costa del Sol, about a half hour's drive from the Malaga airport. It lies on a mountainside, on the outskirts of an ancient village called Benalmádena that originally had been a stronghold against incursions by invading Barbary pirates—the same breed that, nearby, had captured and enslaved a soldier by the name of Cervantes. It has a stunning view of the Mediterranean and, at certain times of the day, of Africa. There I intended to build the most beautiful house in Spain.

CHAPTER SEVENTEEN

*A fool knows more in his own house
than a wise man in the house of another.*

PRAGUE

A city haunted by history. The Charles Bridge over the turgid
Vltava River, Hradcany Castle, Wenceslas Square, all seemed
familiar though one had never before seen them in actuality. The
ancient ghetto where the Rabbi Jehuda Loew had created a golem
to protect the Jews...but in the 16th century he was a trifle premature, since it was four hundred years later that Nazi Germany
would ship Prague's 77,000 Jews to the camps as a way-stop towards
extinction.

Foot traffic was sparse in the city, and pedestrians seemed
hurried, furtive, in scuttling to their destinations. The Soviet threat
hung over the city like a miasma. At my hotel, people in the lobby
or waiting outside slipped notes into my hand or topcoat pockets.
They were invariably messages for relatives in America or pleadings
for a few American dollars in exchange for antiques or other
valuables. "Get rid of those," warned Bözsi. "Assume you're being
watched, because you are. And don't forget they're going to search
every inch of your belongings when you leave."

More travel-wise than I in totalitarian states, she was quite right.

The currency held dangers also. Not one krona (nowadays called
the koruna or crown) could be taken out of the country. All must
be spent before departure or be confiscated at Customs. We'd be
searched, body, bag, and baggage on exit, and all money counted
and accounted for. American dollars held power, and the
Communist administration encouraged leaving them behind.

In the lobby of the Britannia Hotel I noted an oddity—beautiful,
smartly dressed girls who sat about, drinking tea, chatting quietly

with hotel guests or simply looking demure and available. I'd rarely seen such a pod of well-turned-out prostitutes. The secret to their availability, I learned, was the currency. They weren't permitted to be paid in krona, only pounds, dollars, or other "hard" currency — every nickel of which they were to turn over at the end of each day (or night).

Here was Marxist economy in action. Not in theory but at the basic, hormonalogical level. Economy à la lubricity.

The production of *Man of La Mancha* opened at the state-subsidized theatre, with nothing lacking except the spirit of the original. The actors were adequate, the scenic production a discount replica of the original. The audience was warm, if subdued. Fifteen minutes into the performance I realized what was happening — the Czech actors were subtly turning the play into a mirror of their political predicament. Words I'd written in one context were being slanted to serve another.

It was clever. The lines, so far as I could tell, were not being changed, merely the intent. It was clear Don Quixote's madness was of a political nature. It was clear that The Enchanter represented not a personal antagonist of Don Quixote but the repressive forces squeezing freedom from the country.

I was amused, and not at all upset. In a friendly get-together with the cast and director the next day, I asked how long they thought they could get away with it.

"Get away with what?" asked the director, blandly.

Two weeks later they were shut down without notice.

Not long after that the Prague Spring blossomed, when subversion sprang free, with a shout. On August 20, 1968, the Soviet tanks rolled in, forcing Prague into a long silence. Until, in Vaclav Havel, it found voice and leadership once more. In a playwright!

VIENNA

There's no denying the beauty of the city or the countryside, yet I'm always aware they mask a cancer. This is the city of sentimentality, a coin whose reverse side is brutality. Austria is viciously and forever anti-Semitic — historically more so even than Germany. Not far from Vienna is the town of Linz, from which sprang the two Adolfs,

Eichmann and Hitler. Austria has other historical monuments, of course, but these will suffice for our era.

The Theatre an der Wien, where *Der Mann Von La Mancha* opened on the fourth of January, 1968, is exquisite, preserved just as it was when Beethoven conducted its opening concerts. The play had been smartly translated by Robert Gilbert, and the physical production was meticulous. It boasted one memorable item that stood out above all others—the performance of Josef Meinrad as Cervantes/Quixote. Herr Meinrad, a star of the famous Burg Theatre who'd been borrowed for this production, was simply the best Quixote I've ever seen. Not in singing, but in subtlety and range of acting. He opened my eyes, in fact, to a fuller potential of the role. That in fact it was actually four roles—Cervantes the inept government employee; Cervantes the flamboyant stage master; Don Quixote the inspired madman; and Alonso Quijana, the modest country gentleman whose mind had cracked through envisioning a world not as it was but as it might be.

A few others had done it well, but they were the product of talents peculiarly American, the marrying of good acting to good singing in a single performer. Richard Kiley was a performer par excellence in that area. But this combination isn't expected in European theatre; singers are singers, actors actors. Meinrad was a merely adequate singer, but his acting achieved every subtlety of the four incarnations of Miguel de Cervantes and brought joy to my heart. And when he sang, he sang the lyrics of the song, giving them the same value as dialogue, and did not reach for showy vocalization.

I regretted that I couldn't converse with him in depth in my limited German, but I think we understood each other quite well. He was, simply, magnificent.

Nor were other members of this cast far behind. Norman Foster, an American opera singer whose career had blossomed in Germany and Austria, played the Governor/Innkeeper with splendid authority and a soaring baritone, the likes of which wouldn't be heard again for a long time, if ever. Fritz Muliar, a well-known opera bouffe comedian, played Sancho, sweetly. But the performance of Blanche Aubry as Aldonza was curiously different from any I'd seen or even considered. She played the role of my "savage alley cat" in a subdued, beaten, almost catatonic way in its beginning, then changing subtly as the influence of Don Quixote on her psyche takes hold and grows.

The production was a triumph and played for a long run, actually until the actors who'd been "borrowed" from other companies had to return to fulfill contracts with them.

The production at Beethoven's Theatre an der Wien was truly memorable.

TORONTO AND DENVER

Actually, several productions have played the delightful city of Toronto. (Not the least of whose pleasures is one's ability to speak its language.) Road shows from New York, with stars such as Richard Kiley, José Ferrer, and others have settled in for engagements here, almost always at the Royal Alexandra Theatre, under the management of the family Mirvish. But the particular production I was delegated to see in 1993 had requested permission to move on, even into the United States. This required inspection.

It had originated, I was told, in Vancouver, under the direction of Susan Cox, with the direction subsequently taken over by Robin Phillips. It boasted excellent leading performers, Michael Burgess and Susan Gilmour, a husband and wife duo of which the wife, Ms. Gilmour, was one of the best Aldonzas I've ever seen. The production, however, was one of the worst.

The treatment of the play could be labeled as smartass and shocking. It was that bane of playwrights' lives, a work crippled by a "director's concept."

I am quick to confirm that a talented director may introduce a fresh concept to a play, though it's safest done when the play's creator is dead. Mr. Phillips' concept of *Man of La Mancha* consisted in mixing the periods—some of the play took place today, some yesterday, and some in no recognizable period at all. And all of it with thumb at its nose, inviting the audience to applaud its cleverness. Red carpets were rolled out and fireworks exploded from time to time in the production, though I couldn't comprehend why. I recall admiring Burgess and Gilmour and loathing all else. This production had crossed the continent, making stops at such stations as Edmonton and Calgary, but traveled no farther than Toronto.

This "concept" thing turns up frequently as the product of directors hoping to get themselves labeled "creative." Having been a director myself, I'm well aware of the temptation. I don't ask directors to apply a concept, nor to be "creative," which is surely the most abused word in the lexicon. I ask them to interpret the play; I've already done the creating. Good, fresh, imaginative interpretation is difficult, which is why small-time directors prefer to avoid it in favor of tricks that call attention to their wit but serve the play badly.

Other times, dealing with domestic licensing, I've been called upon by the producers or my collaborators to inspect a production of *Man of La Mancha* that seems to have been warped out of shape by someone in charge. Most such productions authors never see, for they're obscure and brief.

One such, however, was The Denver Theatre Centre's production of a "new concept" of the play. The Denver Centre is an estimable cluster of theatres with a good reputation, but after reading alarming reports in the press I went—anonymously—to check it out.

The play's first scene was that of a nun being raped in an elevator. My bewilderment was confirmed by a pair of elderly ladies behind me, one of whom said to the other, "Oh, dear, we're in the wrong theatre," and thereupon they got up and left to find *Man of La Mancha*. Thereafter, to my amazement, I watched a play that took place in present-day Nicaragua and dealt with the malign intervention of the United States upon that benighted country. Spanish language broadcasts informed the audience of American oppression. Actors in camouflage uniforms sat about on bags bearing giant red dollar signs. Here and there, woven into the interstices, were scenes from *Man of La Mancha*.

I didn't get it. On *any* level I didn't get it.

I retained a copyright lawyer who proposed an injunction that would shut them down. "No, no," I said. "That would cost them their run and a million dollar loss." Instead, we arrived at a compromise: the theatre would delete the most offensive material and restore the substance of *Man of La Mancha*.

As a result of the widely publicized brouhaha, the entire run sold out and had to be extended.

Ah, show business.

JOHANNESBURG

An amazing thing happened. After we'd granted rights to South Africa we found out their theatre audiences were, by law, segregated. Whereupon we cancelled their right to present *Man of La Mancha*. Whereupon they informed us they had a law whereby if rights were withheld from them for political reasons they could confiscate those rights and perform the play regardless.

The theatre management in Johannesburg was rather plaintive about it. They really didn't want to take advantage of their laws and cause us to hate them. But they weren't so plaintive that they didn't intend to avail themselves of the law.

I was outraged by the idea that another country could confiscate the property of Americans, even though such property had no home or basis there. My typical reaction in such situations: a Quixotic, "Let's fight it!"

Which we did. We joined forces with the managements of *Fiddler on the Roof* and *West Side Story*, which found themselves in the same pickle. We sent lawyers to South Africa and fought the law in their courts, at great expense. After appeals up through their Supreme Court, we lost.

Man of La Mancha was a hit in South Africa though none of us went to see it or gave a damn.

Not long after, South Africa repealed its law.

MOSCOW

From the *Los Angeles Times*, September 25, 1972: A SOVIETIZED "LA MANCHA"

> One hundred yards from the theater entrance, the stage buffs had started their quiet litany, "Any extra tickets?"
>
> Inside the Academy Theater, the company was performing what Russia considered its first successful effort in duplicating an American musical play, "*Man of la Mancha*."

For those who had seen the American original in either its long New York run or any of the road versions, the Russians' production was a disappointment. But in terms of the Russian theater and its previous efforts with American musicals it was a resounding success and something of a break-through.

There were some subtle changes in emphasis to fit Soviet theater politics, but nothing to seriously damage the story. Russian stage directors are famous for making liberal changes in a writer's work. American authors have no copyright protection in Soviet Union and cannot collect royalties on their works.

One thing was clear about *"La Mancha."* The audience loved the show. They filled the aisles at the close and applauded for nearly a half-hour..."

A letter from Dale Wasserman, addressed to Andrei Goncharov, Director, the Mayakovsky Theatre, Moscow, U.S.S.R.:

Dear Mr. Goncharov,

I am informed that *Man of La Mancha* will be produced at the Mayakovsky under your direction. A dispatch from Moscow further advises that I am being "signally honored" since this will be the first American musical ever to be presented by your theatre.

I regret to say that I feel no more honored than I feel honored by burglars who steal my possessions. In both cases, the applicable word is "theft." Because we are colleagues and because I doubt that you, personally, condone this practice, I wish there were a gentler word for it.

But there isn't. You have neither applied for nor been given the right to do this play. Your country, by reason of its refusal to subscribe to International Copyright Conventions is guilty not only of piracy but of contempt for the very authors it "honors" by the unauthorized and uncompensated use of their works. I will cheerfully forego such honors until the Writers Union of the U.S.S.R., sees fit to link hands with other writers' organizations in the continuing effort to protect the ownership and the integrity of the authors' work.

Even the name of your theatre adds an irony. Vladimir

Mayakovsky, one of the most brilliant of your poet-playwrights, was a militant defender of these same rights. But the revolution, having made use of the artist, abrogated its debt to him, and it is interesting to ponder the implications of the note Mayakovsky left upon his suicide in 1939: "The boat of devotion has crashed upon the rocks of reality." And to consider also the fate of his close friend and fellow-Futurist, Boris Pasternak, who held that the product of a writer's imagination was at least equal in worth to the production of tractors or nuclear armament...

Of course it is possible that these considerations will affect neither your policy nor your conscience. In that event I have a further—and appropriately Quixotic—proposal. You do not have in your possession the correct text or score. Previous productions in the Soviet Union have mangled both, horrendously. Consequently I offer to send you the correct material—on condition that you perform the play exactly as written.

Of course *Man of La Mancha* is propaganda. What play isn't? But its argument may be found salutary. And idealogically speaking, not even dangerous. Unless there is danger in warning the Russian audience that facts may be alien to truth. Or that an impossible dream has virtue because it is impossible. Or that anti-pragmatism may yet be our sole hope of "adding some measure of grace to the world."

Do consider my offer. With good will on both sides, it is possible that something constructive may come of our complicity in the crime.

Sincerely,
Dale Wasserman
"La Mancha"
Benalmádena, Malaga

This letter was widely published in the world press. There was no response. Russia has since joined International Copyright—nominally, at least—and has requested rights to *One Flew Over the Cuckoo's Nest*. But I haven't seen a ruble in royalties, nor do I expect to.

PARIS

Possibly the most famous international star ever to attempt to put his personal stamp on *Man of La Mancha* was the singer-songwriter Jacques Brel. It came about in an odd, spontaneous way, at a time we weren't yet considering France or a production in that language.

We were preparing to open a major road company of the show at the Ahmanson Theatre in downtown Los Angeles when we received word that Jacques Brel was coming to see us. Of course we knew who he was, but we didn't exactly faint at the news; we were more interested in problems we were having with the Ahmanson, which we'd be initiating as a musical theatre and which we'd found to be badly designed for that purpose.

Brel wrote heart-wrenching songs about the heartbreak of love and the burdens of humanity. He'd been long attracting admirers in Europe and a limited audience in New York through a revue of his songs playing in Greenwich Village. I knew and admired his work but wasn't aware that he'd ever been in the States before.

Brel himself was preceded by a bevy of French agents and managers whose mission, it appeared, was to impress upon us the importance of their client and his willingness to travel across an ocean and a continent to make a request directly of the authors. They were somewhat pompous and irritating; we weren't impressed by this figurative fanfare of trumpets announcing the entrance of a Star.

Brel, when he appeared, was less pompous and more forth-coming. Indeed, he was without pomposity at all. He was a small man with very large buck teeth, and I noted that he wore a gray silk suit of exquisite weave and tailoring. He spoke no English at all, but his team translated, singly and severally.

Mr. Brel, we were informed, wanted exclusive rights to *Man of La Mancha* in the French language. He and his managers would mount the production, play major cities in the Francophone areas and then bring the production into Paris for an indefinite run. Further, Mr. Brel would himself do the translation of book and lyrics.

How, I wondered, since he knew no English? The answer: Mr. Brel had a girlfriend, an airline attendant, it appeared, who'd already done a literal translation from which Brel could work.

Would we get much beyond "attachez vos ceintures?" It seemed faintly funny to us until Brel, assuming we were unacquainted with his work (not true), said he proposed to audition for us then and there. And added that he'd never auditioned before, in his entire life—for anyone. Which had to be respected.

Brel took the stage, vast and empty under work lights, guitar in hand, and proceeded to knock us out of our seats with a half-hour performance of his songs. I was not all that unfamiliar with them, though I'd heard them only in recordings. And of course I knew the Off-Broadway *Jacques Brel Is Alive and Well and Living in Paris*. I wasn't fond of the latter, chiefly because of its preciosity and a too-worshipful attitude. But Brel in person had great impact.

The Paris production came into being, though not without considerable wrangling over the French text, which, in a pattern repeated once again, fell into the category of adaptation rather than translation. Albert Marre, by some legerdemain inserted himself not only as the director of the production, but also succeeded in ousting the French actress who'd been engaged to play Aldonza, replacing her as Brel's co-star with Joan Diener, playing the role in French.

L'Homme de la Mancha opened at the Theatre de Champs-Elysées on December 11, 1968, after a break-in engagement at the Royal Monnaie, in Brussels. It was an astonishing production. Brel, on some levels, was the best Cervantes ever, singing the role with unmatched passion. But he had no actor's technique through which to save his energy, and expended himself fearfully in each perform-ance. As I watched him I said, "He cannot last." In the event, he lasted one hundred performances, then collapsed, and the produc-tion closed to sellout houses.

But it wasn't the expenditure of strength that did him in. In October of 1974, Brel, a heavy smoker, learned he had a tumor on his left lung. The prognosis was not good. In December he decided to cross the Atlantic Ocean on his yacht, *Askoy II*, and after cruising in the West Indies and passing through the Panama Canal, he sailed to the island of Atuona in the Marquesas archipelago. His health deteriorating rapidly, he died there October, 9, 1978, and is buried on the Island of Hiva-Oa.

His grave is just a few yards from that of Paul Gauguin's.

Tokyo

What I hold against the Japanese is that they're too good to me. I cannot come to Tokyo without being overwhelmed with attention. Even the flight over will be First Class, at the expense of Toho International, with the JAL crew alerted to show me exceptional courtesies. On the last trip they even replaced the battery in my watch!

Everything is laid on, transportation, hotel, interpreters, tickets to shows, visits to Kyoto, Kobe, Osaka, everywhere *Man of La Mancha* will play, and anywhere else I might wish to go. Not to mention fabulous dinners, with demure geisha to serve each diner and other geisha entertaining continuously on those plangent musical instruments, the koto and the samisen.

An oddity of these nightlong dinners is that normally staid executives get very drunk and proceed to make idiots of themselves, which, my young-lady interpreter hastens to inform me, is considered *de rigueur* in Japan. Once, being irremediably American, I asked her how much it cost to have dinners like this in an exclusive restaurant that few obviously could afford. "Oh, we never speak of such things!" she answered, shocked. But later she whispered, "About fifteen hundred dollars per person."

On a recent occasion, fearing that if I went to Tokyo to receive an award they might again treat me too well, I asked that the award be given in New York. Promptly it was set up that way, with festivities at Town Hall where I was duly given the prestigious Japan Music Award, with its array of goodies ranging from humongous checks (which I donated in turn to the O'Neill Theatre Center) to great Tiffany bowls, bronze sculptures of Samurai, airline tickets to Tokyo (which went unused), plaques, and...I've lost track. One of the most welcome items, however, was a graceful presentation speech by Joan Diener, who I was very pleased to see again.

I have no precise idea why *Man of La Mancha* has had its most successful career in Japan, nor do I understand why it should resonate so powerfully in the Japanese psyche. It's been playing in a continuous cycle there ever since it was born. Every other year it is re-produced, opening first on a multi-city tour including, with variations, Osaka, Nagoya, Kobe, or Kyoto, then moving into one of the grand theatres in Tokyo, either the Imperial or the Nisei.

These houses seat between three and four thousand spectators and are invariably sold out for the entire engagement. The Japanese productions of *Man of La Mancha* are the most meticulous to be seen anywhere on earth, including New York. Japanese theatregoers have become accustomed to treating it as their play, and never fail in response.

The Japanese rights belong to the Toho Company, Ltd., which, barring calamity, intends to continue presenting the play from here to eternity. But the credit for nurture and protection belongs largely to two men, each extraordinary in his own right. The first is Mr. Tatsuo Hirao, the now-retired managing director for Toho, who made the stewardship of *La Mancha* his personal responsibility from inception. Mr. Hirao guarded every detail of the play and its production as though it were his own child, always insisted upon excellence, and never stinted in money or effort to maintain or improve it. The result of his loving labor is a production practically awesome in its perfection. The authors owe this inimitable gentleman profound thanks.

The second is an actor. Somegoro Ichikawa, a Kabuki actor from a famous family, entered upon the role of Cervantes/Quixote in 1969 at the age of 27, and has been playing it ever since. When he graduated to stardom, as is the custom, he was awarded a new name, Koshiro Matsumoto, by which he has been known ever since. In August of 2002, he celebrated both his 60th birthday and his 1,000th performance in the starring role of *Man of La Mancha.* Even more interesting, during the Broadway production's Festival of Foreign Artists, he came from Japan to play the role for six weeks at the Martin Beck Theatre. The marvel is that he didn't speak a word of English but memorized the lines phonetically in that impossibly difficult language, English.

I spent time with Matsumoto in Tokyo, observing him both from the house and also backstage, and can personally testify he's a remarkable man, highly intelligent and deeply caring about his work. Backstage at the Imperial Theatre, post-performance, I witnessed something that astonished me. In the rehearsal hall there was a meeting of the cast immediately following the performance's end and before they'd removed costume or makeup. The meeting was devoted to a short but intense discussion, led by Matsumoto, in which the actors examined their own work—where were we less than we might have been?—where might have we lost concentration?—how do we make it better?

I learned that this was not for my benefit, but a ritual performed at the conclusion of every performance. I was then, and remain, powerfully impressed by the artistry and the esthetic of these devoted theatre people.

CHAPTER EIGHTEEN

I shall impersonate a man...
come, enter into my imagination and see him...

A funny thing happened on my way to make a movie of *Man of La Mancha*—I paused to make another movie, called *A Walk With Love and Death*, for which I was both writer and co-producer. It was not a happy experience. Carter de Haven, one of the investors in *Man of La Mancha*, with whom I got on well, was the primary producer. Its director was John Huston, with whom I got along less well. Huston considered me "difficult," which on occasion could certainly be true, and my opinion of Huston was no warmer than his of me.

But our real problem came with Huston's casting his daughter, Anjelica, in the starring role. Anjelica was 15, about to turn 16, a perfectly nice girl, rather gawky and shy and quite without acting experience. So far as I could tell, Huston was making a *beau geste* in starring Anjelica in a role for which she was neither ready nor right.

We split on this issue, and I left the production, which was shooting in Austria. To Anjelica's credit, she not only later acknowledged her inadequacy but set out to overcome it. She succeeded admirably, a courageous thing to do, given this beginning. I have applauded her success—and regretted the miscarriage of the lovely movie that *A Walk With Love and Death* might have been.

As to Huston himself, I observed him to be frequently cruel, sadistic even, and very much a poseur. Peter Viertel was on target in his roman à clef, *White Hunter, Black Heart*. Actors loved Huston. Writers didn't.

As to the status of the film version of *Man of La Mancha*, knowing that the bidding for rights had passed $3 million, I was surprised to

More important is this: you no longer have *Man of La Mancha*. You have an adaptation of *Don Quixote*. I've seen several such adaptations fail on film and about forty fail on stage. *Man of La Mancha* is a success because I steered clear of *Don Quixote* and invented a play which is original and not an adaptation of the novel. Why is it so difficult for people to see this? Long ago I discovered that one Quixotic adventure exemplifies the man. Ten such adventures leave him to be pitied but not loved.

Further, this script is unpleasantly sadistic. It is also gratuitously homosexual. Speeches and scenes which are the heart of the play have been dropped. Dramatic motivations have been deleted. Having bought *Man of La Mancha* at great expense, you are now allowing it to be altered to something else, and that something else is going to be a ten million dollar fiasco.

Nobody loves a Cassandra, and you will not love me for these comments. But you have a lot of money and devotion invested in this project, so I'll speak loud and clear while there's still time to recover *Man of La Mancha*.

The latest director and screenwriter were dropped, and a new director, Arthur Hiller, engaged. As each director chooses his own screenwriter, Arthur Hiller chose his—which threw me into a quandary since his choice happened to be me.

The quandary was due to my doubts about the filmability of *La Mancha*—but I had considerable respect for Arthur Hiller. Hiller was the director of a dozen feature films, including such winners as *The Americanization of Emily* and *Love Story*, for which he received an Academy nomination. Further, Hiller was one of the best people I've ever known—friendly and forthright, lacking in pose or pretension, an authentic gentleman. Working with Hiller would be a privilege. And so once again I reported to Rome.

The script was by now a confusing patchwork showing the footprints of the several writers and directors who'd trod upon it. Peter O'Toole, Sophia Loren, and James Coco had by now been cast in the leading roles and were already on hand. The pressure of time was severe, shooting must begin, and each day's delay cost heavily.

For me there was no possibility of starting from scratch or "doing my best." My best would be making repairs and restoring continuity as I was best able. I did so, and then, always bored by the actual shooting, which commenced in the summer of 1971, with Hiller's blessing left Rome and resumed furnishing my house in Spain.

The finished picture opened in the winter of 1972. I saw it at its opening in Beverly Hills, one of those $100-a-ticket charitable affairs attended chiefly by society ladies and a sprinkling of film stars.

The movie's opening scene, not written by me, had Cervantes leading a troupe of grotesquely masked actors in a performance of a play satirizing the Inquisition, which leads to arrest by the real Inquisition. The new scene was fearfully confusing to the audience. The march to the prison seems to take an eternity. All that had been dramatically implied on stage was now dully real on the screen.

A good ten minutes elapsed before O'Toole (dubbed by the British actor Simon Gilbert) got to sing "Man of La Mancha." (Loren used her real voice.)

Hiller had done his best at solving the problem of the Cervantes/ Don Quixote transformations by cutting between the "real" scenes in the prison and the "invented" scenes in Cervantes' mind. But this missed the point that both exist in the same time and place.

O'Toole was good but his motivations incomprehensible. Sophia was, as always, beautiful — trying to turn her into "a savage alley cat" was an exercise in futility. Without the benefit of a live audience the actors seemed isolated and uncommunicative. There no longer seemed to be any reason for what they were doing.

Oddly, the best scenes were the ones that had least to do with the story — the dances. Redone by Gillian Lynne, they provided the only moments of action, as in the first half of "Dulcinea" where the men clamber over walls and furnishings, timing their leaps to the editing and giving the viewer a sense of life outside the screen. Later, they did a similar dance to "Little Bird," the kind of male-chorus moment Hollywood has been pulling off for decades, from *South Pacific* to *Seven Brides for Seven Brothers*. It worked here, as well. But nothing worked remotely as well as it did on stage. The medium had defeated the message.

The reviews were generally poor. Gene Siskel, of the Chicago *Tribune*, said it was "...badly choreographed and poorly edited... it looks and sounds hollow." Roger Ebert, his colleague at the *Sun-Times*, called it "...a collection of dialog that would sound incredibly dumb if it weren't in a musical..." United Artists was reduced to quoting *Reader's Digest*, the Cincinnati *Enquirer*, and the Cleveland *Plain Dealer* for their national advertising campaign.

Despite all this, the film opened quite well. It was the top-grossing film for Christmas week, 1972. *Fiddler on the Roof* was number 2, and *1776* number 3—a rare occasion in show business for three movies based upon stage musicals to find themselves in this position. But the expected Academy Awards didn't materialize. There was only one nomination, for Laurence Rosenthal, Best Adapted Score. He didn't win.

An irony: several of the writers who'd done versions of the script applied to the Writers Guild for screen credit. (The Guild has automatic arbitration machinery for determining screen credit when there's more than one writer.) The applications of the other writers were denied, and I, who didn't want it, was "awarded" sole screen credit.

I received a volume of mail on the movie. Some letters were laudatory—not warranted!—and some condemnatory. I've always found the latter interesting. Some ask, with typical show business schadenfreude, how I could so dismally have failed:

> Dear Mr. Wasserman:
>
> I have raved to five of my friends about how good *Man of La Mancha* was as a play, and I "treated" them to see the film. The film began badly with a Prologue that was unnecessary and also removed a wonderful line from the script, "He foreclosed on a church." The lowering of the stairway gave me hope, but that was the high point of the evening. The only scene that worked better in the film than in the play was the death scene.
>
> I have tried to understand why you raped and bastardized your own work. The play worked beautifully. I saw it three times. Why did you take a successful work and damage it so drastically? Don't you recognize a good play when you see one?

And another:

> To be historically accurate, the robes of the Inquisition should have been white. They were Dominicans, not Franciscans. Your researcher missed on that one. I also question the vintage of the armor used. I believe it was from a later period than Cervantes' times...

This one I answered:

> Dear Madam:
>
> My "researcher" is myself. You're not so sharp, either; there was no armor later than the 16th century; the use of armor had ceased. The colors of the Inquisition were white and green, but those colors wouldn't be seen in a prison. The religious order administering the Inquisition was indeed Dominican, though not exclusively. Dominican monks wore black cloaks outside the monastery, brown cloth in ordinary service. But what picky points! I write plays, not scholastic theses.

And to another who said, *"If you are a gentleman you will refund my money..."* I replied:

> Dear Sir:
>
> I am not a gentleman and I would not think of refunding your money. A writer who cares about his work can't afford to be a gentleman. He has to be a fighter. Otherwise, critics would dice him into shreds while offering to shake hands.

The stage play invites the audience to "Enter into my imagination," and the audience does so. Nothing is concealed from them. The magical changes of identity, location, and time are in plain view. All tricks are exposed. The spectators have been asked to supply imagination, and happily they do so, becoming part of the play. The movie asks no such participation. It merely cuts from one sort of reality to another, relegating the audience to passive onlookers. And so they grow bored.

The film version of *Man of La Mancha* now exists as a shabby video, ill-prepared for TV viewing. Requests for remakes of a film come along quite often, but I find no problem in turning them down...until the day an offer comes attached to the right concept for making it. I have my own notion of what that concept is, but will hoard it privately pending other elements falling into place.

Until then, I have the play to keep me warm.

CHAPTER NINETEEN

Many go for wool and come back shorn.

The role of Cervantes in *Man of La Mancha* is one of the prize plums in the musical theatre, so there's little surprise in the desire by eligible leading men to play it, and some ineligible, as well. Actors recognize it as a role doubly showy for being dual. Should they take the trouble to ask me, I'd point out they're mistaken; it isn't a dual role, but, as Josef Meinrad revealed to me, quadruple. First, Cervantes the inept Government employee who offends the Inquisition and is imprisoned. Second, Cervantes the playwright and performer who improvises an entertainment to save his hide and his manuscript. Then there's Don Quixote, the inspired madman of Cervantes' invention and, in the final fifteen minutes of the play, Alonso Quijana, a scholarly country gentleman so addicted to reading books of chivalry that "his brains dry up."

In addition to which he must sing, gloriously if possible.

Lee J. Cobb was the first to play the role, sans music, and he did very well. (When the musical was announced, years later, Lee telephoned me and said two words: "I sing.") Richard Kiley put his stamp irrevocably on the role by being excellent in all departments. He wearied of playing it from time to time, but never able to equal its impact in other roles, he returned periodically to enlist in new tours or revivals. Once he even toured as a one-man show playing Cervantes in a script by Norman Corwin, but it didn't last.

Many actors followed Kiley, even in the original run at the ANTA Washington Square. Jon Cypher, the original Dr. Carrasco and well known to the TV public as Chief Fletcher Daniels of *Hill Street Blues*, played it often and smartly. Lloyd Bridges replaced Kiley for a time, as did one of Broadway's best leading men, John Cullum. José Ferrer headed several national tours. Robert Goulet, Hal Holbrook, and Hal Linden have toured in the play, as have Jack Jones and his father, Allan Jones, in what became a family competition. Both Howard Keel and John Raitt have lent their splendid voices to the role. Laurence Guittard, Bob Wright, Ed Ames (the original Chief Bromden in *Cuckoo's Nest*), and several more have essayed the role in New York or on tour. The names Keith Andes and David Atkinson must be added to the list. Raul Julia tried it—of which more later. Placido Domingo recorded a cast album, badly, in company with Mandy Patinkin, Julia Migenes, and Samuel Ramey. (This recording, with powerhouse performers, demonstrates only that the material isn't proof against error.)

Keith Michell starred in the role in England, alternating runs at the Piccadilly Theatre with Richard Kiley. Michell also played it in an excellent audio recording of the entire play, which I was present to oversee. We recorded at the Beatles' studio outside London.

Some time during the run at the Martin Beck Theatre, following the transfer of the show from Washington Square, our producers had that inspired idea of an International Festival of Don Quixotes. They imported a half-dozen stars of foreign productions of the show, including Charles West from Australia, Keith Michell from England, Claudio Brook from Mexico, Gideon Singer from Israel, and Toshiro Matsumoto—then still known as Somegoro Ichikawa—from Japan, each for a four- to six-week run. Fascinating idea—except that the non-English speakers had accents so extreme that the audience often must have wondered what was being said. One hopes they already knew the play.

It's likely most of them did. *Man of La Mancha* exhibited a welcome phenomenon: repeat business. For several years of its initial run the producers found it unnecessary to take any newspaper advertising except the single line: "What! You've only seen *Man of La Mancha* once?" Ticket buyers came back, again and again.

Special mention must be made of Chev (Shev) Rogers, who played Pedro, the brutal head muleteer. Shev was not only the original, he was a pre-original, for he worked with us during the formative period and did yeoman service singing at the money-raising auditions. He not only played Pedro in the five years of New

York run, but continued playing it in various road companies. He has played just about every role in the show except, possibly, Aldonza. He's an example of that extreme rarity, an actor whose entire professional life has been spent in a single play. When last I saw Shev it was backstage in Palm Springs at a stop of the Robert Goulet company. We fell into each others' arms — 40-year veterans of the Manchegan wars! Like most hulking stage and screen villains, Shev has a heart of pure marshmallow.

Of all the revivals of the show, however, one stands out as wholly disastrous. It was a production of such ghastly ineptitude that ten years later, at the initiation of a new production on Broadway, it was recalled by critics as an example of how low a "classic success" can sink with mishandling.

The paradox is that it was perpetrated by three of the show's original creators. This is a melancholy story that requires a bit of backup history: what happened to the team that had created this "classic"?

The outsized success of the premiere production should logically have led the creative team to new projects, to brave new batterings at boundaries. It didn't. With success they became alienated. Then antagonists. And finally, enemies. They divided sharply, falling into the trap of self-interest, and never worked together again.

The producers, Selden and James, enjoyed their partnership and produced more shows together, including *Hallelujah Baby*, which starred Leslie Uggams and had a good run. *Portrait of a Queen*, at the Henry Miller, ran about 60 performances. *Come Summer* played at the Lunt-Fontanne Theatre in March of 1969, but lasted only seven performances.

Hal James, an extroverted and wholly delightful man who threw an anniversary party at the Players Club on each anniversary of *La Mancha*, was sorely missed after he died suddenly of a stroke in August of 1971. Albert Selden, the more reserved of the two, went on to co-produce shows with various partners until 1980 but actually had little taste for the cutthroat business of Broadway. Disgusted over the brawling on one of his productions, *Irene*, he moved to Santa Fe in 1984, and died there June 10, 1987. With his passing there was no longer anyone in charge of *Man of La Mancha*.

Thereafter the show had no management or headquarters. It has suffered thereby.

Mitch Leigh, as I've already discussed, became an example of the dangers of early success. A clever and a wealthy man with an itch for celebrity, his ego ballooned with the prestige of a wildly successful show. His real talent was for his primary profession, marketing. He was convinced that marketing was the secret of successful showmanship, ironically neglecting the example before him: *Man of La Mancha* in its first incarnation wasn't marketed at all. The audience found it on its own.

In the short biographies in the show's programs, written by the authors themselves, Leigh's begins, "Mitch Leigh is a modern Renaissance man." One wonders, what does he mean—that he's a latter day Medici? A Buonarroti? A Da Vinci?

The success of *La Mancha* made success seem easy. In partnership with Albert Marre, Leigh embarked upon a career of composing, and producing shows financed largely or entirely by his own money. The first of these efforts, with book by Albert Marre and directed by Albert Marre, produced by Leigh and with music by Leigh, was *Cry For Us All*, starring Joan Diener. It opened April 8, 1970, and closed April 15, one week later, having lost an estimated $3 million.

Chu Chem, "A Zen-Buddhist-Hebrew musical" produced by Mitch Leigh, with music by Mitch Leigh, and "Entire Production Staged by Albert Marre," had the distinction of failing three separate times. Its first incarnation appeared in the same 1965 program of musicals in which *Man of La Mancha* was first presented. It was next done at a Yiddish language theatre, downtown. Its final production was at the Ritz Theatre, opening March 17, 1989, and closing May 14, aggregate loss unreported.

Home Sweet Homer, with music by Mitch Leigh, was also produced by Mitch Leigh and financed by Mitch Leigh. "Book and Direction" were by Albert Marre. It starred Yul Brynner in a paraphrase of Homer's *Odyssey*. After a short but troubled tour it opened and closed in New York on the same night, January 4, 1977, at a considerable loss.

An April Song, based on a play by Jean Anouilh, had music by

Mitch Leigh and was produced by Mitch Leigh, but in a rupture of relations between Leigh and Marre closed out of town, loss undetermined.

Saravá, "A Production by Mitch Leigh," with music by Mitch Leigh and financed by Mitch Leigh, was based on Jorge Amado's novel, *Doña Flor and Her Two Husbands*. Starting performances at the eighteen-hundred seat Broadway Theatre on February 12, 1979, it was notable for a Leigh innovation. Observing that opening a show made one vulnerable to bad reviews since critics were known to attend opening nights, Leigh decided not to open the show but just to play it. Therefore, *Saravá* played "previews" while continuously postponing opening.

It was a ploy that didn't sit well with the New York newspapers. The *Times* finally said, snappishly, "Since this show...has been giving public performances for the past month, a review is in order." They thereupon bought tickets for their critics, who thereupon lambasted the show. The other newspapers followed suit.

The title song in *Saravá* was played no less than five times in the course of performance, and as the audience left the auditorium they heard it once more over loudspeakers in the lobby. To no avail; the show ran until June 17, 1979, never officially opening. The loss was estimated at $5 million.

Ain't Broadway Grand was the second try at a musical about flamboyant producer Mike Todd. It was produced by Mitch Leigh with music by Mitch Leigh and was financed by Mitch Leigh. It opened at the Lunt-Fontanne Theatre on April 18, 1993, and closed three weeks later. Unanimously roasted by the critics, its loss was estimated at $7 million.

But the most astonishing thing about this cavalcade of catastrophe was the Mitch Leigh scores. None of the music became popular. None was noted as distinguished. No song became a hit. There were no studios anxious to commit any of the music to recording for the market.

And yet there is that gorgeous score of *La Mancha* and those hit songs for which Leigh has a secure niche in Broadway history.

As 1990 approached it was evident that the 25th anniversary of *La Mancha* might offer an opportunity to reinvigorate the play through presenting a truly fine revival. I passed the thought on to Michael David, whom I considered the best and brightest producer-manager on Broadway, and also to my friend, David Fay, who was then the producing head of Fox Theatricals, in the Midwest. Almost instantly, it seemed, they were at my house in California where, over coffee and corned beef sandwiches, we planned the ultimate, the most elegant production of *La Mancha* ever. It would have new direction, new design, and the most impressive acting ensemble that could be recruited from both sides of the Atlantic. A dream production, no less.

We took into account that previous designs for the show had been forced to conform to the flaws and shortcomings of the ANTA Washington Square Theatre. Subsequent productions had never been freed from those original restrictions, which had been carried forward into proscenium theatres. Now it could be re-imagined. The possibilities were exciting!

I advised my fellow authors, Leigh and Darion, both of whom thought the idea splendid. Leigh rather casually suggested that he'd like to be the producer. I said, "No." We not only had the best producers on Broadway, but as always, I was dead against any of the authors being producer; it would inherently be prejudicial to the other two.

A contract was prepared and submitted to the authors by Michael David's company, David-Strong-Warner, known on Broadway familiarly as "The Dodgers." It was excellent, including the customary percentages of gross royalties to the authors to be divided in the usual ratio.

Whereupon, the thunderbolt. Mitch Leigh appropriated the dream-contract in its entirety, changing only two items: the authors' royalties were increased, and the producer of the show became Mitch Leigh.

I was stunned, and said to Joe Darion, "You're not going to sign that?"

"Well," said Joe, "it's more money."

Mitch produced the most disastrous production of *La Mancha* ever. The old scenery, owned by Leigh, was leased by Leigh to the Leigh production. It was tacky, tired, and too familiar. The direction, again by Albert Marre, excited only a sense of déjà vu. Star of the production was Raul Julia, a fine actor on the spoken stage, but he couldn't sing a lick. He and the orchestra were frequently in keys alien to each other.

The ultimate albatross though, was the co-star, Sheena Easton, a wee popsicle of a girl who could sing but couldn't act. Aldonza, the Spanish slut, puzzlingly was played with a broad Scottish burr when it was played at all, for Easton, chronically ill, missed almost as many performances as she played, and, in a preview on Broadway, walked on stage and fainted dead away. She may have been frightened at where she found herself. Possibly she was genuinely ill. It was certain only that she was not an actress.

Thus we had an actor who couldn't sing and a singer who couldn't act.

Leigh's production of *Man of La Mancha* went on the road prior to Broadway and for the first time in its history got bad reviews. Leigh's talent for marketing was in evidence, but unfortunately for the future of the show the large audiences that saw this production were soured by it, as were the critics.

I sued Mitch Leigh in federal courts prior to the show's opening, hoping to halt a slaughter. His response was to offer to buy out my rights. I had no problem turning it down, but after spending two hundred thousand of my own money on lawyers, saw that I couldn't win, either. The production was already in progress, the damage unstoppable.

The reviews tell the story. "A musty 'Man of La Mancha,'" said the *Los Angeles Times*. "It is to the theatre what reconstituted orange juice is to fresh — a version at least as tired as the weary old knight at its center... What's puzzling is that Leigh, who wrote this rousing score and conducted its overture under a spotlight opening night, can be satisfied to present such a sloppy production, and has the chutzpah to charge a top ticket price of $55 for it. Not only does the public deserve more bang for the buck, but Leigh should be trying for a much better class of impossible dreams."

Daily Variety, reviewing the show at the Pantages Theatre, Los Angeles: "This 25th-anniversary tour of *Man of La Mancha* suffers from the kind of high-tech casting that turns out to be more of an obstacle than it's worth. The production has a stilted, plodding feel…Librettist Wasserman objected to this revival and tried to stop it. Unfortunately composer-producer Mitch Leigh has not come up with a production that even slightly outweighs Wasserman's objections."

Headlines continued to tell the story.

La Costa, California:
'MAN OF LA MANCHA' FAILS TO ACHIEVE ITS POTENTIAL

The Orange County Register:
MAN OF LA MANCHA IS IMPOSSIBLY MISCAST

Los Angeles Daily News:
LA MANCHA REVIVAL NOT CHARMING

The Chicago Sun-Times:
LA MANCHA QUEST FAILS TO TURN UP ENERGY

Chicago Examiner:
TO STAGE THE IMPOSSIBLE PLAY…
MAN OF LA MANCHA SLIGHTS CERVANTES

The Boston Herald:
LA MANCHA LACKS FIRE

USA Today:
FRESH LA MANCHA AN IMPOSSIBLE DREAM

The Washington Times:
QUIXOTIC CASTING KILLS 'LA MANCHA'

New York Post:
A 92 LA MANCHA? YOU MUST BE DREAMING

New York Daily News:
LOOK, IT'S THE PAN OF LA MANCHA!

The reviews were fully as hostile as the headlines indicate.

The production opened at the Marquis Theatre on Broadway on April 26, 1992, and played for two weeks before closing. The damage lasted for ten years and, in some ways, forever.

For five years I didn't speak to Joe Darion. It may be a comment on my own naivete, but I was deeply shocked by his agreement to this production. After five years of non-communication, we pasted over our differences and resumed a friendship, at least nominally. Joe is gone now, and I miss him greatly. But it's nonsense to say one forgives and forgets. One forgives, but it's impossible to forget.

Does *Man of La Mancha* have true importance? If so, it lies in its importance as a pivotal show—literally—in the history of the American musical theatre. It was the last show of one cycle, and first of the next. Lacking objectivity in this judgment, I shall again resort to an analysis and judgment from that independent chronicler of the musical theatre, Robert S. Sennett:

> Because of its dependence on narrative and staging, and its conventional order of book scenes, character songs and show stopping numbers, *Man of La Mancha* is very much in the mold of the classic, Golden Age musical. Yet it is also one of the very first, if not the first, works of musical theater to be properly called conceptual—to contain one overriding conceit which, in effect, places quotation marks around the entire experience and brings the audience into complicity with the creators. In this sense, it has more in common—at least on the surface—with the big thematic musicals of the 1980s such as *Cats* (1982) where the entire Winter Garden was transformed into a trashy litter box, or, to choose an example of higher artistic achievement—Sondheim's *Sweeney Todd* (1979), where the elements of horror and dislocation of the story overspread the music, the set, and eventually the audience as well.
>
> *Man of La Mancha* has its feet planted firmly between both camps. It is a crafted musical play, in the most professional sense of the phrase, needing no trick set or multi-million dollar investment to achieve its effects. Yet it invites—even necessitates— deconstruction, that curious term so appropriate to our age. Nearly

everything about *Man of La Mancha* both seems and is. It is a play within a play within a play. The irony, the great stakes, and the ambiguity of the final message of the play most certainly point to *Man of La Mancha* as being one of the first great musical plays of the Post-Golden Age.

In this curious position *Man of La Mancha* stands alone—a singular example of a truly revolutionary work which proved to be overwhelmingly popular. Its shades and colors come and go with the seasons—operatic or folkloric, spectacular or tawdry, holy or profane, depending upon which production you see and which critic you read.

One thing is certain, the work will live on.

On December 5, 2002, the brave new production I'd envisioned ten years earlier opened on Broadway. It had a tough young producer, David Stone, who allowed no compromise; a director, Jonathan Kent, with a fresh new vision for the play; a designer, Paul Brown, with an equally fresh vision of the physical production; and a dream cast headed by Brian Stokes Mitchell, Mary Elizabeth Mastrantonio, and Ernie Sabella.

I am content.

CHAPTER TWENTY

Every man is as God made him,
and most of the time a good deal worse.

FRAGMENTS AND AFTERTHOUGHTS: I own one piece of wisdom, acquired empirically, regarding the creation of musicals. It's a perfectly obvious point, which some, nevertheless, disregard. A musical may succeed if its foundation is a work sturdy enough to stand on its own. Here's the Wasserman Test: if you strip a musical of its music, will it be worthy to perform as a play?

If not, proceed at risk. *My Fair Lady* is, of course, *Pygmalion*. *Miss Saigon* is a geographically dislocated *Madame Butterfly*. *Phantom of the Opera* is a classic novel and play. *Rent* (which I happen to detest) is a high-decibel *La Bohème*. *Oklahoma!* is *Green Grow the Lilacs*. *Carousel* is *Liliom*. *Porgy and Bess* is Du Bose Heyward's novel...And *Les Misérables*...well, you know that one.

Are there exceptions? Surprisingly few.

I have observed that the more sophisticated the critic—or the rag he writes for—the more compelled he will feel to denigrate *Man of La Mancha*, or at least to feel the obligation to do so. I ascribe this to the embarrassment of sophisticates at feeling or expressing emotion. I observed that pattern in London; the Brits are uneasy with emotion, it's somehow unseemly, so they resist. In America it's a given that publications like *The New Yorker* or *The New York Times* will deplore *La Mancha*'s emotion as "kitsch."

I do not see *Man of La Mancha* as kitsch, though a poor production will allow it to appear so. I think of *The Sound of Music* as kitsch, as Teutonic sentimentality nesting comfortably with Hummel figurines and cuckoo clocks.

People who hate the play hate it not mildly but with passion. This in itself is curious and isn't true of kitsch, which isn't hated but treated with Pecksniffian distaste. Among critics, the curious case of Mr. Gottfried has already been addressed, but joining him in Boston is Kevin Kelly. Both men froth at the mouth in print when the show is even mentioned.

The reverse side of this coin is those who love it. Their devotion is paid not merely to a show but to a philosophy...or more accurately to an alternative view of existence. It's the rare customer or critic who is neutral. I've yet to hear anyone say, upon seeing a performance of *Man of La Mancha*, "Yeah, it's sorta okay." But often one hears, "It's like a religious experience."

To me, this aspect of the play is interesting, for I've never acknowledged faith in any religion. To the contrary, my customary mode takes the shape of a wary skepticism. I have no belief in the Faulknerian cliche, "Mankind will prevail." I believe that if there's a potential vandalism to be committed by our own species upon this earth, we will commit it or we already have.

So why, then, did I write *Man of La Mancha*? I don't know. It was an involuntary blurt. Involuntary blurts aren't subject to planning. They're involuntary.

Because my plays have gone to almost all eligible countries in the world, I'm sometimes asked which peoples are the best and which the worst to deal with. The answers are easy. Best, in my experience, are the Japanese. I've found them honest, ethical, and unfailingly respectful. Worst are the French. I've found them immoral, unprincipled, felonious, corrupt, crooked, incredibly greedy, and utterly without conscience. Worse, they're serenely smug in their belief that all of these are entitlements permitted them because they're French and the rest of the world isn't. I've never had any dealings with the French that didn't produce some form of chicanery, abuse, or outright theft.

Their crookedness of mind extends to their culture, which they regard as the only culture on Earth worthy of the name. I'm amused to recall an argument I had with Jacques Brel over his translation of

Man of La Mancha. "Why," I inquired of Brel, "have you changed Cervantes' line from, 'I am a poet,' to 'I am almost a poet.'"

"Because," explained Brel, "in France to say 'I am a poet' would be presumptuous. Poets are revered in France. They have very high status."

"Cervantes was not in France," I said. "Cervantes was Spanish."

"But this play will be performed in France."

I maintained my position and Brel maintained his. Later he was to state that this argument had so depressed him that he cut the run shorter than it might have been, presumably in retaliation for my brutish insensitivity to French culture.

Brel, by the way, was not French; he was Belgian.

I'm asked why I choose to live in Arizona. It's because Arizona is the only state that refuses to accept daylight saving time.

I like mavericks. I like maverick states, countries, plays, and people.

Not being a New Yorker I've observed New Yorkers to be the most provincial people in America. To New Yorkers there's their city, and then there's a vast outback, the Great American Cultural Desert, where nothing of importance happens other than a certain marginal activity in Hollywood.

I think of New York as less a place than a time of life. New York is the season wherein one struggles to succeed at some difficult, competitive profession. If successful one has a choice—to enlist permanently in the Militia of New York, establishing a bivouac on the upper West Side—or to take one's talent to other venues, to territories where one may exercise his expertise in behalf of institutions it may benefit.

The case of the theatre is a case of acute snobbery. The hundreds of regional and not-for-profit theaters throughout the country are crippled by their slavish "Direct from Broadway" fixation, which they consider a necessary lure to their subscribers. Most often, of course, their offerings are extremely *indirect* from Broadway, layered with a multiyear patina of dust upon arrival. Nor were they necessarily good or even successful when they played New York.

The problem in the regional theatres is their fear of originating theatre literature, a fear given fangs by financial risk and a paucity of talent. Sometimes these are overcome, but too seldom and with difficulty.

I know because, although I choose to remain remote from New York, I haven't stopped writing. In the past few years I've written and overseen productions of a number of new plays and musicals. There's *Western Star*, for instance, a musical that grew out of my backpacking into the Rocky Mountains where I observed ghost towns, their crumbling structures being sucked back into the earth. Who were the people who built them? What did they hope for? Why did they fail? I visualized them, not the celluloid pioneers of Hollywood manufacture but the real people who came west—the jailbirds, bankrupts, and failures, the runner-awayers seeking new lives—their voices both pathetic and brave, in music ranging as broadly as their range of aspirations.

Or *An Enchanted Land*, a play distilled from memories of my residence in Haiti and interest in the religion of Vodoun. This play was well-received in London in a fine production by Stephen Glover, but has yet to be welcomed in the United States.

Or *Beggar's Holiday*, the only musical boasting a Duke Ellington score not yet heard. The play is as satirically wicked as its ancestor, *The Beggar's Opera*, with a view of American morality as slantwise as was John Gay's of England.

Or *A Walk in the Sky*, a musical based upon an original television play of mine, much as was *Man of La Mancha*. The play and the musical exist side by side, both frequently produced. But as with *La Mancha* the musical spans a wider range of emotion than is possible with the play.

As I write this, another in the endless parade of movies attempting to dramatize *Don Quixote* has bitten the dust. This one sadly died a'borning, Terry Gilliam's *The Man Who Killed Don Quixote*. Budgeted originally at forty million dollars, it lost eight million dollars of its financing, withdrawn just before shooting commenced in Spain. Thereafter, plagues which struck the production included the roar of F-16 jets from a nearby NATO base, a hailstorm, torrential rains, and then its star, the French actor, Jean Rochefort, being crippled by a double herniated disc, plus...

That was sufficient. The company that insured the movie cried, "Enough!" and pulled the plug. What has been salvaged is a documentary called *Lost in La Mancha: The Story of a Movie Which Never Got Made*. As I viewed the documentary, tears came to my eyes in sympathy for the disasters suffered by Gilliam and Company, and empathy also, for I've been there. In particular I'd have warned them, do not cast an actor of the age of Quixote in the role. Whether on stage or in film, playing it requires the athleticism and stamina of a much younger man. Younger actors can be made up to look the age; older actors cannot survive the demands.

The plot of *The Man Who Killed Don Quixote*: a young advertising executive (to have been played by Johnny Depp) is transported centuries into the past to encounter Don Quixote for whom he becomes his Sancho Panza. Thereafter the story flips backwards and forward in time, rather like *A Connecticut Yankee in King Arthur's Court*.

Terry Gilliam is talented and imaginative and indeed might have made something of it, but unfortunately the idea is already weary. Personally, I have encountered it a number of times. Periodically I am asked if I will invent a TV series based on a Don Quixote in collision with our modern world and all the amusement such a collision will cause. I have said "no" to all of them. For me, Don Quixote belongs in his original period and milieu. He was already an anachronism when Cervantes invented him; as Dr. Carrasco argues, "There have been no knights for three hundred years." Transported to other times, Quixote becomes merely quaint, the subject of a one-joke syndrome.

There are two immensely popular targets in converting classics: one is *Don Quixote*, the other *Lysistrata*, both favorites of college undergraduates who find it immensely clever to transplant their respective protagonists to alien corn.

In assembling news stories of the debacle that spawned *Lost in La Mancha*, I noted, with amusement one constant: every news story or review applied the phrase "The Impossible Dream" in either its text or headline. Two of them described the phrase as, "In

Cervantes' immortal words..." They are not Cervantes' words; they're mine. But I hereby deed them to The Master, a small installment on an enormous debt. Of course, the words will stubbornly be attributed to him, regardless.

More movie versions of *Don Quixote* will inevitably be attempted, but I believe a definitive version to be impossible. It was a conclusion I came to long ago, in the ponderings that led me to write *Man of La Mancha*. I watch the ongoing attempts with interest and sympathy, but have discovered no reason for a change of mind.

I cannot close this account without comment on the latest "revival" of *Man of La Mancha*. (How can a play be a "revival" when it has never stopped playing?) It opened in Washington D.C. in October of 2002, and in New York at the Martin Beck Theatre (always the Martin Beck!) on December 5th of the same year. I admire this production and applaud its radical, utterly fresh approach in both direction and design. I admire its leading performers, Brian Stokes Mitchell, whose singing lifts the audience to its feet in transports of delight; Mary Elizabeth Mastrantonio, who brings different dimensions to the role of Aldonza; and Ernie Sabella, who was born to play Sancho. I'm *happy* about this one.

Which some may find peculiar, since I have not seen the production and in all likelihood never will.

Some time ago I made a decision against further long-distance travel. Having led a gypsy life and attained a full quota of years, I felt myself entitled to abjure airports and air travel. If people want to talk with me in person, they come to my home in Arizona. Jonathan Kent, director of the new *La Mancha*, did so, twice. During his visits we discussed, compared ideas, and evolved a fresh approach to the production. Of course there is no substitute for studying the performance itself, but by demanding reviews of people who see it I learn a good deal. Such reviews are more perceptive and of greater value to me than those of professional critics.

In my lifetime I have heard the phrase "stopping the show" hundreds of times, but I have never known it literally to happen. Not until Brian Stokes Mitchell's singing of "The Quest," also known as "The Impossible Dream," upon the conclusion of which the audience rises to its feet for an ovation, which stops the show dead in its tracks. Stokes has the most beautiful voice ever brought to the Cervantes/Quixote role, nor do I think it will be matched in this generation. In addition to which he is an amazingly modest and down-to-earth fellow, as I have discovered in our periodic late night post-performance telephone chats.

I believe that what keeps *Man of La Mancha* alive is not only its philosophy but its accessibility. It can be performed in a myriad of ways, in all sorts of spaces and at many levels of professionalism. It is almost immune to indifferent actors. It "works," even in the hands of amateurs and arty directors. I have seen it performed in a tent adjacent to a thundering freeway; on a stage bare of all scenery but projection screens; in the midst of a war with interruptions of exploding grenades; in almost every conceivable environment. In California it is being played to the musical accompaniment not of an orchestra but of a single guitar in the hands of a lone musician who wanders a bare stage...As I write, a production now in the twentieth week of an open-end run.

So it is not an "impossible musical" after all. Merely improbable.

Once upon a time I invented a phrase, "the impossible dream." People think it comes from a song, but it doesn't. It's from my original television play, *I, Don Quixote*. The phrase has gone into the language and traveled far and wide. It's been used (and abused) countless times, and will continue into the future. I invented it simply to explain Don Quixote's quest — indeed, the song's proper title is "The Quest." But the public seized upon the eponymous phrase and won't let go.

"The impossible dream" has been used to promote everything under the sun and some in the shade. It's been used in sales pitches by General Mills, General Motors, and General Westmoreland. Also, by baseball teams and bidets and by sleazy politicians and by charlatans of all breeds and vocations.

Sometimes I'm sorry I invented it. Sometimes I feel I opened a verbal Pandora's box and wish it could be slammed shut again.

The odd thing about this little phrase is that everyone seems to misunderstand it. "The impossible dream" is customarily applied to ventures that may be somewhat difficult but perfectly possible. A pennant for the Mets. A new spike in the company sales chart. An even faster computer (who needs it?) or possibly the latest burp in technology. When I see these references—and I see them every day—my impulse is to holler, "Pay attention, damn it, the operative word is not 'dream,' the operative word is 'impossible!'"

Of course no one listens. But "impossible" is exactly what I meant: the dream, to be valid, must be impossible. Not just difficult. *Impossible.* Which implies an ideal never attainable but nevertheless stubbornly to be pursued. A striving for what cannot be achieved but still is worth the effort. As, for instance, peace on earth. Or a gentleness for all who breathe, and breathing, suffer. Or a hope that we may mitigate the horrors paraded for us on the news every hour of every day of every week. That we may reduce the tidal surge of wars, crimes, cruelties to humans and to animals, and the orgies of atrocities that sicken the earth.

These are impossible dreams. Still, quixotically, they must be dreamed.

I, DON QUIXOTE

A PLAY BY DALE WASSERMAN

© *1960 Renewed 1988*

Here follows the script of *I, Don Quixote* with its faults and defects plainly visible to the clinical eye. Since this is an account of beginnings as well as endings, I present this infancy of *Man of La Mancha* for the curious who are interested in grubs before they become butterflies. Enjoy!   —D.W.

THE PEOPLE

(Note: Each character plays two or more roles. These are their permanent identities, in the prison.)

MIGUEL DE CERVANTES In age about 50. Tall, thin, with a short graying beard. Manner courtly, voice courteous and leavened with gentle humor. Face life-worn. Eyes remarkable—a child's eyes, grave and curious, endlessly interested.

ESCALANTE (Aldonza) A splendid alley cat, survivor if not always victor of many back-fence tussles. She is vital, half-savage, with an aura of natural sexuality. Black hair in tangled profusion. A ripe body threatening to burst its ragged clothes.

SANCHO (Manservant) Short, rotund, cheery, mixing peasant naivete and pragmatism is odd proportions.

THE DUKE (Dr. Carrasco) A handsome young man of elegance and fearful ennui. English. His mordant cynicism marks the frustrated idealist.

JUDAS MACABEO (Padre) An old man with little square spectacles. Unctuous and pedantic. Kindly and faintly ironic of manner.

MONIPODIO (Governor) A born boss, jovial, clever, amoral. Knows every iniquity and is practiced in all. He limps.

GRACIOSA (Antonia) A girl of 18, vacuously pretty, with a streak of malice. Not terribly bright; sometimes cunning.

THE SCORPION (Pedro) A surly cutthroat with a hook in place of one hand. Bull-like and dangerous.

LOBILLO (Anselmo) A swarthy, affable pimp. He plays guitar and sings well.

EL MÉDICO (Barber) A grinny little man; evil and sprightly.

MOTHER BANE (Housekeeper) A hoarse-voiced hag of many years and misdeeds.

THE GYPSY A dark, lithe and ragged boy of 13.

CAPTAIN OF THE INQUISITION

FOUR MASKED MEN OF THE INQUISITION (non-speaking)

THE SETTING

A vast stone prison vault whose furthest reaches are lost in shadow. There are skeletal platforms at various heights, used by the prisoners for sleeping—and by us for playing certain scenes. There are two qualities of light used: the scant cold rays which sift into the prison from a grille overhead; and the warm suffusion which lights the Don Quixote scenes.

Although the walls of the prison are seemingly solid stone they will, in the "playing" scenes, become transparent and give way to the hot sun and landscape of La Mancha; or on occasion to night sky with stars.

THE PLACE

A prison in Seville in 1594.

ACT I

*There is music. It sweeps and rolls with the bombast and blind
arrogance of Spain at the end of the 16ᵗʰ century. A confident march
to nowhere.*

*The curtain rises on a one-way traveler which moves wall-like
across stage, an art-work panorama of Spain. It is a profile of the
wide, empty region called La Mancha framed in the distance by the
burned hard lines of the sierra. A highway winds across the plains.
These are some of the things we may see:*

A country home set bleakly in the fields.

A shepherd escorting his flock in rolling clouds of dust.

A crossroads gibbet with a hanged man dangling from its beam.

A march of soldiers led by men playing bugles and kettledrums.
They haul cannon and carry guns of the period.

A turreted castle, disintegrating, — springing from crags.

*A procession of hooded monks carrying tall crosiers, escort
for a prelate in a sedan chair.*

*The decorated wagon of a troupe of strolling players. The
actors themselves riding, or walking behind in costume.*

A cluster of windmills.

Muleteers with long coiling whips freighting goods over the road.

A roadside inn. And finally,

*The massive and ornate gates of Seville and, seen through
and above them, the city itself.*

*On this last image the music has given way to the muffled drums
and chanting of the* MEN OF THE INQUISITION. *The sound is
inimical, chilling. Then the lights come up in the vast prison vault
which occupies the entire stage.*

The GYPSY *is dancing a "seguiriya gitana" with epicene sensuality.*
LOBILLO *sings and beats the rhythm on a sanbomba.* GRACIOSA
wields a palm broom in dry, shuffling accompaniment. JUDAS

MACABEO *tinkles with a spoon on an iron bar, nodding his head in
dignified, approving manner.*

The DUKE *is to one side, leaning against the wall, stiff in his
armor of indifference.* SOME *of the other* PRISONERS *may be seen,
dimly, sleeping or huddled in the shadows.*

*There is little vitality in the dance or accompaniment. Jaded, born
of boredom.*

The JAILER *enters down right, followed by a* MANSERVANT
burdened with a sizable, shabby straw trunk. HE *pauses to look back.*

JAILER (*Brusquely, to someone following*) Well?

> (MIGUEL DE CERVANTES *enters carrying a bulky
> package under one arm.* HE *is hesitant; his eyes canvass
> the surroundings.*)

Anything wrong? The accommodations?

CERVANTES No, no, they appear...interesting.

JAILER (*slyly*) For a consideration, I could arrange something more
    private.

CERVANTES No, no, I *like* company.

JAILER If you change your mind, just shout...if you are able.

> (HE *exits*)

MANSERVANT (*Nervously*) What did he mean by that?

CERVANTES Calm yourself. There is a remedy for everything but
    death.

MANSERVANT That could be the one we need!

CERVANTES Good morning, gentlemen...ladies. I regret being

thrust upon you in this manner and I hope you will not find my company objectionable.

> (*Silence. The* PRISONERS' *eyes glitter like snakes into whose den a rabbit has been thrust*)

I'm not really a stranger to these surroundings, my friends. I have been in prison before—oh, yes, more than once! And on occasion I've thought the whole world a prison, a very large one where all have desires and practically none are fulfilled.

> (HE *laughs courteously—alone. Movement begins, a slow surround by the* PRISONERS, *approaching, circling. The* SCORPION *slithers to the floor from his sleeping place, his iron hook ready.* MOTHER BANE *comes creeping from upstage*)

But how thoughtless of me to complain in the face of your misfortunes. Does one speak of the rope in the house of the hanged? Let me say, rather—take heart! Remember that the light of hope is most clearly seen in the dark. I have always believed—

> (*With a yell the* PRISONERS *pounce. The* SCORPION *leaps on* CERVANTES' *back, bending him into an arc with the iron hook about his throat. The* GYPSY *and* LOBILLO *rifle his pockets, ripping them inside out. The* WOMEN, *shrieking like harpies, tear open the trunk and sack and plunder the contents. The* MANSERVANT *too is smothered in the attack.*
>
> THE DUKE, *unmoving, smiles remotely at the entertainment.*
>
> MONIPODIO, *who has been sleeping, rolls over, blinks at the doings, sits up*)

MONIPODIO (*a roar*) Basta! Enough!

> (*Action freezes.* HE *slides to the floor, grumbling and scratching*)

Noise, trouble, fights. Kill each other if you must, but for God's sake do it quietly.

> (HE *becomes aware of* CERVANTES *still held by the iron hook*)

Who are you?

> (CERVANTES *makes a strangling sound*)

Eh?

> (CERVANTES *gurgles desperately.* MONIPODIO *snaps his fingers at the* SCORPION, *who sullenly releases* CERVANTES)

CERVANTES Cervantes. Miguel de Cervantes.

MONIPODIO (*With mock respect*) A gentleman!

CERVANTES It has never saved me from going to bed hungry.

MONIPODIO (*Of the* MANSERVANT) And that?

CERVANTES My servant. May I have the honor—?

MONIPODIO They call me "The Governor."

CERVANTES (*Bows*) Your Excellency.

MONIPODIO Are you mocking me?

CERVANTES (*Sincerely*) No, señor. I have known several governors, and all deserved this place more than you.

MONIPODIO I doubt that. What's your stuff?

CERVANTES My—?

MONIPODIO (*Impatiently*) Your specialty, man. Cutpurse? Highwayman?

CERVANTES Oh, nothing so interesting! I am a poet.

THE DUKE (*With his first sign of interest*) They're putting men in prison for that?

CERVANTES Oh, no!

THE DUKE (*Losing interest*) Too bad.

MONIPODIO Well, what *are* you here for?

CERVANTES I am to appear before the Inquisition.

(*A reaction among the* PRISONERS — *this is bad*)

MONIPODIO Heresy?

CERVANTES Not exactly. You see, I had been employed by the government as a tax-collector—

MONIPODIO Tax-collector! You must be rich!

CERVANTES (*A doleful denial*) I have the misfortune to be honest.

(*A whistle of incredulity from the* PRISONERS)

MONIPODIO (*Trying hard to stay with it*) How does a tax-collector get in trouble with the Inquisition?

CERVANTES By making assessments against the church.

MONIPODIO (*In disbelief*) You did . . . *what?*

CERVANTES (*Defensively*) The law says tax all property equally.

MONIPODIO (*Helplessly*) The *law*.

THE DUKE This gentleman has empty rooms in his head.

MONIPODIO They'll burn him at high noon and if I were there I'd light the fire.

> (*Pulls himself together. Briskly*)

Well. Let's get on with the trial.

> (*This is the signal for a burst of activity from the* PRISONERS. THEY *scurry about pulling benches into position, setting up a table and stool for* MONIPODIO. CERVANTES *views this in growing bewilderment*)

CERVANTES Excuse me. What trial?

MONIPODIO Yours, of course.

CERVANTES What have I done?

MONIPODIO (*Cheerfully*) We'll find something.

CERVANTES That's not fair!

MONIPODIO Fair is for the innocent. You're guilty.

CERVANTES You don't seem to understand. I'll only be here a few hours. The Inquisition—

MONIPODIO (*Patient but firm*) My dear sir, no one enters or leaves this prison without being tried by his fellow-prisoners.

CERVANTES And if I'm found guilty?

MONIPODIO Oh, you will be.

CERVANTES What kind of a sentence...?

MONIPODIO We generally fine a prisoner all his possessions.

CERVANTES All of them...

MONIPODIO Well, it's not practical to take more.

CERVANTES One moment! These things are my livelihood.

MONIPODIO (*Puzzled*) I thought you said you were a poet.

CERVANTES Of the theatre.

> (MONIPODIO *crosses to the trunk, digs out a sword, pulls it from its scabbard*)

MONIPODIO False!

CERVANTES Costumes and properties. You see, actually I am a playwright and an actor. These are the trappings of my profession, so of course they could not possibly be of any use to... to...

> (*Halts as* HE *looks at the inimical faces. The* PRISONERS *fling the trappings about, making a game of it*)

(*Helplessly clutching the package*) Very well, take them. Only leave me this.

> (*The package is snatched from him and tossed to* MONIPODIO)

MONIPODIO Heavy! Valuable?

CERVANTES To me.

MONIPODIO We might let you ransom it?

CERVANTES I have no money.

MONIPODIO How unfortunate.

> (*Raps with his "gavel"*)

Hear ye, hear ye—

CERVANTES (*Desperately*) Your Excellency!

MONIPODIO Now what?

CERVANTES I demand a jury.

MONIPODIO (*A gracious wave at the* PRISONERS) You have one.

CERVANTES (*Looks them over*) A man...a man should know those who will judge him.

MONIPODIO (*Cheerfully*) Certainly. Why not?

> (*Making the rounds*)

The Scorpion. Cutthroat and murderer.

THE SCORPION (*Presenting his iron hook*) Here is my sting.

CERVANTES (*A hand at his throat*) Ah, yes...

MONIPODIO Mother Bane.

CERVANTES Your specialty, Mother?

MOTHER BANE The Evil Eye!

CERVANTES (*A compliment*) It is superbly evil.

MONIPODIO El Médico.

CERVANTES I have always envied doctors. The only ones who can take our lives without fear of punishment.

MONIPODIO (*Chuckling, to* EL MÉDICO) Show him how you operate.

> (EL MÉDICO, *grinning, raises his clenched right fist. A wicked little blade springs out of a ring and* EL MÉDICO *jerks it across an imaginary throat.* CERVANTES *recoils*)

Anyone you want scarred? The Doctor charges by the inch.

> (*Moving on*)

The Gypsy. Pickpocket.

THE GYPSY I can steal your watch while you're looking at it!

CERVANTES How fortunate I do not own one.

MONIPODIO Judas Macabeo. Jew and professional slanderer.

CERVANTES The first crime is self-evident. But professional slanderer...?

JUDAS MACABEO Engage my services and I will spread stories about your enemy that will ruin his business, his reputation, and the good name of his wife.

CERVANTES A difficult way to make a living. So much competition!

MONIPODIO Lobillo, the Little Wolf. He is a...businessman.

LOBILLO (*Wounded*) A broker.

CERVANTES (*To* LOBILLO) May one ask the nature of your merchandise?

LOBILLO (*Snaps his fingers, smiling. The* TWO GIRLS *come to his either side. Introducing them:*) Graciosa. Escalante.

CERVANTES Escalante. The Ladder...? Why is she called that?

LOBILLO She is so frequently climbed.

MONIPODIO (*Cheerfully*) A jury to hang the whole human race!

CERVANTES And the judge?

MONIPODIO Highly qualified. I have spent more time in court than most lawyers.

CERVANTES (*Is looking curiously at* THE DUKE) There is a gentleman I have not met.

MONIPODIO The Duke.

(*A dismissal with a tinge of distaste*)

Not really one of us.

THE DUKE (*As* CERVANTES *crosses toward him; not looking*) Name, James William Fox. Nationality, English. Profession, traitor.

CERVANTES You deal in treason?

THE DUKE I sell false information about one country to others too stupid to believe it.

CERVANTES (*Considers*) It seems a sound proposition. What brought you here?

THE DUKE A lapse of judgment. I told the truth. Whereupon your King Philip had me arrested on the painfully obvious charge of heresy.

CERVANTES You are for the Inquisition?

THE DUKE (*Remotely*) How annoying to be charged with false gods when one has none at all.

CERVANTES (*Sympathetically*) I am sorry.

THE DUKE I shan't be called. A traitor has friends.

CERVANTES Do you enjoy your profession?

THE DUKE Oh, quite.

CERVANTES Then why do you despise yourself?

THE DUKE (*Turns his eyes upon* CERVANTES *for the first time*) I despise all men.

CERVANTES I have noticed that men often jeer what they love best. Their country. The world.

THE DUKE (*Carefully*) The world is a dung heap and we are
   maggots that crawl upon it.

CERVANTES (*With ingenuous interest*) And yet you told the truth
   when you should have lied.

THE DUKE A moment of weakness!

CERVANTES Or was it morality? Yes I think that within you there
   is so stern a moralist he forced you to betray yourself.

THE DUKE (*Coming upright*) I believe I could learn to
   dislike you.

   (*With venom*)

   Poets. Spinning nonsense out of nothing! Are you a good
   poet or bad?

CERVANTES (*With humor*) Well, a play of mine once took first
   prize in a competition.

THE DUKE What was the prize?

CERVANTES Three silver spoons.

THE DUKE And that was the pinnacle of your success?

CERVANTES I have written ballads for blind beggars to sing
   on the streets.

THE DUKE How utterly loathsome.

   (*To* MONIPODIO)

   Governor—if you don't mind, I should like to prosecute
   this case.

MONIPODIO (*Rapping on the package*) Very well, I declare this court in session!

THE DUKE (*Strolls into the arena*) Miguel de Cervantes. I charge you with being an idealist, a bad poet, and an honest man. How plead you?

CERVANTES (*A pause as* HE *looks over the expectant faces*) Guilty.

MONIPODIO (*Crowing*) Excellent! It is the sentence of this court—

CERVANTES Your Excellency! What about my defense?

MONIPODIO But you just pleaded—

CERVANTES Had I said "innocent" you would surely have found me guilty. Since I have admitted guilt the court is required to hear me out.

MONIPODIO (*Puzzled*) For what purpose?

CERVANTES Extenuation. The jury may choose to be lenient.

MONIPODIO (HE *considers this odd argument. Then* HE *begins to chuckle*) Clever!

THE DUKE He is trying to gain time!

CERVANTES Is there a scarcity of that?

MONIPODIO (*To the* PRISONERS) Any urgent appointments?

(*A hollow groan is the answer.* HE *waves* CERVANTES *permission to proceed*)

CERVANTES It is true I am guilty of these charges. An idealist? Well I do not have the courage to believe in nothing.

(THE DUKE *snorts disdainfully*)

A bad poet? This comes more painfully—

THE DUKE Don't forget those odes for blind beggars.

CERVANTES (*Smiling*) Hunger drives talent to do things which are not on the map.

THE DUKE You were also charged with being an honest man.

CERVANTES Not my fault! I lack the training for professions like yours. But more than anything, I am guilty of bad luck.

MONIPODIO (*Dryly*) Worse than ours?

CERVANTES You chose your misfortunes. Mine were assigned me by fate. My family decayed nobility, too poor to indulge their pretensions, too proud to give them up. Only two careers were possible—the pen or the sword. I doubted my ability with words and so I became a soldier. I fought for the first time at Lepanto, against the Turks.

MONIPODIO I was there! This crippled foot...

CERVANTES This crippled hand.

(HE *raises his gloved left hand, smiling*)

I gave my left hand for the greater glory of the right. They tell me I fought well. I do not know. I remember only that nothing was left undamaged that day but human hatred. They gave me letters of praise and sent me home. My ship was in sight of the Spanish coast, when out of the south came the galleys of Barbary pirates. And for the next five years I was a slave in Africa.

(EL MÉDICO *giggles as though this were an uncommonly fine joke*)

Yes. Ironic. The letters I carried led the Moors to believe I was someone of importance—and so they set an impossibly high price on my freedom. Five years, while my family begged, borrowed, sold all they owned in order to raise the ransom.

MONIPODIO You never tried to escape?

CERVANTES Seven times. And seven times caught. But I was too valuable to kill, so each time others paid the penalty for my attempt.

THE DUKE Ah, then you *were* lucky.

CERVANTES I wept for those who were killed or tortured in place of myself. Then suddenly I was ransomed. I came home with joy in my heart—and found there was no employment for a disabled soldier, no reward for hardship. My mother died, poor and alone. My brother, also a soldier, fell in Flanders. My two sisters, penniless and without hope of marriage, were forced to adopt—

(*A bow to the* TROLLOPS)

—your profession. I was broken sick at heart, sick of life. All that sustained me was the knowledge that there is no memory to which time does not put an end, no pain which death does not abolish.

MONIPODIO (*Skeptically*) There's a saying, Cervantes: "A stout heart breaks bad fortune."

CERVANTES I can no more avoid bad luck than I can strike the sky with my fist!

THE DUKE (*Laughs*) How very touching.

CERVANTES And so I turned to the pen. I joined a troupe of strolling players, writing, acting in my own plays. I grew to know every road, every village in Spain every audience that pelted us with rotten eggs. And then—I fell in love.

THE DUKE The final disaster.

CERVANTES She was an actress in the company. Lovely... laughing...and fickle. I learned that love is a happy torment. A sweet poison. I learned that beauty looked at too closely vanishes like a dream. She left me with a keepsake of our affair—an infant daughter. The girl is grown up now but no comfort to me nor I to her.

THE DUKE You looked for the wrong things in life, Cervantes.

CERVANTES What should I have sought?

THE DUKE There's only one thing worth the struggle. Gold! It never betrays. It doesn't sicken. Bullets cannot do it harm. And how it propagates!

CERVANTES I know a better currency than that.

THE DUKE Name it.

CERVANTES Imagination.

THE DUKE You won't spend much of it in this place.

CERVANTES (*Taps his head*) I create in here. I invent other lives. I live them all. And in that moment—I am God.

THE DUKE (*Sincerely*) I believe you must be mad.

CERVANTES Possibly. But I have invented a man who was. A
man who...come—enter into my imagination and see him!
His name is Alonso Quijana. He is a country squire...no
longer young...bony and hollow-faced...eyes burning with
the fire of inner vision. Being retired he has much time for
books. He studies them from morn to night—and through
the night as well. And all he reads oppresses him...fills him
with indignation at man's murderous ways toward man. He
broods...and broods...and broods...and finally, from
so much brooding his brains dry up. He lays down the
melancholy burden of sanity and conceives the strangest
project a man ever imagined. He will become a knight-errant
and sally forth into the world to right all wrongs!

> (*The* PRISONERS *chortle appreciatively.* CERVANTES
> *moves quickly now, selecting props and costume elements
> from his trappings, falling into character as* HE *dons
> them; and his* SERVANT *assists*)

He hunts out an old rusted suit of armor or as many pieces
as he can find. He scrubs and oils them. He fits them on his
aging bones. Breastplate...cuisse...shoulder plates...
gauntlets...casque! But there is something missing. Of course!
A proper knight must have a squire.

> (*Looks about, crooks a finger at the* MANSERVANT,
> *who scurries to his side*)

He finds one—a peasant from a neighboring farm. They
conspire secretly to take their leave. And one morning...
before their families are awake...they steal out of their
homes...

> (*The action is played. The* MANSERVANT —*now*
> SANCHO PANZA, *brings two stick-horses, one with a
> mournful nag's head, the other with an ass's*)

They mount their trusty steeds. Softly, they make their way to the highway...

> (MUSIC COMING UP — *and the lighting is altering, prison walls giving way to the hot sweep of Manchegan sky*)

Now he is no longer Alonso Quijana — but a dauntless knight, known as — *Don Quixote de la Mancha!*

> (MUSIC UP, *and* THEY *ride*)

DON QUIXOTE (*Singing*)
> Never was knight so served
> By any noble dame
> As Don Quixote was
> When down the road he came
> With queens to wait on his every need
> While princesses cared for his steed.

> (*Pulls up suddenly*)

Sancho!

SANCHO Your Grace?

DON QUIXOTE (*Looking ahead*) How long since we sallied forth?

SANCHO (*Looks at the sun*) About two minutes?

DON QUIXOTE So soon!

SANCHO Eh?

DON QUIXOTE So soon shall I display the valor of my good right arm! Sancho, on this, the first day of our venture, I shall

perform deeds that will be written down in the book of
fame for centuries to come!

Sancho I don't quite follow Your Grace.

Don Quixote (*Pointing into the distance*) Do you see where
yon dust cloud rises? Mark it well, Sancho—for beneath
it marches a vast army!

Sancho No! What kind of army?

Don Quixote (*He cranes in his saddle*) Men of all nations!
I see Moors, Arabians, Medes, Parthians, Persians, Franks,
Greeks, and Ethiopians. And look—look who commands!

Sancho (*Frightened*) Who?

Don Quixote Alifanfaron, the evil Emperor, Lord of the
Isle of Trapobana!

Sancho God help us all!

Don Quixote He is that same wizard that stole the
Princess Pentapolin and sealed her in a tower guarded
by forty ogres!

Sancho Is Your Grace sure?

Don Quixote You see his coat of arms? A cat, crouching on a
field tawny, and beneath it the inscription: "Miau"!

Sancho We'd better run!

Don Quixote Don Quixote run from a mere army? Take up
thy bugle, Sancho. Blow me a blast that will strike fear into
yon craven hearts!

(SANCHO *takes the battered bugle which hangs by a cord around his neck and blows a frightened bleat*)

DON QUIXOTE (*Bellowing*) Ho, false knight! Blackhearted betrayer of maidens! Prepare to meet thy doom!

(HE *levels his lance*)

SANCHO (*Excitedly, grabbing his arm*) Your Grace! Wait! I see them now!

DON QUIXOTE So do I.

SANCHO It is only a flock of sheep!

DON QUIXOTE (*Annoyed*) What nonsense is this?

SANCHO I vow to God! No Moors, no Ethiopians, no cats — nothing but sheep. Listen!

DON QUIXOTE (*Cocking an ear*) I hear the sound of trumpets and the rolling of drums!

SANCHO Maybe Your Grace is hard of hearing.

(HE *lifts the flap of* DON QUIXOTE's *casque. The baaing of many sheep is heard*)

And see? There is the shepherd, the one Your Grace thought was All-what's-his-name.

DON QUIXOTE (*Bitterly, lowering his lance*) Ah, Sancho, this is the work of my enemy.

SANCHO What enemy?

DON QUIXOTE The Enchanter. Envious of the glory I was to

achieve in this battle, he changed the army into sheep and Alifanfaron into a shepherd.

SANCHO He sounds dangerous!

DON QUIXOTE He is dangerous. But one day we shall meet face to face, and then...

SANCHO (*Sensibly*) I wouldn't be upset, Your Grace. As I always say, have patience and shuffle the cards. I don't know who this enemy is, but if we keep traveling we're bound to meet him somewhere along the way. Furthermore—

DON QUIXOTE Silence.

SANCHO What?

DON QUIXOTE I am trying to think!

SANCHO Very well, Your Grace, but as Your Grace knows I am naturally talkative and it will be Your Grace's own fault if all the things I have to say begin to rot on the end of my tongue.

DON QUIXOTE *Silence!*

(**SANCHO** *claps a hand over his mouth*)

It comes to me, Sancho. How my enemy was able so easily to deceive me.

(*A groan of self-recrimination*)

Oh, knave that I am. To violate the first rule of chivalry and then complain. Sancho—I beg you keep it secret from the world—but Don Quixote has committed a grievous error.

(*Silence*)

Sancho? I spoke to you.

(SANCHO *dumbly indicates the hand over his mouth*)

Sancho!

SANCHO Your Grace said to be silent.

DON QUIXOTE Do not anger me, Sancho, I warn you I am terrible in anger!

SANCHO Very well. What was Your Grace saying?

DON QUIXOTE I have been punished for committing a sin against the order of knighthood.

SANCHO Which sin was that?

DON QUIXOTE I had no right to offer nor accept a challenge since I have never properly been dubbed a knight.

SANCHO That's no problem. Just tell me how it's done, Your Grace, and I'll be glad to take care of this drubbing.

DON QUIXOTE Dubbing. Thank you, friend Sancho, but it is a ceremony which may only performed by another knight.

SANCHO (*Whistles in dismay*) There's a problem—I've never *seen* another knight.

DON QUIXOTE The lord of some castle would do. Or a king, or a duke.

SANCHO Very well, Your Grace. I'll keep an eye out for any kings or dukes as we ride.

DON QUIXOTE (*Gratefully*) Thank you, my friend.

(THEY *ride on.* DON QUIXOTE *pulls up sharply*)

Aha! See who approaches!

SANCHO Doesn't look like royalty to me.

DON QUIXOTE But notice what he wears on his head!

SANCHO (*Squinting into the sun*) That is a peculiar hat...

DON QUIXOTE Oh joyous moment! Oh, glorious undertaking!

SANCHO (*Apprehensively*) Oh, dear. What now?

> (*The* BARBER — *played by* EL MÉDICO — *comes
> capering along, singing a lively seguidilla. Now and
> then* HE *cracks his heels in the air just for the devil
> of it.* HE *carries over one shoulder a bundle of his
> equipment.* HE *holds his brass shaving-bowl on his head
> to shield his eyes from the sun, and it gleams brightly*)

DON QUIXOTE (*Handing over his lance*) Remain well apart,
Sancho. This encounter may be perilous.

> (HE *draws his sword as the little* BARBER *approaches
> unaware, singing and capering.* SANCHO *blows a
> cracked blast on the bugle as* DON QUIXOTE *presents
> his sword point-first. In tones of thunder:*)

Hold, thou varlet! Stand and deliver!

> (*The* BARBER'S *song dies on a questioning note.*
> HE *comes to a stop, goggling in disbelief*)

BARBER By the beard of St. Anthony—

> (*Points a shaking finger*)

I could swear I see before me a knight in full armor!

Ridiculous. There *aren't* any knights.

> (DON QUIXOTE *roars in anger, raises his sword. The* BARBER *falls to his knees*)

I was wrong!

DON QUIXOTE Address me properly ere I bloody my sword on thy unworthy carcass!

BARBER Forgive me, Your bigness. I thought I'd been touched by the sun!

DON QUIXOTE Thou wilt be touched by worse if thou do not speedily hand over that golden helmet!

BARBER Golden helmet? What—where—?

> (*Beginning to comprehend,* HE *takes the basin from his head. Wonderingly:*)

This? Why, this is nothing but a shaving-basin! And you thought—ha! Ha ha!

DON QUIXOTE (*Thundering*) Thou darest laugh at Don Quixote de la Mancha?

BARBER No, no I wasn't laughing! If Your Bigness will let me explain—I am nothing but a poor barber who plies his trade from village to village. And this—I was wearing it on my head to ward off the rays of the sun.

DON QUIXOTE (*With fine contempt, to* SANCHO) Observe how glibly the rascal lies.

SANCHO (*Critically*) I must say, it *does* look like a shaving basin.

BARBER (*Timidly*) Perhaps Your Highness would like his beard trimmed?

DON QUIXOTE (*A roar*) Hold thy tongue!

(*The* BARBER *flinches, is silent. To* SANCHO:)

Here is an example of how to the untrained eye one thing may appear to be another. Know thou what that really is?

(*Impressively*)

The Golden Helmet of Mambrino. When worn by one of pure heart and noble birth it renders him invulnerable to all wounds!

(*The* BARBER *examines the basin, impressed*)

SANCHO (*Equally impressed*) Say—that sounds like a very handy thing. I wonder how *he* got hold of it?

DON QUIXOTE How indeed! Misbegotten thief! Where didst thou steal it?

BARBER Your Worship, I swear—

DON QUIXOTE Enough! Defend thyself, wretch, or else render unto me that which is justly mine!

BARBER (*Blankly*) What?

SANCHO He means, hand it over.

BARBER But, Your Worship, it cost me half a crown!

behind—not the castle of Don Quixote de la Mancha, but
the residence of a country squire known as Alonso Quijana...

(HE *and the* OTHERS *are shifting the essential props into
position. He will cue the* PEOPLE *who play the roles*)

CERVANTES Imagine the shock to his niece—Antonia—

(*Played by* GRACIOSA)

—to his housekeeper—

(*Played by* MOTHER BANE)

—and to the neighborhood padre, who has known
him all his life—

(*Played by* JUDAS MACABEO)

—as the dreadful...the unbelievable news reaches them!

(*The scene is set, the lighting changing.* ANTONIA *begins
sobbing brokenheartedly. The* HOUSEKEEPER *stands
grimly by, taking righteous pleasure in catastrophe. The*
PADRE *paces back and forth*)

PADRE (*Marveling*) Extraordinary. An *extraordinary* occurrence.
From whom did you hear about it?

HOUSEKEEPER (*Answering for* ANTONIA) The farmer, Garcia, met
them on the road.

PADRE Them?

HOUSEKEEPER The Master and Sancho Panza.

PADRE Ah, yes, Sancho Panza.

(*Shakes his head*)

He wouldn't be much help.

HOUSEKEEPER Garcia was astonished to see the Master dressed as he was, and spoke to him. Señor Quijana said — "I beg you to address me in the proper way. I am Don Quixote, knight-errant in the service of all that is good on earth."

PADRE (*Musing*) "In the service of all this is good on earth." It doesn't seem such a *terrible* madness.

ANTONIA (*Angrily*) It's still madness!

PADRE I suppose you are right. Have you notified your fiancé?

HOUSEKEEPER I sent for Doctor Carrasco as soon as I heard the news.

PADRE Then let us wait before deciding upon a course of action.

(*Marveling*)

Alonso Quijana... the good Alonso... the studious...

ANTONIA (*Bursting out bitterly*) Studious! That's what did it! Look at those *books!* They ought to be marked "Poison!"

PADRE (*Demurring*) Oh, now —

ANTONIA Reading day and night, that's all he did. How many times have I heard him, pacing the floor, talking out loud. Arguing with himself! I'd say, "Uncle, please go to bed." He wouldn't even hear me!

PADRE (*Has taken a book from a pile, opened it*) "Tales of Chivalry." I know this one.

(*Smiles, reading*)

Not a bad story!

HOUSEKEEPER *All* books are bad.

PADRE (*Mildly*) Let us at least exclude the Scriptures.

ANTONIA She's right!

(*Wildly, flinging a stack of books to the floor*)

They should be burned like heretics!

PADRE (*Sighs, closing the one* HE *holds*) Very well, my child. Tomorrow we shall have a public auto-da-fe. In the meantime—

ANTONIA (*Catches sight of* DR. CARRASCO—*played by the* DUKE— *who has just entered*) My darling!

(SHE *flies to his arms.* CARRASCO *carries his own self-importance as though afraid of breaking it.* HE *takes* ANTONIA *in his arms but with a certain remoteness*)

PADRE Have you heard?

DR. CARRASCO On my way here I was informed by at least ten people.

(*To* ANTONIA)

My dear, your uncle is the laughing-stock of the entire neighborhood.

ANTONIA Oh-h…

(*And begins sobbing afresh*)

DR. CARRASCO Padre? What do you know of this?

PADRE Only that the good Señor Quijana has been carried away by his imagination.

DR. CARRASCO (*Stiffly*) Señor Quijana has lost his mind and is suffering from delusions.

PADRE (*Quizzically*) Is there a difference?

DR. CARRASCO Exactitude of meaning. I beg to remind you, Padre, that I am a Bachelor of Science, graduate of the University of Salamanca.

PADRE Very well, Doctor. What shall we do?

DR. CARRASCO (*Detaching himself from* ANTONIA) I am afraid the damage has already been done.

ANTONIA Damage?

DR. CARRASCO My dear, we must recognize a certain danger.

ANTONIA But Uncle Alonso isn't *dangerous*.

DR. CARRASCO The danger is to us. To our future. It has been scientifically established that the taint of madness may recur in future generations.

ANTONIA You mean our marriage? You want to—?

(*Stricken*)

Oh. Oh-h!

PADRE (*Alarmed at this drift*) Oh, come, come, Doctor!

DR. CARRASCO Padre, we are modern men. We face facts.

HOUSEKEEPER (*A sibyl*) The innocent must pay for the sins of the guilty.

PADRE (*Roused*) Guilty of what? A gentle delusion!

DR. CARRASCO How do you know it is gentle? By this time who knows what violence he has committed! He was armed?

ANTONIA (*Hopelessly*) With sword and lance.

DR. CARRASCO (*Throws up his hands, resigning*) Why should this fall upon *me*?

ANTONIA (*Recognizes a crisis, and an ancient female cunning stirs in her. Her voice becomes forlorn and wistful*) Sanson. I had hoped for so much for us. For you, really.

DR. CARRASCO (*Lost in self-pity*) I know...

ANTONIA Everything was to be for you. My dowry... you would have been free to continue your studies.

DR. CARRASCO (*Suffering*) Yes...

ANTONIA This house. These lands...

DR. CARRASCO House? Lands?

ANTONIA (*Simply*) I am uncle's only heir.

PADRE True. They would all come to you.

ANTONIA To us.

PADRE (*The Devil's Advocate*) Consider, Doctor. After all, if one is to serve science, one must have the means.

DR. CARRASCO (*Musing*) I suppose that is a consideration.

PADRE Definitely. But not as great as the other.

DR. CARRASCO The other?

PADRE Think what cleverness it would take to wean this man from madness! To argue him from his course and persuade him to return home. Difficult, Doctor. Perhaps impossible.

DR. CARRASCO Hmmm...that is a challenge...

PADRE Extraordinary.

DR. CARRASCO (*To the* PADRE) He can't have gotten far?

PADRE No more than a day's journey!

DR. CARRASCO We shall go after him.

PADRE (*Cheerfully, to* ANTONIA) You see, child? Stop worrying!

ANTONIA I can't help it. I keep thinking of him out there in the wilderness helpless hungry—maybe even in pain.

(*Sobbing*)

Oh, my poor uncle. My poor, suffering uncle...

(*A cross-fade in the light as this scene disappears and we see* DON QUIXOTE *and* SANCHO *lolling in a shady glen off the road. All is lovely, idyllic with the sound of songbirds and the splashing of a little cascade nearby.*

> QUIXOTE *lies in the cool grass, waving a fan-leaf as* HE *hums a tranquil tune.* SANCHO *is eating*)

DON QUIXOTE (*With a happy sigh*) Ah, Sancho, is it not lovely? See how Nature conspires to delight the soul. What more could a man possibly need?

SANCHO (*Proffering*) An onion?

DON QUIXOTE No, thank you, my friend.

> (*A pause of pure euphoria.* DON QUIXOTE *smiles dreamily, his eyes on the horizon*)

How this place puts me in mind of the Golden Age. Was there ever such a time? In those days there were not yet such words as "mine" and "thine," and no labor was required of man but to reach forth and take the nourishment which God so generously gave. There were clear-running rivers and springs, trees that bore fruit the year round, and men lived in harmony for no one had taught them to quarrel. There was love then, simple as the simple hearts from which it sprang. Deceit, hatred, and envy had not yet commingled with truth, and in all mankind there was delight in creation, a joyous embracing of life.

> (*A shadow crosses his face*)

Then did it change. The pleasures of that life passed like the shadow of a dream, and out of the darkness crawled another kind. These were the enchanters, they of cold thought and shriveled spirit. They are among us now, Sancho, and their disguise is clever, for they look like other men. Yet you may know them, for their eyes are blind to beauty, their ears deaf to music, and where they walk the earth is blighted. These are the ones I fight. The men against life—the shepherds who are wolves—the spoilers of the dream!

(He *rises to his feet, eyes burning with a vision of combat*)

Come forth, ye magicians! Come forth, ye wizards and make ready for battle! Ye are many and strong and this is but one man who defies thee, but beware! For the sword of Don Quixote points to the stars!

(He *holds, exalted. Then, unmistakably, the sound of a snore.* He *discovers* Sancho *curled up and sleeping.* He *prods him disgustedly with a toe*)

Sancho. Sancho!

Sancho (*Wakes with an assortment of subhuman noises*) Huh? What—? Oh, excuse me, Your Grace, I was dreaming.

Don Quixote (*With irony*) Of high adventure?

Sancho Of home, and my wife Teresa.

(*Smiling fondly*)

I can see those little black mustaches of hers now.

Don Quixote Come. We'd best be riding.

Sancho (*Rising*) Does Your Grace know where we're going?

Don Quixote Wherever the road may lead.

Sancho (*Philosophically*) Well, they say no journey is a bad one unless it be that which leads to the gallows.

Don Quixote Do you never run out of proverbs?

Sancho No, Your Grace, I was born with a bellyful of them. I always say—

DON QUIXOTE (*Suddenly, as* HE *hears a noise*) Sh-h!

(*The sound again, cries faintly heard*)

Someone is in distress!

SANCHO It may be something private.

DON QUIXOTE What anguish is private from Don Quixote?

(*Unsheathes his sword.*

LIGHTS UP *on a shadowy place in the woods where a* FARMER *played by* LOBILLO *is lashing a ragged* BOY)

ANDRES (*Played by the* GYPSY) Oh! Ow! Please! Don't!

FARMER Bungler! Whelp! Loafer!

ANDRES I won't do it again, sir! Ow!

FARMER Hold your tongue!

ANDRES Oh! I swear it!

FARMER There! There! And there!

ANDRES Ow! Help! Help!

DON QUIXOTE (*In ringing tones*) Stay thy hand!

(*The* FARMER *uncertainly raises the switch*)

Stop, base lout! I say—desist!

(*The* FARMER *looks around. His hand is paralyzed in*

mid stroke by the sight of DON QUIXOTE. *The* BOY, *too, gapes at the apparition.* DON QUIXOTE *advances upon them*)

FARMER Who...who are you?

DON QUIXOTE The terror of rascals like thyself!

(*Leans on his sword as* SANCHO *comes puffing on scene. Coldly:*)

I will hear thy explanation — and thou have one.

FARMER Explanation? Why should I—?

(*Stops, intimidated by* DON QUIXOTE'S *cold, level look*)

I am a farmer, sir. This boy works for me, in charge of my flock. Twice now he has allowed sheep to get lost. Therefore I am bound to punish him.

DON QUIXOTE (*Coldly*) So say you.

(*Turns to the* BOY)

ANDRES (*Apprehensively*) Sir, I...I...

DON QUIXOTE Be not afraid, boy. Speak up.

ANDRES My name is Andres, sir. It is true that I let the sheep stray, but only because he refuses to pay me.

FARMER I hold him responsible for the sheep that are missing!

ANDRES He is a miser and will not give me my pay!

FARMER (*Cholerically*) You insolent little rascal, I'll—

DON QUIXOTE Stop!

(*With contempt*)

Coward and bully. To strike one powerless to defend himself! Release the lad. Instantly!

(*The* FARMER *sullenly looses the* BOY's *hands*)

(*To* ANDRES:) Now, then. How much does he owe you?

ANDRES For nine months' work, sir, at seven reales a month.

DON QUIXOTE (*Not awfully strong on arithmetic*) Nine months at seven reales...that would be...

SANCHO (*Also figuring*) Eighty...

FARMER (*Anguished*) Sixty-three!

DON QUIXOTE Very well. Pay him.

FARMER But, sir—

DON QUIXOTE Pay him or by the God who rules us I'll make an end to thee here and now!

FARMER (*Digs in his pocket, starts counting money into* ANDRES' *hand*) Twenty—forty—sixty—

ANDRES (*Boldly*) And three.

DON QUIXOTE Are you satisfied, Andres?

ANDRES Oh, yes, sir. Thank you!

DON QUIXOTE (*To the* FARMER) Take warning, miser. Lay not a hand on that boy again.

FARMER Yes, sir.

DON QUIXOTE You swear it?

FARMER (*Piously*) I swear.

DON QUIXOTE And you, boy. Should any ask who it was that came to your aid, tell them it was Don Quixote de la Mancha!

ANDRES Don Quixote de la Mancha!

DON QUIXOTE Righter of wrongs and defender of the weak!

ANDRES Righter of wrong and defender of the weak!

> (DON QUIXOTE *presents his sword in a salute, turns and goes*)

ANDRES Good-bye, sir! Good-bye!

> (*Turns to the* FARMER. *Boldly*)

From now on you'd better watch yourself

FARMER (*His attention on the departure*) Oh, I will.

ANDRES Because if you don't that knight will come back and slice you up like a lemon!

FARMER (*Not really listening*) True.

ANDRES And another thing. I don't get paid enough.

FARMER Hmmm?

> (*Turns to him, satisfied* THEY *are gone*)

What did you have in mind?

ANDRES Well, some kind of a bonus.

FARMER A bonus? Certainly!

> (*Hand in pocket. Hungrily*)

Come here, my boy.

ANDRES (*Approaching, becomes a little nervous*) You haven't got anything funny in mind, have you? Because if you have I'm warning you—

FARMER (*Pounces, claps a hand over* ANDRES' *mouth*) Give me back that money!

> (ANDRES *struggles, makes strangled noises. The* FARMER *wrests it from him. With satisfaction:*)

Now, you whelp. You ungrateful cur. I believe you mentioned a bonus.

DON QUIXOTE (*As* HE *and* SANCHO *mount*) Tell me, Sancho, have you ever seen a knight more cool, more firm, more valiant than I?

SANCHO I must say, Your Grace handled that situation very nicely.

DON QUIXOTE Thank you. Still, the credit is not all mine. Remember, Sancho—evil always surrenders to virtue, and in the end justice always prevails.

(THEY *ride on*)

FARMER (*Beating* ANDRES *twice as vigorously as before*) There!
There! And there!

ANDRES (*Howling in vain*) Ow! Oh! Mercy! Help! Help!

> (*The laughter of the* PRISONERS *rises... and then is
> stilled as another sound is heard. It is the slow-march
> roll of drums, and a chanting which echoes from distant
> corridors.* ALL *fall silent. The lighting chills and dims to
> the prison setup.* CERVANTES *moves center, uncertainly*)

CERVANTES That sound...?

MONIPODIO The Men of the Inquisition.

CERVANTES (*With the beginning of apprehension*) What does it
mean?

MONIPODIO They're coming to fetch someone. They'll haul him
off, put the question to him. Next thing he knows—he's
burning.

CERVANTES (*Voice unsure*) Are they coming for me?

MONIPODIO (*Cheerfully*) Who knows?

CERVANTES (*To the* DUKE) But perhaps...for you.

THE DUKE (*Smiling coolly*) Never for me.

> (*The drums approach, growing louder. Echoes bounce
> and clash from the stone walls.* CERVANTES *is beginning
> to sweat, body rigid, face drawn. The sound grows to
> almost unbearable volume, then cuts off, seemingly just*

outside the vault. There is the sound of the adjoining cell being opened, then there is a scream, rising to a pitch of terror, as abruptly choked off)

MONIPODIO (*Cheerfully, to* CERVANTES) Well! Not this time.

THE DUKE (*Smiling*) Were you afraid, Cervantes?

(CERVANTES *sinks to a bench, shaking and undone*)

THE DUKE What, Cervantes? No courage? Or is that in your imagination, too?

(*The drums crash into their death march again, now receding.* CERVANTES *flinches, covers his face with his hands. The* DUKE'S *laughter rings out in malicious triumph.*)

END OF ACT I

ACT II

There has been no time lapse.

The drums are receding. CERVANTES *is crouched as we last saw him, head in hands.*

MONIPODIO *goes upstage, fetches a goatskin of wine, pokes* CERVANTES *and hands it to him.* CERVANTES *takes it in trembling hands, drinks deeply.*

MONIPODIO (*With amused good nature*) Better?

CERVANTES (*Still shaky as* HE *hands it back*) Thank you.

MONIPODIO Let's get on with your defense!

CERVANTES (*Apologetically*) If I could rest for a moment...

THE DUKE This place he calls La Mancha—is it real?

MONIPODIO Oh, yes! I've been there myself

LOBILLO So have I!

THE SCORPION (*Proudly, pointing to himself*) Three months in jail at Argamasilla!

MONIPODIO An empty place. Great wide plains.

LOBILLO The songs of the people wail and cry.

MOTHER BANE And the weather—nine months of winter and three months of hell!

JUDAS MACABEO A desert.

MONIPODIO A wasteland!

THE DUKE (*Dryly*) Which apparently grows lunatics.

CERVANTES (*Looking up*) I would say, rather...men of illusion.

THE DUKE Much the same.

CERVANTES La Mancha is a wasteland, true. The sky is too high for comfort, the horizons too wide. Most men are frightened by them. They drop their eyes to the ground and presently the ground reaches up and enfolds them. But if they have courage they turn their eyes upward—and see there a world not yet made.

    (HE *rises*)

These are the men of La Mancha. They have discovered reality for what it is; a strangler-vine that crushes the human spirit. Each man makes his own world in La Mancha. Illusion grows on that land. Imagination soars to unimaginable heights!

    (*The lighting alters to the Manchegan sky. The* PRISONERS *fall back, isolating* CERVANTES *as* HE *becomes* QUIXOTE)

To the men of La Mancha reality is illusion and only illusion real. They look away from life and they choose a dream. Then they ride forth over the boundless plain of the human spirit, searching, each in his own way...

DON QUIXOTE (*Halting*) Sancho!

SANCHO (*Startled out of a doze*) Your Grace?

DON QUIXOTE (*Pointing triumphantly*) There!

SANCHO It may be that the sun has melted my brains, but all I see is more of this road.

DON QUIXOTE *What?*

SANCHO If Your Grace would give me a hint—?

DON QUIXOTE In the distance. A castle!

SANCHO (*Looking vainly*) Castle.

DON QUIXOTE Rockbound amidst the crags.

SANCHO Crags.

DON QUIXOTE And see the turrets!

SANCHO How many?

DON QUIXOTE (*Counts*) Nine.

SANCHO That's a lot!

DON QUIXOTE And the banners—ah, the brave banners flaunting in the wind!

SANCHO Anything on'em?

DON QUIXOTE (*Shielding his eyes*) I cannot quite make out the device, but it must be the insignia of some great lord.

SANCHO Oh, that's fine, Your Grace. Maybe this is where you can get yourself drubbed.

DON QUIXOTE Dubbed. Yes, Sancho, I have no doubt there will

be earls, dukes, brave knights and gentle maidens without
number. Perchance even some princess lying under an
evil spell. Here may I plunge my arms up to the very elbows
in adventure!

(*To* SANCHO)

Blow thy bugle that a dwarf may mount the battlements and
announce our coming!

SANCHO (*Under his spell, lifts the bugle to his lips. Hesitates*) But I
don't see a castle.

DON QUIXOTE Thou and thy peasant eyes!

SANCHO (*Doubtfully*) I do see something... maybe it's an inn.

DON QUIXOTE (*Sadly*) An inn.

(*Resigned*)

Come, Sancho. We shall ride straight to the drawbridge and
there, perchance, thy vision will improve.

(THEY *ride out of view as lights come up on the courtyard
of the "inn." An improvised table at which sit* THREE
MULETEERS *of loud voices, crude humor, lusty appetites*)

MULETEERS (*Boisterously, banging on the table*) Food!
We starve!
Soup!
Meat!
Cheese!
Wine!
Olla podri-i-i-da!

(*This last in a falsetto wail followed by appreciative*

guffawing. PEDRO, *the leader—played by the*
SCORPION — *who sits at the head of the table, strikes
up a song of Rabelaisian flavor. The* OTHERS *join in,
a cheerful bedlam.* MARIA, *the Innkeeper's wife—
played by* MOTHER BANE — *comes hurrying from the
kitchen with baskets of bread*)

MARIA It comes! It comes! Everything—be patient!

MULETEERS We're dying!

Bring the stew!

MARIA (*Shrieking toward the kitchen*) Aldonza! Hurry! Bring the
stew!

MULETEERS The stew! The stew!

MARIA (*Frantic*) Where is that slut! Aldonza!

MULETEERS (*Picking it up*) Aldonza! Aldonza! *Aldonza!*

ALDONZA (*Emerging from the kitchen with a huge, smoking tureen.*
SHE *is played by* ESCALANTE) Shut up or you'll get this over
your lousy heads!

(*A cheer of approval from the* MULETEERS *as* ALDONZA
marches to the table with the tureen. SHE *sets it down
with a crash*)

There, swine, feed.

PEDRO (*Reaching for a convenient portion of her anatomy*) Aldonza...

ALDONZA (*Eluding him lithely*) I'll be back!

(SHE *exits, muttering imprecations to herself.*

The INNKEEPER *enters—played by* MONIPODIO)

INNKEEPER (*Rubbing his hands*) There we are, gentlemen! Everything in order.

JOSÉ (*Played by* EL MÉDICO) Did you feed the mules?

INNKEEPER They're eating as well as you!

TENORIO (*Played by* LOBILLO) God forbid.

INNKEEPER (*Chuckling*) He jokes!

JOSÉ (*Mouth full, growling*) Wine.

INNKEEPER No wine! Maria—to the kitchen!

PEDRO (*Shouting after her as* SHE *goes*) Send it out with Aldonza!

INNKEEPER (*slyly*) You like that one, eh?

PEDRO A man has to do *something* about these cold nights.

JOSÉ (*A shout*) Bring the wine!

ALDONZA (*Off*) Stop yelling, for God's sake, I'm bringing it!

> (PEDRO *waves the* INNKEEPER *away as* ALDONZA *comes to the table with a decanter of wine. Grumbling:*)

Bellies that walk like men!

> (SHE *starts filling cups as the* MEN *eye her with frank appetite*)

TENORIO (*Lasciviously*) I've been thinking of you, Aldonza.

ALDONZA (*Pauses*) You promised to bring me a comb from Toledo.

TENORIO (*Grinning*) That was last time.

ALDONZA It was, eh? Then last time was *your* last time.

> (SHE *moves on, pouring wine for* JOSÉ. HE *continues eating, but one hand is reaching slyly under her skirt. Without change of expression* ALDONZA *shifts the stream of wine from the cup to* JOSÉ*'s head.* HE *yells, tumbles over backward from the bench*)

And you, little dog—never!

PEDRO (*Laughing, as are the* OTHERS) Aldonza! Sweetheart. Come here.

ALDONZA (*Approaching sullenly*) Keep your hands where I can see 'em.

PEDRO Come here, come here.

> (*Pulls her close. Confidentially*)

I've marked out a nice thick bed of hay in the stable.

ALDONZA (*As confidentially*) Good. Eat it.

PEDRO I had something else in mind.

ALDONZA I know what you had in mind,

PEDRO You wouldn't refuse Pedro?

ALDONZA Try me.

PEDRO My *mules* are not as stubborn as you!

ALDONZA Then go lie with your mules!

(*Scathingly, of* TENORIO)

He was going to bring me a comb from Toledo.

PEDRO (*Changing tones*) Aldonza.

> (HE *reaches in his pocket, deliberately drops one two, three coins on the table.* ALDONZA *hesitates, then reaches for them.* PEDRO *imprisons her hand beneath his*)

Tonight?

ALDONZA (*Sullenly*) When I'm through in the kitchen.

> (PEDRO *smiles, releases her hand.* SHE *snatches up the coins, exits, followed by the guffaws of the* MEN)

JOSÉ Payment before delivery? She won't show up!

PEDRO She'll be there.

TENORIO All *I* had to pay was a promise!

> (THEY *laugh.*
>
> DON QUIXOTE *and* SANCHO *have appeared at the far side of the stage.* QUIXOTE *gestures to* SANCHO *who raises his bugle and blows a horrible, off-key blast.*
>
> The MEN *drop their implements and gape*)

JOSÉ What in the name of—?

INNKEEPER (*Hurrying in as* SANCHO *blows another blast.* HE *is* *non-plussed a moment, then lights up*) The pig-butcher! I didn't expect him until tomorrow.

(*Hurrying to the "gates"*)

Coming, Señor Butcher, coming!

DON QUIXOTE (*Haughtily, as the* INNKEEPER *swings open the "gates"*) Is the governor of the castle at hand?

(*No reply from the flubbergasted* INNKEEPER)

I say, is the Castellano here?

INNKEEPER (*With an effort*) I am in charge of this place.

DON QUIXOTE We waited, sire, for a dwarf to mount the battlements and announce us but none appeared.

INNKEEPER The...the dwarfs are all busy.

DON QUIXOTE Then know ye that Don Quixote, knight-errant, defender of the right and pursuer of lofty undertakings, implores the boon of hospitality!

(*The* INNKEEPER *looks open-mouthed at the* MULETEERS, *who look back in kind*)

Well, sir? Is it granted?

INNKEEPER (*Pulling himself together*) Absolutely! This inn — I mean, this castle — is open to everybody.

DON QUIXOTE Thank you, my lord.

(HE *clucks Rocinante forward and rides through the gates. The arch is too low, it knocks him off his horse*)

INNKEEPER (*Hurries to him, horrified*) Oh dear—are you hurt?

DON QUIXOTE (*With total dignity*) These little mishaps are all part of my profession.

> (*With the* INNKEEPER'*s aid* HE *gets to his feet and limps to the* MULETEERS)

How my heart is gladdened by the sight of such fair company! Good morrow, brave knights, gentle warriors.

> (*Seeing* MARIA)

Hail, oh Empress of La Mancha! Thou hast but to command, and my good right arm is ready to serve.

> (MARIA *turns a frightened look on the* INNKEEPER)

MARIA He's a madman!

INNKEEPER Madmen are the children of God!

> (*To* DON QUIXOTE)

You must be hungry, sir knight.

DON QUIXOTE Aye, that I am.

INNKEEPER There's food aplenty, and for your squire, too.

> (*Crossing to* SANCHO)

I'll just help him stable your animals.

DON QUIXOTE I thank thee, Sir Castellano.

> (*Approaching the* OTHERS)

Fair knights — gentle lady — I have ridden far, have
encountered many and fearful adventures, and there are
great tales to relate. Only this morning while crossing
the burning plains of La Mancha —

> (ALDONZA *has emerged laden with things for the table.*
> *Stops, puzzled, at the silence.*
>
> DON QUIXOTE *is gazing at her, stricken*)

Dear God, it is she.

> (ALDONZA *stares incredulously.* HE *lays hand to sword,*
> *flings a challenge to the sky*)

Let the whole world tremble if the whole world does not
confess that in the whole world there is not a damsel more
beautiful than this!

> (ALDONZA *turns astounded eyes to Maria, who gestures*
> *urgently:* Humor him! *When there is no answer to*
> *his challenge,* DON QUIXOTE *sweeps the barber's basin*
> *from his head, kneels to* ALDONZA, *eyes lowered*
> *worshipfully*)

Sweet lady...fair virgin...

> (*A strangled snort from the* MULETEERS)

I dare not gaze full upon thy countenance lest I be blinded
by beauty. But I implore thee — speak once thy name.

ALDONZA (*Prompted by a gesture from* MARIA. *A growl:*) Aldonza.

DON QUIXOTE My lady jests.

ALDONZA Aldonza!

DON QUIXOTE (*Smiling, eyes on the ground*) The name of a kitchen-scullion, or mayhap my lady's serving-maid?

ALDONZA I told you my name! Now get out of the way or by Christ I'll—

> (*A shriek from* MARIA *restrains her from bashing him over the head*)

DON QUIXOTE (*Humbly*) Forgive me, lady, for offending thy modesty. Be charitable—for I assure thee that from this moment on thou art sovereign of my captive heart.

INNKEEPER (*Returning*) Come along, Señor Knight! I'll show you to your quarters.

> (DON QUIXOTE *rises, keeping eyes averted from* ALDONZA, *follows the* INNKEEPER *off.*
>
> ALDONZA *is angry and confused*)

PEDRO (*Swooning across the table*) Dear God, what vision is this?

JOSÉ (*Languishing*) What princess? What queen?

TENORIO (*In falsetto*) Sweet lady...

PEDRO Divine maiden...

JOSÉ Fair...virgin?!

> (THEY *explode, hee-hawing like their mules*)

ALDONZA (*Furious*) Apes! Asses!

PEDRO (*Using a table knife for sword. Declaiming:*) Let the whole world tremble if the whole world does not confess—

ALDONZA (*Clawing at him*) Son of a castrated goat!

JOSÉ—that in the whole world there is not—

ALDONZA Filthy swine!

TENORIO—a damsel more beautiful—

> (**ALDONZA,** *nearly out of her mind, seizes a loaf of bread from the table and belabors them, cursing, as* **THEY** *dodge about, laughing and jeering.*
>
> *Lights out; up on one of the raised levels which is now* **DON QUIXOTE'S** *room in the inn.* **HE** *is seated, writing, as* **SANCHO** *comes up the stairs, whistling*)

DON QUIXOTE Is it thou, Sancho?

SANCHO Yes, Your Grace.

> (*Entering, depositing saddle-bags*)

Everything's fine. Rocinante's in the stable eating like a whole herd. Now if Your Grace doesn't mind I'll go do the same.

DON QUIXOTE (*Dreamily*) Ah, Sancho, Sancho...did you see her?

SANCHO Her?

DON QUIXOTE She with the eyes of a dove...hair like the raven's wing...

SANCHO Oh, *that* one.

> (*Nudges* **DON QUIXOTE,** *man to man*)

Nice piece of goods.

(DON QUIXOTE *turns shocked eyes upon him, rises tall and terrible.* SANCHO *backs off in dismay*)

What did I say?

DON QUIXOTE Vile-tongued wretch!

SANCHO I'm sorry!

DON QUIXOTE I warn thee, Sancho!

SANCHO Your Grace *knows* my tongue throws out the first thing it gets hold of.

DON QUIXOTE Never let it sully the fair name of woman!

SANCHO What I meant, I wonder if it's a good idea to get mixed up with them.

DON QUIXOTE Know you not that a knight without a lady is like a body without a soul? To whom shall he dedicate his conquests? What name give strength to his right arm? What vision sustain him when he sallies forth to do battle with ogres and with giants?

SANCHO (*Tentatively*) A woman?

DON QUIXOTE A *lady*.

SANCHO Well, if Your Grace puts it that way...

DON QUIXOTE Is there any other?

SANCHO (*Considers*) No.

DON QUIXOTE (*Turning back to the desk, folding a paper*) My friend, I would entrust thee with a most delicate errand.

(*Lights fade out on* QUIXOTE *and up on* ALDONZA, *who is scrubbing pots and pans, her skirts hiked up on her thighs.* SHE *is bawling out a ditty as* SHE *works*)

ALDONZA (*Singing*) "For a red-headed lad of old Seville, my heart is all aflame, For a little brown lad I know, any girl would part with her good name..."

(SHE *becomes aware of* SANCHO *approaching, falls silent and watches him with hostile eyes*)

What do *you* want?

SANCHO My master sent me with a missive.

ALDONZA (*Suspiciously*) Missive? What's a missive?

SANCHO A kind of a letter. He warned me to give it only into your hand.

ALDONZA (*Darkly*) Let's see it.

(SHE *takes the folded sheet from* SANCHO, *inspects both sides. Sullenly*)

I can't read.

SANCHO Neither can I. But my master, foreseeing such a possibility, recited it to me so I could commit it to heart.

ALDONZA (*Angrily*) What made him think I couldn't read?

SANCHO Well, as he explained it, highborn ladies are so busy with their needlework—

ALDONZA *Needlework?*

SANCHO Embroidering devices on banners for their knights. He said they had no time for study.

ALDONZA (*Contemptuously*) What's it say?

SANCHO (*Takes the letter from her, holds it before him, closes his eyes and recites:*) "Most lovely Sovereign and Highborn Lady—"

ALDONZA Ha.

SANCHO "The heart of this, thy vassal knight, faints for thy favor."

ALDONZA Ho.

SANCHO "Oh, fairest of the fair, purest of the pure, incomparable Dulcinea—"

ALDONZA Who?

SANCHO "Incomparable Dulcinea—"

ALDONZA Why, that letter isn't even for me!

SANCHO I assure you—

ALDONZA My name is Aldonza!

SANCHO (*Patiently*) My master calls you Dulcinea.

ALDONZA (*Glowering*) Why?

SANCHO I don't know, but I can tell you from experience that knights have their own language for everything, and it's better not to ask questions because it only gets you into trouble.

LEFT Myself, a career hobo at age 16, in a pause between freight trains in West Allis, Wisconsin. **BELOW** I am caught in the act of directing the opera, *Ouanga* at the Academy of Music, Philadelphia, circa 1956.

LEFT This photo proves that I am capable of extreme skepticism. **BELOW** Contemplation, at home in Spain, 1975.

Top In an argument with my
dog, at home in the Casa La Mancha,
Benalmadena, Malaga, Spain.
Difficult, because I'm speaking
English and my dog knows
only Spanish. **Left** At work, 1976,
Spain; but actually I am gazing
across the Mediterranean at Morocco.

THIS PAGE: **Right** Deep thinking in my studio, Spain. **Below** We call this one "The Pencil Eater." At home in Arizona, 2002.

OPPOSITE PAGE: **Top** With Mel Ferrer, at my home in Spain. We are plotting a production in Paris. **Lower Left** This is Martha Nelly Garza, a.k.a. Mrs. Dale Wasserman for the past 26 years. We met in the midst of a movie. **Lower Right** Kirk Douglas in the first production of *One Flew Over the Cuckoo's Nest*, New York, 1963, a less than ecstatic experience.

OPPOSITE PAGE: The Broadway production of *Man of La Mancha* at the Martin Beck Theatre 2002/2003. Mary Elizabeth Mastrantonio was a splendid Aldonza with a surprise singing voice.

THIS PAGE: **Right** Jamie Torcellini as the Barber, backed by sudden sunflowers on the extraordinary set designed by Paul Brown. Martin Beck Theatre, 2003. **Below** Brian Stokes Mitchell, the most musical Don Quixote ever, at the Martin Beck Theatre, 2003.

"The Impossible Dream." Mary Elizabeth Mastrantonio as Aldonza listens to
Brian Stokes Mitchell as Don Quixote, at the Martin Beck Theatre, 2003.
Mitchell's rendition literally stopped the show at every performance.

(ALDONZA *gestures: "Go on"*)

"I beg thee grant that I may kiss the nethermost hem of thy garment—"

ALDONZA Kiss my *which?*

SANCHO If you keep interrupting the whole thing will be gone out of my head! "—and swear to be thy knight forever. Lady, do not deprive me of the beauty that renders life joyful, the grace which charms it, the modesty which gives it measure. Know that thou, dearest enemy, holds me submissive to thy every wish. Thine until death, Don Quixote de la Mancha."

ALDONZA (*A pause*) That's all?

SANCHO He said to tell you he would be trembling and languishing upon your reply.

ALDONZA What was that name again...?

SANCHO Don Quixote de la Mancha.

ALDONZA The other one.

SANCHO Dulcinea.

ALDONZA (*With sudden violence*) Your master's a crackbrain!

SANCHO Oh, no!

ALDONZA Oh, yes!

SANCHO He's the best and bravest man in the whole world.

ALDONZA He's crazy!

SANCHO (*Stubbornly*) Well, if he is I'll just have some of the same.

ALDONZA You're crazy, too!

SANCHO (*Patiently*) My master said there would be a reply.

ALDONZA I'll give him a reply. Tell him I may be a stupid kitchen-wench, but nobody makes fun of me!

SANCHO My lady—

ALDONZA Don't you "my lady" me, or I'll crack you like an egg. Now get out of here.

> (*As* HE *hesitates,* SHE *picks up pots and pans, flinging them at him*)

Out! Out!

> (SANCHO, *dodging in panic, disappears*)

(*Sneering:*) Dearest enemy! Kiss the hem of thy garment! Incompar-able—

> (*A hesitation*)

—Dulcinea...

> (*Uncertainly,* SHE *picks up the letter and studies it, forehead knitted, as though it might yield some further secret.*

> *The lights fade out. They come up on* DON QUIXOTE *pacing his room as* HE *waits*)

INNKEEPER (*As* HE *ascends the stairs*) Señor knight. Señor knight!

DON QUIXOTE (*Excited*) Sancho?

(*Disappointed*)

Ah, what is it, my lord?

INNKEEPER (*Puffing*) Two gentlemen.

DON QUIXOTE (*Puzzled*) They inquire for *me*?

INNKEEPER They say: one who calls himself Don Quixote
de la Mancha.

DON QUIXOTE (*Pleasure lighting his face*) So soon has my fame
spread abroad!

INNKEEPER They probably need your help.

DON QUIXOTE Some high enterprise. A perilous adventure
or a challenge to be met. An exploit which can only be
accomplished by me!

(*Briskly*)

Thank you, my lord. I shall attend upon them.

(*Lights go up on the* PADRE *and* DR. CARRASCO *in the
central courtyard. The* PADRE *is nervous,* DR. CARRASCO
calm as HE *removes his travel cloak and beats dust from it*)

PADRE I confess I shall not know what to say to him.

DR. CARRASCO In that case leave it to me.

PADRE But how does one deal with an old friend who is...who...

DR. CARRASCO (*Calmly*) To one of my training there is
no problem. The procedure must go according to the
phenomena.

PADRE We are not in the laboratory!

DR. CARRASCO All the world is a laboratory.

PADRE And men merely specimens?

(DR. CARRASCO *shrugs*)

He may not even know us!

DR. CARRASCO I am prepared for that contingency. Should he fail to recognize us —

(HE *stops, realizing that* SOMEONE *has entered*)

DON QUIXOTE (*Entering, strikes a pose. In ringing tones:*) Who is it crieth help of Don Quixote de la Mancha? Is there a castle beleaguered by giants? A king who lies under enchantment? An army besieged and awaiting rescue?

PADRE (*Quavering*) Alonso...

DON QUIXOTE (*Surprised*) What is this?

(*With cordial welcome*)

My friends!

DR. CARRASCO (*Taken aback*) You know us?

DON QUIXOTE (*Equally puzzled*) Should a man not know his friends? You are the Bachelor, Sanson Carrasco. And you —

(*With great warmth, taking his hand*)

— Padre Perez!

PADRE Then you are not—?

DON QUIXOTE Not what?

DR. CARRASCO Out of your head!

DON QUIXOTE What foul rumor is this?

PADRE (*In deep relief*) Ah, Señor Quijana—

DON QUIXOTE (*In cool reproof*) I should prefer that you address me properly. I am Don Quixote, knight-errant of la Mancha.

> (*The* PADRE *quails*)

Now, then. What dire circumstance has led you to seek my aid?

DR. CARRASCO The dire circumstance is your family.

DON QUIXOTE My family is all mankind.

DR. CARRASCO We ask you to return home.

DON QUIXOTE My home is the whole wide world.

DR. CARRASCO (*Grimly*) He knows us, Padre, but not himself!

DON QUIXOTE Wrong, Doctor. I know who I am...and who I may be if I choose.

DR. CARRASCO Señor Quijana—

DON QUIXOTE Don Quixote.

DR. CARRASCO There are no giants. No kings under enchantment.

No castles. No chivalry. No knights. There have been no knights for three hundred years.

Don Quixote (*Indifferently*) So say you.

Dr. Carrasco These are *facts.*

Don Quixote Facts are the enemy of truth!

Dr. Carrasco Would you deny reality?

Don Quixote (*Coolly*) Which — mine or yours?

Dr. Carrasco There is only one!

Don Quixote (*Smiles calmly*) I think reality is in the eye of the beholder.

(*As* Dr. Carrasco *would answer*)

No, my friend, it is useless to argue. Give me my way and let the devil take those who have no more use for imagination than a rooster for his wings.

(Dr. Carrasco *turns away, angry*)

Padre (*Fascinated*) *Why* do you do this?

Don Quixote In the service of God...and my lady.

Padre I have some knowledge of God — but this other?

Don Quixote My lady Dulcinea.

Dr. Carrasco (*Pouncing*) So there's a woman!

Don Quixote A *lady!*

(*Softening*)

Her beauty is more than human. Her quality? Perfection. She is the very meaning of woman...and all meaning woman has to man.

PADRE (*A pause. With a sad smile:*) To each his Dulcinea.

DR. CARRASCO And when will this...enterprise...be finished?

DON QUIXOTE When I have conquered my enemy.

DR. CARRASCO What enemy?

DON QUIXOTE The Great Enchanter.

DR. CARRASCO A man?

DON QUIXOTE He may appear as a man.

DR. CARRASCO (*Intently*) How will you know him?

DON QUIXOTE I will know him. And I will fight him. And I will win!

DR. CARRASCO (*Studies him a moment. Then in a businesslike tone:*) Come, Padre. It's a long way home.

PADRE (*Hesitates a moment*) Go with God.

(*Follows* DR. CARRASCO, *pauses to look back*)

There is either the wisest madman or the maddest wise man in the world.

DR. CARRASCO He is mad.

PADRE Or is the word...possessed?

Dr. Carrasco You know a distinction?

Padre One could say Jesus was possessed. Buddha... Saint Francis.

Dr. Carrasco Jesuit!

Padre (*Curiously*) Strange. You are angry.

> (Dr. Carrasco *makes a brusque gesture, thinking. The* Padre *sighs, giving up*)

Well... in any case, we have failed.

Dr. Carrasco Not necessarily. We know the sickness. Now to find the cure.

> (They *go. The* Innkeeper *enters, bringing wine*)

Innkeeper (*Seeing* Don Quixote *alone*) Your friends have departed?

> (Don Quixote, *deep in thought, does not notice him*)

Señor Knight?

Don Quixote Forgive me. I am troubled.

Innkeeper (*Heartily*) Have a glass of wine!

Don Quixote (*Drops to one knee suddenly*) Sir Castellano —

Innkeeper (*Alarmed*) Here, what's this?

Don Quixote I would make a confession.

Innkeeper To me?

DON QUIXOTE I would confess that I have never been dubbed a knight.

INNKEEPER Oh! That's bad.

DON QUIXOTE (*Anxiously*) And yet I am well qualified, my lord. I am brave, courteous, bold, generous, affable, and patient.

INNKEEPER (*Judiciously*) Yes...that's the list.

DON QUIXOTE Therefore I would beg of thee a boon.

INNKEEPER Anything! Within reason.

DON QUIXOTE Tonight I would hold vigil in the chapel of thy castle, and at dawn receive from thy hand the ennobling stroke of knighthood.

INNKEEPER Hmmm. There's one small difficulty. No chapel.

DON QUIXOTE No...chapel?

INNKEEPER That is—it's being repaired. But if you wouldn't mind holding your vigil some place else—?

DON QUIXOTE (*A happy thought*) Here in the courtyard. Under the sky...

INNKEEPER Fine. At sunrise you'll be dubbed a knight.

DON QUIXOTE I thank thee, I thank thee!

INNKEEPER Now—how would you like some supper?

DON QUIXOTE Before a vigil? No, my lord. On this night it is better that I fast and compose my spirit.

(*Lights out in the courtyard and up dimly on a level—
the stable loft—where* PEDRO *and* JOSÉ *play cards
while* TENORIO *touches his guitar and sings. The song is
lonely and sentimental.*

Lights up on another level, where ALDONZA *is combing
her hair by the reflection of a fragment of mirror.
Her movements are slow and automatic.* SHE *puts the
comb down, picks up* DON QUIXOTE's *letter, studies
it, brows knitted. Flings it aside, irritably, picks up
a rebozo, puts it on her head. Is caught by her image
in the mirror. Leans forward curiously, gazing at
herself. With the rebozo her face is softened, almost
madonna-like*)

ALDONZA (*Almost soundlessly*) Dulcinea...

(*Lights come up in the courtyard... moonlight from a
full moon on an attendance of stars.* DON QUIXOTE *is
there, lance on his shoulder as* HE *paces slowly back and
forth.* HE *is keeping vigil over his armor, which lies on a
watering trough. An atmosphere of serenity. Of mystery.
The guitar and singing are heard softly*)

DON QUIXOTE (*Musing*) Now must I consider how sages of the
future will describe this historic night.

(HE *strikes a pose*)

"Long after the sun had retired to his couch, darkening the
gates and balconies of la Mancha, Don Quixote with
measured tread and lofty expression held vigil in the courtyard
of a mighty castle!"

(*Hears the pompous echo of his voice, bows his head,
ashamed*)

Oh, maker of empty boasts. On this of all nights to give way to vanity! Nay, Don Quixote. Now is the time to take a deep breath of life and consider how it should be lived.

(*Eyes closed*)

Call nothing thine own except thy soul.

Love not what thou art, but only what thou may become.

Avoid self-contempt for this is the nearest thing to hell on earth.

Be a father to virtue and a stepfather to vice.

Do not pursue pleasure for you may have the misfortune to overtake it.

Be brave in spirit rather than body, and remember that most courage is but fear of censure by others.

Remain always at odds with the majority, for men singly may be right but in unison are always wrong.

Respect all gods except them that are cruel or jealous.

Look always forward; in last year's nest there are no birds this year.

(ALDONZA *has entered the courtyard en route to her rendezvous with* PEDRO. *She stops, watching* DON QUIXOTE *and listening*)

Be just to all men, yet remember that charity is even better than justice.

Be courteous to all women.

Keep ever before thee a vision of that one for whom great deeds are performed...she that is called Dulcinea.

ALDONZA (*Harshly*) Why do you call me that?

DON QUIXOTE (HE *opens his eyes, quickly kneels*) My lady!

ALDONZA Oh, get up from there. Get up!

(DON QUIXOTE *rises worshipfully*)

Why do you call me by that name?

DON QUIXOTE Because it is thine.

ALDONZA My name is Aldonza!

DON QUIXOTE (*Shakes his head respectfully*) I know thee, lady.

ALDONZA My name is Aldonza and I think you know me not.

DON QUIXOTE All my years have I known thee. Thy virtue. Thy nobility of spirit.

ALDONZA (*Laughs scornfully, whips the rebozo from her head in a defiant gesture*) Take another look!

DON QUIXOTE (*Gently*) Shall I trust my eyes when my heart knows better?

ALDONZA Your heart doesn't know much about women!

DON QUIXOTE It knows all, my lady. They are the soul of man, and the radiance that lights his way.

ALDONZA Oh, God, you *are* mad.

Don Quixote A woman is... glory!

Aldonza (*Anger covering uncertainty*) What do you want of me?

Don Quixote Nothing.

Aldonza Liar!

Don Quixote (*Bows his head*) I deserved the rebuke. I ask of my lady—

Aldonza (*Scornfully*) *Now* we get to it.

Don Quixote —that I may be allowed to serve her. That I may hold her in my heart. That I may dedicate each victory to her and call upon her in defeat. And if I give my life I give it in the sacred name of Dulcinea.

Aldonza (*Draws her rebozo about her shoulders, backs away uncertainly*) I must go... Pedro is waiting...

(*Vehemently:*)

Why do you do these things?

Don Quixote What things, my lady?

Aldonza These ridiculous—the things you do!

Don Quixote I hope to add some measure of grace to life.

Aldonza Life stinks like a rotten fish—and *you* won't change *that!*

Don Quixote (*Gently*) My lady knows better in her heart.

Aldonza What's in my heart will buy a load of hellfire and

damnation. And you, Señor Don Quixote—you're going to take such a beating!

DON QUIXOTE Whether one wins or loses does not matter.

ALDONZA (*Jeering*) What does?

DON QUIXOTE Only that he fights—and follows the quest.

ALDONZA (*Spits in vulgar contempt*) *That* for your quest!

> (**SHE** *turns from him, marches away. Stops. Comes back. Sullenly:*)

What does it mean...quest?

DON QUIXOTE The mission we follow.

ALDONZA *We?*

DON QUIXOTE Surely it is yours as well as mine.

> (**HE** *lifts his eyes to the stars*)

To dream the impossible dream.
To fight the unbeatable foe.
And never to stop dreaming or fighting.
This is man's privilege and the only life worth living.

ALDONZA (*Silent a moment. Then pleading suddenly:*) Once—just once—would you look at me as I really am?

> (**DON QUIXOTE** *lowers his eyes from the sky, gazes into hers*)

DON QUIXOTE I see beauty. Purity. I see the woman each man holds secret within him. Dulcinea.

(ALDONZA *moans in inexpressible despair.* SHE *backs away from the steady eyes, shaking her head.* SHE *turns to run—and gasps as* SHE *collides with* PEDRO *who has appeared unseen.* HE *grips her in fury*)

PEDRO Keep me waiting, will you?

ALDONZA I wasn't—I didn't—

PEDRO (*Shaking her*) Next time I'll know better than to pay in advance!

ALDONZA I swear I was—

PEDRO (*Mocking ferociously*) My lady. My princess. My little flower. Here's a kiss for Dulcinea!

(*And* HE *slaps her so that* SHE *goes spinning to the ground*)

DON QUIXOTE (*A roar of outrage*) Monster!

PEDRO Stay clear!

DON QUIXOTE (*Advancing*) Thou wouldst strike a woman?

PEDRO Get back or I'll break your empty head!

DON QUIXOTE Oh, thou heart of flint and bowels of cork! Now shall I punish thee!

PEDRO I warn you—*ai-e-ee!*

(DON QUIXOTE, *clubbing his lance, catches* PEDRO *alongside the head, sending him sprawling*)

DON QUIXOTE Impudent beast! Get to thy feet that I may strike again!

PEDRO (*Groaning*) Oh-h-h, I am killed.

(*In a yell, staying on the ground*)

José! Tenorio! Muleteers!

DON QUIXOTE Rise! Up, that I may teach thee courtesy! Oh, thou unmannerly, ignorant, impudent, backbiting, insolent monster of Nature!

PEDRO (*Scrambling away but staying prudently on the ground*) José! Tenorio! Muleteers—to the rescue!

MULETEERS (*Approaching at the run*) Hold, Pedro!
We come!
We come!

(ALDONZA, *back on her feet, has sheltered herself behind the watering trough*)

DON QUIXOTE (*Facing the reinforcements*) Come one, come all! Don Quixote will vanquish armies!

PEDRO Beware the lance!

TENORIO (*Pulling up*) Stone him! Stone him!

ALDONZA (*Stepping out*) Leave him be!

PEDRO Back, whore!

(*The* MULETEERS *pick up stones and, keeping distance from* DON QUIXOTE's *lance, fling stones at him.* HE *is struck, staggers back with a cry of dismay*)

ALDONZA I said leave him be! He's worth a thousand of you!

PEDRO (*Diverted from* DON QUIXOTE) You want the same, eh?

> (HE *lurches toward her.* ALDONZA *snatches* DON
> QUIXOTE's *sword from the watering trough, swings it in
> a mighty arc, and the flat of the blade sends* PEDRO
> *bowling butt over elbow*)

ALDONZA (*Exultant*) There's a kiss for *you!*

> (*To the* OTHERS, *eyes blazing*)

Come on, brave men—who's next?

DON QUIXOTE (*Bawling it to the sky*) For God—and for
Dulcinea!

> (HE *charges back into the fray.* HE *wields the lance,*
> ALDONZA *swinging hugely with the sword. The battle
> rages for a while, then the tide turns and the* MULETEERS,
> *with cries, groans and howls of pain, fall hors de combat.*)

(*Gasping but triumphant*) Victory!

ALDONZA (*Brandishing the sword*) *Victory!*

INNKEEPER (*Roused from sleep, comes rushing up wearing nightgown
and bedcap. Aghast:*) What is this? All the noise!

> (HE *sees the* MULETEERS *where they lie groaning or
> crawling away*)

Oh! Oh! What dreadful thing...?

ALDONZA What *glorious* thing!

DON QUIXOTE (*Gasping*) Sir Castellano—I would inform you...
that the right has triumphed.

Sancho (*Coming on the run*) Your Grace! Are you hurt?

Don Quixote No, Sancho. A little weakness, perhaps... temporary and of no—

(He *collapses suddenly,* Sancho *catching him*)

Aldonza Oh, he is hurt!

(She *drops the sword and hurries to help*)

Innkeeper Oh, what a terrible thing...

Aldonza (*Tenderly, as* She *and* Sancho *help* Don Quixote) Gently, my lord. Gently...gently...so...

(Maria, *frightened and in nightclothes, comes running out*)

Maria What is it?

Innkeeper Fetch me hot water. Bandages. More light!

Maria (*Sees* Quixote) The madman! I knew it!

Innkeeper Hurry, Maria!

(He *helps set* Don Quixote *against the trough*)

Aldonza (*Tenderly*) There. Poor man!

(Maria *hurries in with water and bandages*)

Give me those!

(She *snatches the cloths, dips one and begins cleansing the wounds*)

There...oh,—what they did to you! Poor warrior...

MARIA (*Bitterly*) Poor lunatic!

INNKEEPER (*Wearily*) Go back to bed, Maria.

MARIA I warned you what would happen if—

INNKEEPER *Go to bed.*

    (**MARIA** *sniffs, exits haughtily.* **DON QUIXOTE** *stirs, moans*)

SANCHO He's coming around!

DON QUIXOTE (*Opens his eyes and is looking at* **ALDONZA**. *Weakly but with pleasure:*) Ah...might I always wake to such a vision!

ALDONZA Don't move.

SANCHO I must say, Your Grace, you certainly did a job out here.

DON QUIXOTE (*Coming to fully*) We routed them?

ALDONZA Ho! There's not a man in that bunch'll walk straight for a week!

DON QUIXOTE (*Distressed, tries to rise*) My lady—

ALDONZA Sit still!

DON QUIXOTE It is not seemly to gloat over the fallen.

INNKEEPER (*Agitated, to* **DON QUIXOTE**) Sir, I am a tame and peaceful man. I have a wife and responsibilities. Please, Sir Knight—I don't like to be inhospitable—but I must ask you to leave as soon as you are able.

Don Quixote (*With dignity*) I am sorry to have offended the dignity of thy castle and I shall depart with daylight. But now, my lord, I must remind thee of thy promise.

Innkeeper Promise?

Don Quixote True, it is not yet dawn, but I have kept vigil and proven myself in combat. Therefore I beg that thou dub me knight.

Innkeeper (*Remembering*) Oh-h. Certainly. Let's get it over with.

Don Quixote Sancho, wilt be good enough to fetch my sword?

> (**Sancho** *looks for it.* **Don Quixote** *rises weakly,* **Aldonza** *assisting*)

(*Warmly:*) Lady, I cannot tell thee how joyful I am that this ceremony should take place in thy presence.

Aldonza (*As* **He** *sways a little*) Be careful, now!

Don Quixote It is a solemn moment which seals my vocation...

Aldonza (*Worriedly*) You shouldn't be on your feet!

> (**Sancho** *has found the sword, hands it to the* **Innkeeper**)

Innkeeper (*Handing the sword gingerly*) Are you ready?

Don Quixote (*Firmly*) I am.

Innkeeper Very well, then. Kneel.

> (**Don Quixote,** *with* **Aldonza** *and* **Sancho** *assisting on either side, gets down to his knees*)

Don Quixote de la Mancha—according to the rules of chivalry and my authority as lord of this castle, I hereby dub thee knight.

(HE *touches him with the sword on each shoulder*)

DON QUIXOTE Your Lordship.

INNKEEPER Didn't I do it right?

DON QUIXOTE (*Humbly*) Your Lordship, it is customary at this time to grant the new knight an added name.

INNKEEPER Oh...of course.

DON QUIXOTE Would Your Lordship devise such a name for me?

INNKEEPER (*Reflects, looks down at the battered face*) Don Quixote, I devise and proclaim that you shall henceforth be known as the Knight of the Woeful Countenance!

DON QUIXOTE (*Simply, bowing his head*) I thank thee.

INNKEEPER (*Handing the sword to* SANCHO) Now, Sir Knight, I am going to bed. And I advise you do the same!

(*Exits*)

DON QUIXOTE (*Still on his knees; raptly*) Knight of the Woeful Countenance...

ALDONZA (*Near tears*) It's a beautiful name.

SANCHO (*Practically*) Come, Your Grace. Let's get you up to bed.

(DON QUIXOTE *holds out his hands and* SANCHO *and* ALDONZA *help him to his feet*)

This way.

DON QUIXOTE (*Holding back*) Not yet. I owe something to my enemies.

ALDONZA *That* account's been paid.

DON QUIXOTE No, my lady. I must yet raise them up and minister to their wounds.

ALDONZA (*Aghast*) *What?*

DON QUIXOTE Nobility demands.

ALDONZA It does?

DON QUIXOTE Yes, my lady. Therefore I shall take these —

ALDONZA (*Firmly, reaching the bandages before him*) No, you won't. *I'll* take them. *I'll* minister.

DON QUIXOTE But, my lady —

ALDONZA (*Simply*) They were my enemies, too.

DON QUIXOTE (*With emotion*) Oh, blessed one...!

SANCHO Come, Your Grace.

> (HE *helps* DON QUIXOTE *toward his room.* ALDONZA *climbs to the stable loft, where the* MULETEERS *lie about, moaning and muttering curses over their wounds.* SHE *calmly sets down the pot of water, begins tearing bandages from her underskirt. The* MEN *stare at her blankly.* PEDRO *gapes in disbelief*)

PEDRO What are you doing here?

ALDONZA (*Matter-of-factly*) I'm going to minister to your wounds.

PEDRO You're...what?

ALDONZA Nobility demands.

(*To* TENORIO)

Turn over, you poxy goat.

> (SHE *goes to work on him.* PEDRO's *eyes light up with
> cat-and-mouse savagery and* HE *comes to his feet.*
> ALDONZA *is unaware as* HE *approaches from behind.*
> HE *grips her by her hair, yanks her upright.* ALDONZA
> *cries out, the cry cut off as* HE *strikes.* SHE *falls back,
> moaning.* PEDRO *seizes the cloth, whips it around her
> head, ties it tight, gagging her.* JOSÉ *leaps upon her, ties
> her hands.* PEDRO *stands up*)

PEDRO Nobility, eh?

(HE *kicks her savagely. To the* MEN:)

We're leaving.

TENORIO (*Pointing to* ALDONZA) What do we do with that?

PEDRO (*Grimly*) We take it along—and have a little sport
as we go.

> (JOSÉ *slings* ALDONZA *over his shoulder like a sack of
> meal. The* MEN *descend quietly from the loft.*
>
> *In* DON QUIXOTE's *room* SANCHO *is helping him to a
> reclining position.* QUIXOTE *leans back with a sigh*)

DON QUIXOTE Ah, Sancho, how I do envy my enemies.

SANCHO Well, I wouldn't unless they're feeling better than you.

DON QUIXOTE But they are, my friend. Oh, lucky enemies! To know the healing touch of my lady Dulcinea.

(HE *smiles rapturously.*

The MULETEERS *are crossing the stage, carrying* ALDONZA, *whose moans are anguished, though muffled*)

END OF ACT II

ACT III

It is eating time in the prison. The JAILER *officiates, ladling soup from a tub, tossing about chunks of bread. The* PRISONERS *sprawl or sit about cross-legged.*

LOBILLO (*Inspecting the contents of his bowl*) You call this soup? Scum!

THE SCORPION What's *this*?

JAILER (*Cheerfully*) Bread, Señor Scorpion.

THE SCORPION Fungus!

MOTHER BANE (*Indignantly*) Look! A worm!

JAILER Very nourishing, madam. More, Señor Judas?

JUDAS MACABEO (*Mournfully, as* HE *holds out his bowl*) An insult to the belly.

JAILER Buen apetito!

(MONIPODIO *rises, flings aside his bowl and crosses to* CERVANTES)

MONIPODIO (*Affably*) Eat up, fellow. Let's get back to your crazy cavalier.

THE DUKE (*Pensively, as* HE *plucks pieces from his chunk of bread and tosses them aside*) Curious.

JAILER The bread?

THE DUKE No, that's merely revolting.

(*To* CERVANTES)

Why are you poets so fascinated with madmen?

CERVANTES Are we?

THE DUKE There's a writer chap in my country—Will Shakespeare, of the Globe Theatre?

CERVANTES I do not know of him.

THE DUKE Never a play of his without its lunatic.

CERVANTES (*With humor*) I suppose artists and madmen have much in common.

THE DUKE They both turn their backs on life.

CERVANTES They both select from life what pleases them.

THE DUKE (*With irony*) You find that preferable to sanity?

CERVANTES To me it *is* sanity.

THE DUKE A man must come to terms with life as it is!

CERVANTES (*Sets down his bowl*) I am more than fifty years of age and I have seen life as it is. Misery, pain, sorrow, hunger cruelty beyond belief. I have heard the singing from taverns and the moans from bundles of filth on the streets. I have been a soldier and seen my comrades fall in battle—or die more slowly under the lash in Africa. I have held some of them in my arms at the final moment. These were men who saw life as it is—yet they died despairing. No glory, no gallant last words. Only their eyes filled with confusion, whimpering the question: "Why?" I do not think they asked why they were dying, but why they had lived.

(HE *rises, and will move into the character of*
DON QUIXOTE)

No, madness lies down other roads. To be practical is madness. To surrender dreams—this is madness. To seek treasure where there is only trash. Too much sanity is madness. And maddest of all, to see life as it is and not as it should be...

(DON QUIXOTE *and* SANCHO *are back on the road. It is bright morning but* DON QUIXOTE *is moody*)

SANCHO (*Singing merrily but not beautifully*)
I have danced at all the dances,
Many serenades I've sung,
But I always was unwelcome,
Spurned by maidens old and young.
One I loved was named Teresa,
She lived up there on the hill;
Said I kissed her like an angel
But I was a monkey still!

DON QUIXOTE Sancho.

SANCHO (*About to launch another verse*) Your Grace?

DON QUIXOTE Have the goodness to be silent.

SANCHO I was trying to cheer you up!

DON QUIXOTE (*Sighs gustily*) I cannot bear it, Sancho. To find and then lose her!

SANCHO Well, you know what they say. "Never put to the test what's sure to fail."

DON QUIXOTE Do not condemn before thou knowest!

SANCHO She ran off with those muledrivers, didn't she?

DON QUIXOTE (*Loyally*) But undoubtedly with some high purpose.

SANCHO (*Stubbornly*) High or low she could have said good-bye. And there's another thing. Suppose you conquer some kings or giants. Naturally you'll send them to the Lady Dulcinea?

DON QUIXOTE Aye.

SANCHO Well, how are they going to find her? I can see them now, wandering around like a bunch of nitwits!

DON QUIXOTE (*Gloomily*) Verily, that is a problem.

SANCHO You see? And I'll tell you something else, Your Grace—

DON QUIXOTE (*Halting suddenly*) Sancho!

SANCHO (*Startled*) What ails you?

DON QUIXOTE There!

> (HE *points to the road ahead. Emerging from darkness are* FIVE MASKED FIGURES *standing atop a Players' wagon, their costumes blowing eerily in a wind. At the center is* DEATH, *robed in black and skull-faced. To his right a figure dressed as* LOVE, *and a* CLOWN. *To his left an* ANGEL *and a* DEMON)

SANCHO (*Peering vainly*) Where?

DON QUIXOTE Dost not see them?

DEATH (*Raises his arm, finger leveled straight at* DON QUIXOTE)
Stand, Sir Knight. Prepare to deliver that for which thou wilt
have no further use — thy body.

DON QUIXOTE (*Quaveringly*) Who…who art thou?

DEATH I am the incurable wound, the sickness without remedy.
The final victor of each battle!

> (*He laughs, and the others echo his laughter, a sound like
> wind among trees*)

SANCHO Master…who are you talking to?

DON QUIXOTE (*Bravely, raising his voice*) I flee neither phantom
nor man. Whoever or whatever ye are — prepare to do battle
with Don Quixote de la Mancha!

> (HE *levels his lance*)

DEATH (*Quickly*) Halt! Hold, sir. We did not know!

DON QUIXOTE Did not know my name?

DEATH Nay, sir. We thought you were one of us.

DON QUIXOTE (*Perplexed*) How should I be one of you?

DEATH An actor! You see, sir, because of your costume —

DON QUIXOTE (*Outraged*) Costume?

DEATH (*Amending quickly*) We *thought* it was a costume. We
deemed you one of our profession and thought to have a
little fun.

DON QUIXOTE (*Darkly, but unsure*) Methinks I do not trust this tale. Why should actors wear their trappings on the highway?

DEATH (*Easily*) Oh, I can explain that, sir. Today is Corpus Christi and we play the same piece in three different villages. Therefore we do not change costumes between.

DON QUIXOTE What is the name of thy play?

DEATH "The Parliament of Death."

SANCHO (*Bemused,* HE *plucks at* DON QUIXOTE's *sleeve*) Master — what...?

DON QUIXOTE Silence!

(*To the* FIGURES)

Tell me what ye represent, and I will then decide whether to slay thee or not.

(DEATH *gestures to his* TROUPE *to comply*)

DEMON (*Steps forward, flicking his whip*) I am a Demon, sir. There is at least one of me in every man, and with this whip I flog him toward his heart's desire. In some I am lust for fame. In others, lust for power or possessions. In many, simply lust.

DON QUIXOTE Do men know thou art within them?

DEMON Oh, yes, but they always call me by some virtuous name!

DON QUIXOTE I think I would do well to kill thee first.

DEMON But why?

DON QUIXOTE Thou art a foul enslaver!

DEMON Oh, no, sir, it's the other way around. Men seek me out if I do not find them first. They beg that I shall enter into them. They suffer when I do not scourge them with this whip!

(HE *cracks it smartly*)

DON QUIXOTE (*To the* ANGEL) And thou?

ANGEL I am what men hope to be after they have dealt with *him*.

(SHE *indicates* DEATH)

DON QUIXOTE And are they not?

ANGEL Oh, yes, sir, most of them are. They enter my land where there is neither pain nor ecstasy. No striving, no passion, no darkness and no light. Just one eternity after another.

DON QUIXOTE This land of yours sounds more like Hell!

ANGEL Yes, sir. That's what it *is*.

(DON QUIXOTE *looks to the* NEXT *who steps forward without bidding*)

LOVE (*Timidly*) I am love, sir. But I have no lines to speak.

DON QUIXOTE Love — silent?

LOVE Yes, sir, everyone's so busy talking about me I can't get in a word.

DON QUIXOTE Thou art obviously the victim of malicious gossip.

(*To the* CLOWN)

But what place has laughter in a Parliament of Death?

CLOWN (*Exuberantly*) Everything! Why, without me, sir, the performance would be *ghastly*. Wise men call me the highest attribute of intelligence. Others say I am the only certain way to tell animal from man. And regardless, sir, if it weren't for me, how could you ever bear with *them*?

(HE *points to the* OTHERS *and his derisive laughter rings out*)

DEATH (*Steps forward*) I am the Director and General Understudy.

DON QUIXOTE (*Puzzled*) General Understudy?

DEATH A theatrical term. It means that I may change costume and play the roles of any of these others.

DON QUIXOTE Is the audience not aware?

DEATH No, sir, they don't know there's been a substitution—at least not until the performance is over. Then it's too late, sir, because I've taken their money and gone.

DON QUIXOTE I wonder would it be a kindness were I to slay thee now?

DEATH (*With humor*) Well, sir, it would be a terrible disappointment to the next village.

DON QUIXOTE Only if thou art truly actors as thou claim. Remove thy mask.

DEATH I warn you, sir—

DON QUIXOTE (*Leveling his lance*) Remove it, or by all the gods—

(DEATH'S *hand goes to his mask.* HE *removes it. Beneath it is an identical skull-face. The* CLOWN'S *laughter burbles*)

IXOTE Wretch that I was to doubt her even for a
ent!

To the sky)

nea—queen of my heart—forgive me! If it be possible
y prayers to reach thine ears, forgive the weakness that
s me unworthy of thy favor!

ou think she hears you?

xote She hears! She hears! Ah, Sancho, my heart is
restored to joy.

hat's fine, Your Grace. Now if you want to do
hing for *my* heart, you'll just get down to business
nquer a few kingdoms.

xote Have no fear!

Stubbornly) Well, we've been riding a long time and I'm
 anxious.

xote I assure you there will be conquests and kingdoms
y. The fortunes of war—

tops suddenly)

poke I not truly?

hat? Where?

ote (*As the shadows of great vanes revolve across the*
here before you, Friend Sancho! Twenty or more
giants with whom I mean to do battle!

NCHO *lifts himself in the saddle to peer ahead)*

DON QUIXOTE Now shall Don Qui

SANCHO (*Bewildered*) Master—!

> (DON QUIXOTE *charges. Bu*
> *fading and his charge meets*
> SANCHO *hurries to him, ho*

Master, who are you fighting?

DON QUIXOTE Saw thou not?

SANCHO I didn't see anybody.

DON QUIXOTE It was Death hims

SANCHO Oh—that's a very bad or

DON QUIXOTE (*Getting up*) Nay,
dost know what that encounte

SANCHO Of *what*?

DON QUIXOTE My faith. Had I fl
should have been the end of I
very soul of courage.

> (*Modestly*)

Didst note my poise? How g

SANCHO I didn't note a thing!

DON QUIXOTE Know thou what
lady.

SANCHO (*Surprised*) Dulcinea?

**DON QU
    mon

    Dul
    for r
    mak

**SANCHO

**DON QU
    again

**SANCHO
    some
    and

**DON QU

**SANCHO
    gettin

**DON QU
    aplen

    (

Aha!

**SANCHO

**DON QU
    scene)
    lawles

    (S

SANCHO *What* giants?

DON QUIXOTE Be happy, for I shall deprive them of their lives, and with the spoils from this encounter you shall have your kingdom!

SANCHO But look, Your Grace, those are not giants.

DON QUIXOTE (*Scornfully*) Not giants? See their long arms whirling in rage!

SANCHO Why, they're nothing but windmills. And what you call arms are just their sails turning in the wind.

DON QUIXOTE If thou art afraid, Sancho, go off to one side and say thy prayers. For I am about to engage these giants in fierce unequal combat!

SANCHO Your Grace—

DON QUIXOTE (*Shouting*) Accursed breed, I shall remove thee from the face of the earth! Nay, do not seek to flee, cowards and vile creatures! This is but one single knight who challenges thee! Rocinante—charge!

> (HE *goes charging out of sight, lance leveled. There is a fearful crash and* HE *comes spinning back minus lance*)

SANCHO Master—!

DON QUIXOTE (*Gaining his feet, unsheathing his sword*) Yea, cry, shout, flourish thy arms! It will avail thee naught! For God— and for Dulcinea!

> (HE *charges again*)

SANCHO (*Clutching his cheeks*) Oh! Oh!

(DON QUIXOTE *comes sailing back to land with a crash. His sword is corkscrewed*)

Oh!

DON QUIXOTE (*Staggering erect*) Surrender, thou monsters! Thou art beaten, I tell thee!

(*Back to the attack*)

Yield or I shall show thee neither pity nor—

(HE *comes spinning back, goes head over heels, and this time* HE *does not rise*)

SANCHO I told him they were windmills!

(*Hurries to his aid*)

Didn't I tell you? Didn't I say, "Your Grace, those are windmills?"

DON QUIXOTE (*Hollow-voiced*) The fortunes of war.

SANCHO Can Your Grace get up?

(HE *helps him and* DON QUIXOTE *gains his feet with considerable pain and difficulty*)

DON QUIXOTE Sancho, you have seen a perfect example of the work of my enemy.

SANCHO The Enchanter?

DON QUIXOTE Jealous of my success, he changed those giants into windmills at the last moment. He will stop at nothing in order to deprive me of glory.

SANCHO (*Doubtfully*) I don't know, Your Grace. He seems a lot tougher than you are. One of these days he might get you killed.

DON QUIXOTE (*Roused*) How can he prevail against *me*?

SANCHO He's doing a pretty good job.

DON QUIXOTE Because he hides! He skulks and slinks behind his magic. But there will come a time when we meet face to face. And then—

(HE *groans, the result of too violent a gesture*)

SANCHO Is Your Grace in pain?

DON QUIXOTE (*Nobly*) Nothing... nothing.

SANCHO We'll go back where we can get some help.

(*Lights fade on them.*

Lights up on the courtyard of the inn. The INNKEEPER *is crossing toward the stable, singing.* HE *hears the bleat of* SANCHO'S *bugle.*

HE *turns a haunted face toward the gates.* MARIA *comes crashing from the inn. The bugle again, and* SANCHO *and* DON QUIXOTE *are seen*)

MARIA (*A shriek*) Don't open the gates! Don't let him in!

INNKEEPER (*His face clearing*) Of course! It's the pig-butcher!

MARIA No, no! Don't open!

INNKEEPER The pig-butcher. Don't you remember? We expected him yesterday.

(HE *swings open the "gates."* MARIA *screams and runs off. A wail*)

Not again?

(*Trying to bar the way*)

This place is closed.

SANCHO But—

INNKEEPER This castle has gone out of business!

DON QUIXOTE (*Feeble, but stern*) What, sir? Deny the right of sanctuary?

INNKEEPER I *hate* to, but—

DON QUIXOTE And to a knight dubbed by thy own hand?

INNKEEPER (*Wavering*) It *doesn't* seem right, does it?

DON QUIXOTE Not by any rule of chivalry!

INNKEEPER (HE *sighs, yielding*) Bring him in.

(SANCHO *helps* DON QUIXOTE *to a bench at the table*)

Knight of the Woeful Countenance, it appears I named you well.

(*Bringing* DON QUIXOTE *wine*)

More muleteers?

SANCHO (*As* DON QUIXOTE *drinks*) No, sir. My master fought a dreadful encounter with twenty giants.

INNKEEPER *Giants?*

SANCHO But at the last moment, just as he was about to overcome them, they changed into windmills.

INNKEEPER Oh. And you lost.

DON QUIXOTE To a mere handful of giants? Why, it is not an unheard-of-thing for a single knight to rout an entire army. Nay, sir, I was upset by enchantment.

> (*In the far background, unseen,* ALDONZA *enters*)

INNKEEPER No one doubts your bravery—only your discretion. Why not declare a truce?

DON QUIXOTE And allow wickedness to flourish?

INNKEEPER I'm afraid wickedness wears thick armor.

DON QUIXOTE It cannot withstand courage!

INNKEEPER You won't overthrow it by tilting at windmills.

DON QUIXOTE (*Roused*) Wouldst thou have me stop trying? Nay, for a time virtue may be thwarted but in the end evil must give way. Let a man be overthrown ten thousand times, still he must rise and again do battle. The Enchanter may twist the outcome but the effort remains sublime!

ALDONZA Lies. Madness and lies.

DON QUIXOTE (*As* ALL *turn to her, startled*) My lady!

ALDONZA Enough of that!

> (SHE *advances toward them, eyes burning with fury and*

disillusionment. SHE *has been badly beaten and worse.* HER *face is bruised, hair matted, clothing in tatters)*

INNKEEPER (*Horrified*) Aldonza! What happened?

ALDONZA Ask *him.*

(*Crying in rage*)

Oh, how they beat me. How they used me!

DON QUIXOTE (*Rising, pale*) I shall punish them that did this crime.

ALDONZA Crime. You know the worst crime of all? Being born. For that you get punished your whole life!

DON QUIXOTE Dulcinea—

ALDONZA Get yourself to a madhouse! Rave about nobility and inner calls where no one can hear.

DON QUIXOTE (*Pleading*) My lady—

ALDONZA I am not your lady. I am not any kind of a lady. I was spawned in a ditch by a mother who left me there. My father? An unknown regiment. I grew up on the garbage heaps of La Mancha. I have been starved, kicked, beaten, violated, more times than memory can count. I slave in kitchens, and when my luck is good I earn a few coins from casual bridegrooms. You want to know me better? Cross my palm with silver and I'll teach you all of me there is!

DON QUIXOTE Thou art my lady Dulcinea.

ALDONZA Still he torments me!

(*Shrieking*)

I am Aldonza. Aldonza the kitchen-wench. Aldonza the slut. Aldonza the whore!

DON QUIXOTE (*Steadily*) Now and forever, thou art my lady.

ALDONZA (*Collapses, weeping*) Oh, God, leave me be. Leave me be...

> (DON QUIXOTE *limps toward her, extends a compassionate hand—but suddenly, off, there is a fanfare of trumpets. Brazen, warlike, ominous in quality*)

A VOICE (*Harsh and clangorous*) Is there one here calls himself Don Quixote de la Mancha? If there is—and he be not afraid to look upon me—let him come forth!

> (SANCHO *is the first to move.* HE *crosses and looks outside the gates*)

SANCHO (*Backing away from what* HE *sees*) Master. Oh, master...!

> (*Fear chokes him. There is another fanfare*)

THE VOICE Come out from thy hiding-place, Don Quixote. Come face me if thou dare!

> (DON QUIXOTE, *as in a dream and with premonition behind his eyes, crosses slowly. Entering to meet him is a* KNIGHT. *Behind him are* LIVERIED RETAINERS. *The* KNIGHT *is tall and terrifying in jet-black armor.* HE *wears a chain-mail tunic on which are mounted tiny mirrors that glitter and dazzle the eyes. On his head a closed casque, only his eyes visible through the slit. From*

the crest of the casque spring great plumes accentuating what seems already incredible stature. On his arm a shield turned away from view. And in his hand a naked sword. We will know him as the KNIGHT OF THE MIRRORS)

DON QUIXOTE (*At length, voice shaking*) I am Don Quixote, Knight of the Woeful Countenance.

KNIGHT OF THE MIRRORS Come forth, Don Quixote. Stand before me!

(DON QUIXOTE *advances to face the strange* KNIGHT. *The* OTHERS *move closer, awed and silent. The* KNIGHT's *voice is magnified and metallic within the casque*)

Now hear me, thou charlatan, thou sickly poltroon! Thou art no knight but a foolish pretender. Thy pretense is a child's mockery, and thy principles dirt beneath my feet!

DON QUIXOTE (*Trembling with anger*) Oh, false knight! Discourteous and with heart black as thy armor! Before I chastise thee, speak thy name.

KNIGHT OF THE MIRRORS Thou shalt hear it in due course.

DON QUIXOTE Then say why thou seekest me out!

KNIGHT OF THE MIRRORS (*Mockingly*) Thou called upon me, Don Quixote. Thou reviled me and threatened.

DON QUIXOTE The Enchanter!

(*A moan from* SANCHO. *The* KNIGHT OF THE MIRRORS *chuckles evilly*)

I know thee now. My enemy. He that cripples each effort and bewitches victory from my grasp. Thou art The Enchanter!

(*The* KNIGHT *chuckles louder.* DON QUIXOTE, *enraged, tears off his left gauntlet and flings it at the feet of the* OTHER)

Behold at thy feet the gage of battle!

SANCHO (*Anguished*) Master—no!

(HE *runs, scrabbles for the gauntlet, but the* KNIGHT *pins it with his sword*)

KNIGHT OF THE MIRRORS (*Suddenly very cold*) On what terms do we fight?

DON QUIXOTE Choose thine own!

KNIGHT OF THE MIRRORS Very well. If thou art beaten thy freedom shall be forfeit and thou must obey my every command.

(DON QUIXOTE *bows coldly*)

And thy conditions?

DON QUIXOTE If thou art still alive thou shalt kneel and beg mercy of my lady Dulcinea.

KNIGHT OF THE MIRRORS (*Mockingly*) Where shall I find this lady?

DON QUIXOTE There she stands.

(*The* KNIGHT OF THE MIRRORS *turns his eyes to*

ALDONZA — *her rags, her bruises, her ruined face.* HE *begins to laugh in cruel derision.*

(*Enraged:*) What means this?

KNIGHT OF THE MIRRORS (*Gasping*) Thy...lady...!

DON QUIXOTE The fairest upon earth!

KNIGHT OF THE MIRRORS Thy lady is an alley-cat!

DON QUIXOTE (*Drawing his sword in fury*) Foul caitiff! Defend thyself!

KNIGHT OF THE MIRRORS (*Steps back. Commandingly*) Hold!

(*As* DON QUIXOTE *pauses*)

Thou asked my name, Don Quixote. Now I will tell it. I am called — The Knight of the Mirrors!

(*With the words* HE *swings his shield forward. Its surface is burnished steel, a brilliant mirror.*

DON QUIXOTE *flings up an arm before his eyes and falls back, blinded by reflected sun. The* KNIGHT *moves upon him, slowly, inexorably*)

Nay, do not flinch, Don Quixote. Look upon my device. Gaze deeply — for this is the mirror of reality and it tells things as they truly are.

(DON QUIXOTE, *trying to avoid the blaze of light, raises his sword*)

Look!

(*Again the shield blinds him, and that of the* ATTENDANTS, *too*)

What seest thou, Don Quixote? A gallant knight? Naught but an aging fool.

(*Again* DON QUIXOTE *raises his sword*)

Look!

(*And again falls back before the shield*)

Thou wilt see there is no Don Quixote. Naught but an old man—weak of brain. Seest thou? The face of a madman!

(DON QUIXOTE *raises his sword in one final trembling effort*)

Look!

(*And* HE *strikes at* DON QUIXOTE's *sword, which goes flying from his hand*)

The masquerade is ended!

(HE *crashes his shield against the* OTHER's *chest.* DON QUIXOTE *reels back into the dust.*

ALDONZA *cries out, stifles the cry.*

The KNIGHT OF THE MIRRORS *stands over* DON QUIXOTE, *sword point at the* FALLEN MAN's *throat*)

Confess! Thy lady is a trollop and thy dream the nightmare of a disordered mind!

DON QUIXOTE (*Dazedly, uncertain*) My lady is the lady Dulcinea...and the dream...the dream...?

(*His eyes wander and for the first time* HE *seems to realize what has happened*)

Oh, God—I am vanquished...

(*The* KNIGHT OF THE MIRRORS *steps back and waves his* ATTENDANTS *to bring forward a wooden cage which has been concealed behind them*)

SANCHO (*Hurrying forward, lifts* DON QUIXOTE's *head. Anguished*) Master—are you hurt?

DON QUIXOTE Vanquished...

SANCHO You couldn't help it!

DON QUIXOTE Vanquished...

(TWO *of the Attendants lift him roughly to his feet.* THEY *shove him toward the cage.* DON QUIXOTE *holds back when* HE *sees it*)

KNIGHT OF THE MIRRORS Remember the terms!

(DON QUIXOTE *dazedly enters the cage. The door closes behind him*)

It is done!

(*And* HE *sweeps the casque from his head*)

SANCHO (*Thunderstruck*) Your Grace! See! It is Doctor Carrasco! It is only Sanson Carrasco!

Dr. Carrasco Forgive me, Señor Quijana. It was the only way.

Don Quixote (*After a long, slow look*) I would rather you had killed my body... for when the spirit dies...

> (He *starts to cry, nakedly, broken. His head bends down between the bars and* He *sinks, weeping to the floor.*
>
> Aldonza *starts forward, her face devastated by loss and pity.*
>
> The Captain of the Inquisition *enters, crossing the forestage.* He *comes to the door, rattles it jarringly*)

Captain (*Shouting*) Cervantes? Cervantes!

> (*The* Prisoners *look at him blankly, from another mood. The* Jailer *recalls himself, hurries to open the door*)

Prepare to be summoned.

Cervantes (*Confusedly, crawling out of the cage*) By whom?

Captain The judges of the Inquisition!

> (He *slings a bundle of cloth across to* Cervantes)

You are to wear this.

Cervantes (*Takes the bundle, lets it fall open. It is a black robe with an imprint of yellow flames rising from the bottom*) What is it?

The Duke (*With relish*) Oh, very fashionable these days. To be worn at burnings.

CAPTAIN (*Maliciously*) Don't laugh, Señor Englishman. I think there is an order for you, too.

THE DUKE An order for freedom!

MONIPODIO Captain? How soon?

CAPTAIN Soon!

> (HE *exits*)

MONIPODIO But not yet.

> (*To* CERVANTES, *with satisfaction*)

Good. You'll have time to finish the story.

CERVANTES But the story is finished.

MONIPODIO *What?*

THE DUKE (*Cheerfully*) Of course. *Quite* the proper ending.

MONIPODIO (*Coldly*) I don't think I like this ending. I don't think the jury likes it, either.

> (CERVANTES *turns to look at them. Their faces are cold and hostile*)

THE DUKE Cervantes — you've failed!

MONIPODIO (*With a rap of his gavel*) How says the jury?

CERVANTES (*In panic*) Wait! Could I have a little more time?

MONIPODIO Oh, *I'll* grant it — but the Inquisition?

CERVANTES (*Harassed*) A moment only. Let me think...

> (*A pause. Music establishes a somber mood, a ticking of
> time.* CERVANTES *slowly removes the remnants of his
> armor, moves to an area where the* PRISONERS *establish
> an improvised bed.* HE *puts on a dressing gown which*
> MONIPODIO *holds for him. His armor, sword atop the
> heap, is laid atop a table. The lighting alters to shafts of
> dying sun as* CERVANTES *lies down on the bed...and as*
> ANTONIA, *the* PADRE, *the* HOUSEKEEPER *and* DR.
> CARRASCO *move into positions of attendance. We are in*
> DON QUIXOTE's *bedroom.*
>
> QUIXOTE's *eyes are open but deep-hollowed and remote,
> windows on a mind that has retreated to some secret place.*
>
> *There is silence a while but for the music*)

ANTONIA (*Voice low, to* CARRASCO) Can you do *nothing*?

PADRE (*With soft compassion*) I'm afraid there'll be more need of
my services than his.

> (*Waves a hand slowly across* QUIXOTE's *unseeing eyes*)

Where is he, I wonder? In what dark cavern of the mind?

DR. CARRASCO According to recent theory —

PADRE Doctor. Please.

DR. CARRASCO (*Offended*) I was only going to —

PADRE I know what you were going to.

DR. CARRASCO (*Resentfully*) Don't you think I did right?

(*The* PADRE *throws up his hands.*

SANCHO *enters timidly, hat in hand*)

ANTONIA You again!

DR. CARRASCO Tell him to go away.

PADRE (*Wearily*) What harm can he do?

ANTONIA Yes—it's all been done!

(SHE *lets him pass, grudgingly*)

PADRE Good evening.

SANCHO (*Bobbing his head*) Your Reverence.

(*Diffidently*)

Could I talk to him?

PADRE I'm afraid he won't hear you.

SANCHO Well, then I won't say much.

(*The* PADRE *rises, leaving his chair for* SANCHO)

DR. CARRASCO Not too long, please.

SANCHO Oh, he likes to hear me talk! Why, when we were out adventuring—

(*Stops, as* HE *gets a hard look from the* OTHERS)

(*To* DON QUIXOTE:) Good evening, Your Grace.

ANTONIA (*Bitterly*) Your Grace!

SANCHO (*Gaining confidence, to* DON QUIXOTE) Oh, what a time
I've been having since I got back! You know my wife Teresa,
how strong she is? Muscles like a Miura bull! Well, she beat
me, Your Grace. She hit me with everything but the house
itself. And she yells: "Where's all them gold and jewels
you were going to bring me? Where's that kingdom you were
supposed to get?" Well, Your Grace, I just kept a dignified
silence because there are some questions you can't answer. Like
when a man says, "What are you doing with my wife?" that's
one of those questions you just can't answer. Of course I hit
her back, Your Grace, but as I say, she's a lot stronger than I
am, and whether the stone hits the pitcher or the pitcher hits
the stone it's going to be bad for the pitcher.

> (*The* PADRE *is listening with a smile. His eyes turn to*
> DON QUIXOTE, *and there is sudden interest at what*
> *they see*)

But things might be worse, Your Grace. Because even if I
didn't get that kingdom I didn't come home with completely
nothing. What I means is, on the way back I saw two baskets
of wheat sitting all alone in a field with nobody near them,
and I said to myself— "Sancho Panza, when they offer you a
heifer, come running with a halter." So I just took those two
baskets along. I know it wasn't exactly honest, Your Grace, but
I made up for it by giving one basket to the church. "Steal the
pig," I say, "but give the feet to God," and the Padre himself
can tell you that the fat of Christianity is four fingers deep on
my soul. Well, Your Grace—

DON QUIXOTE (*Smiling a little, barely audible*) Sancho.

SANCHO (*Politely, as the* PADRE *warns the* OTHERS *to silence*) Did
Your Grace say something?

DON QUIXOTE You're a fat little bag stuffed with proverbs.

SANCHO Yes, Your Grace. Well, as I was telling you—

ANTONIA (*A cry as* SHE *runs to him*) Uncle!

DON QUIXOTE (*Feebly*) My dear

    (*His eyes go to the* OTHERS)

Good morning, Padre. Or is it evening?

PADRE Alonso...

DR. CARRASCO How do you feel, sir?

DON QUIXOTE Not well, my friend.

DR. CARRASCO Can you speak your name?

DON QUIXOTE Should a man not know his own name?

DR. CARRASCO If you would say it—?

DON QUIXOTE (*In surprise*) Alonso Quijana.

DR. CARRASCO (*With a look of triumph at the* PADRE) Thank you!

ANTONIA (*As* DON QUIXOTE *closes his eyes and is silent. Anxiously:*)
Uncle?

DON QUIXOTE (*Faintly*) Forgive me, dear. When I close my eyes I
see a pale horse...and he beckons me—mount.

PADRE No, Alonso. You will get well!

DON QUIXOTE (*Smiling*) Why should a man get well when he is dying? 'Twould be such a waste of good health.

(*Gestures feebly*)

Come closer, my friends.

(THEY *come to the bedside*)

In my illness I dreamed most strangely. Oh, such dreams. It seemed that I was a...no, I dare not tell lest you think me mad.

ANTONIA Put them from your mind!

DON QUIXOTE (*Deeply weary*) They are gone, my dear—nor do I know what they meant. Padre—

PADRE Here, beside you.

DON QUIXOTE If you please...I should like to make a will...

PADRE Speak, my friend, and I shall write.

DR. CARRASCO (*As* DON QUIXOTE *remains silent*) Señor Quijana?

DON QUIXOTE (*Opens his eyes*) Yes...yes...

(HE *summons strength*)

I, Alonso Quijana, aware of the approaching end to my earthly existence—

(*The* PADRE's *pen scratches busily. From the front of the house is heard the thudding of the door knocker*)

ANTONIA (*To the* HOUSEKEEPER, *as* SHE *goes to see*) Don't admit
anyone.

DON QUIXOTE — do hereby make the following disposition of my
estate. The bulk I bequeath to my beloved niece, Antonia
Quijana —

>   (*From off comes a racket of* VOICES *in vehement
>   argument*)

— With the exception of certain personal bequests which are
as follows —

>   (*The* HOUSEKEEPER *backs in, pushed roughly by*
>   ALDONZA)

HOUSEKEEPER You cannot! I say you cannot!

ALDONZA Get out of my way, you hag —

ANTONIA (*Angrily*) What is this?

HOUSEKEEPER I tried to stop her! She threatened to —

ALDONZA — tear your eyes out! And if you touch me again, by
God —

ANTONIA Sanson!

DR. CARRASCO It's that slut from the inn.

>   (*Advancing on* ALDONZA *grimly*)

Get out of here.

ALDONZA Not before I see him!

Dr. Carrasco I'm warning you—go quietly or I shall—

Don Quixote (*Voice weak but commanding*) Let be.

Dr. Carrasco Señor Quijana—

Don Quixote Let be, I say! In my house there will be courtesy.

> (Carrasco *is balked, but stands between* Aldonza *and the bed*)

Let me see her.

> (Carrasco *reluctantly steps aside, and* Aldonza *and* Don Quixote *are looking at each other*)

Come closer, girl.

> (Aldonza *approaches, losing her bravado*)

What did you wish?

Aldonza (*Incredulously*) Don't you know me?

Don Quixote (*Puzzled*) Should I?

Aldonza I am Aldonza!

Don Quixote (*Blankly*) I am sorry. I do not recall anyone of that name.

Aldonza (*Looks about wildly. Sees* Sancho. *Points to him*) He knows!

> (Don Quixote's *eyes go to* Sancho, *who steps forward as though to speak.* Dr. Carrasco *warns him fiercely with a gesture.* Sancho *closes his mouth, shrugs feebly*)

ALDONZA (*Panicky, to* DON QUIXOTE) Please, my lord!

DON QUIXOTE (*Curiously*) Why do you say "my lord?" I am not a lord.

ALDONZA You are my lord Don Quixote!

> (*A gasp from* ANTONIA. *The* PADRE *stills her with a warning gesture*)

DON QUIXOTE Don Quixote.

> (*Rubs his forehead, troubled*)

You must forgive me, my dear. I have been ill...I am confused by shadows. It is possible that I knew you once— I do not remember.

> (ALDONZA *is stunned.* DR. CARRASCO *smoothly steps forward, takes her by the arm*)

DR. CARRASCO (*Moving her along*) This way.

> (ALDONZA *allows herself to be led. But* SHE *stops, pulls loose suddenly, and in a rush comes back and flings herself to her knees beside the bed*)

ALDONZA Please! Try to remember!

DON QUIXOTE (*With helpless compassion*) Is it so important?

ALDONZA (*Anguished*) Everything. My whole life. You spoke to me and it was different.

DON QUIXOTE I...spoke to you?

ALDONZA And you looked at me! And you didn't see me as I was!

(*Incoherently*)

You said I was sacred, and lovely. You said I was a a vision of purity, and a radiance that would light your path. You said a woman is glory!

DON QUIXOTE Glory...

ALDONZA And you called me by another name!

DR. CARRASCO I'm afraid I must insist—

DON QUIXOTE Leave her be!

(*Deeply disturbed, his mind stirring*)

Then perhaps...it was not a dream...

ALDONZA You *spoke* of a dream. And about the inner call. How you must fight and it doesn't matter whether you win or lose if you follow the inner call. And our mission!

DON QUIXOTE (*With growing alertness*) Mission?

ALDONZA You said it was mine as well as yours!

DON QUIXOTE The words. Tell me the words!

ALDONZA (*Her eyes shining*) "To dream the impossible dream. To fight the unbeatable foe. And never to stop dreaming or fighting—!"

DON QUIXOTE "—This is man's privilege—and the only life worth living."

(He *turns to her, his eyes catching fire*)

Dulcinea!

Aldonza (*Seizes his hand, kisses it*) Thank you, my lord!

Don Quixote But this is not seemly, my lady. On thy knees?
To me?

(He *gets up, raising her*)

Aldonza (*In protest*) My lord, you are not well!

Don Quixote (*Growing in power*) Not well? What is sickness to
the body of a knight-errant? What matter wounds? For each
time he falls he shall rise again—and woe to the wicked!

(*A lusty bellow*)

Sancho!

Sancho Here, Your Grace!

Don Quixote My armor! My sword!

Sancho (*Delighted, claps his hands*) More misadventures!

Don Quixote *Adventures*, old friend! And let there be a mount
for the lady Dulcinea—from henceforth she rides by my side!

(*Takes the sword from* Sancho *and stands firm, eyes
glowing and visionary with the old purpose*)

Now does Don Quixote sally forth again. Now let the good
take heart and the evil beware, for he shall perform the most
astounding deeds of chivalry this world has known.

(*In growing exaltation*)

Avaunt, ye Enchanters! Tremble, ye men against life! Cry terror and flee, for this is Don Quixote, Knight of the Woeful Countenance, and he is invincible! Cry, quake, gnash thy teeth—it will avail thee not. He shall win! For the sword of Don Quixote points—

(HE *wavers suddenly*)

ALDONZA (*A cry of apprehension*) My lord—!

DON QUIXOTE (*In a whisper*) To the stars!

(*The sword falls from his hand and* HE *crumples to the floor*)

ANTONIA Uncle!

(CARRASCO *brushes her aside, swiftly moves to* DON QUIXOTE, *places a hand on his heart. In a moment* HE *looks up at* ANTONIA *in confirmation*)

He is dead. My poor uncle...

(HER *eyes turn to* ALDONZA, *gathering fury*)

You killed him. You with your stories. Your lies. He was sane. He was himself again. And you—!

(SHE *flies at* ALDONZA, *frenziedly striking and scratching*)

Slut! Kitchen trull! Harlot!

(ALDONZA *reels under the attack, but does not defend herself*)

Dr. Carrasco (*Catching* Antonia, *holding her back*) It's too late now.

Antonia (*Struggling, spits at* Aldonza) Filthy animal! Out! Out!

> (Aldonza *silently leaves the area of the room.* Antonia *starts to cry in* Carrasco's *arms. The* Padre, *kneeling by* Don Quixote's *side, makes the sign of the cross.*
>
> *The lights begin to fade but remain up on* Aldonza *where* She *stands alone.*
>
> Sancho *leaves the room.* He *is blubbering, his fat face wet and foolish.* He *sees* Aldonza *where* She *leans against a post, eyes closed.* He *goes to her*)

Sancho He is dead. My master is dead.

Aldonza (*Without emotion*) A man died. He seemed a good man but I did not know him.

Sancho But you *saw*...

Aldonza Don Quixote is not dead. Believe, Sancho. Believe.

Sancho (*In confused hope*) Aldonza...?

Aldonza (*Gently*) My name is Dulcinea.

> (She *leaves him, serene and transfigured.*
>
> *Off, we hear the snarling roll of the drums of the Inquisition.*
>
> *The lighting becomes that of the prison once more and in a moment the* Captain *enters, crossing the stage at the head of* Four Hooded, Chanting Men. *They fall*

silent, remaining outside as the JAILER *opens the door
and the* CAPTAIN *steps inside*)

CAPTAIN (*Unrolling a scroll*) Under authority of the Holy Office
of the Inquisition!

(*Reading*)

By reason of certain offenses committed against His Majesty's
Most Catholic Church the following are summoned to give
answer and submit their persons for purification if it be so
ordered. Don Miguel de Cervantes.

(CERVANTES *nods, almost with relief*)

James William Fox.

(HE *slings a bundled black robe straight at the* DUKE,
*who catches it automatically, comes upright in a paralysis
of shock*)

CERVANTES (*With wry bravado*) How popular a defendant I am.
Summoned by one court before I've quite finished with
another. Well? How says the jury?

MONIPODIO (*Of the package*) I think I know what this contains.
The history of your mad knight?

(CERVANTES *nods, smiling*)

Plead as well there as you did here and you may not burn.

CERVANTES (*Accepting the package*) I've no intention of burning.

(*To* THE DUKE, *cheerfully*)

Your Lordship? Shall we go?

(THE DUKE's *face is white, eyes glazed. The* MAN *is in the grip of total, abject terror.* CERVANTES *understands, comes to him. Voice low:*)

Courage.

(*No response.* HE *takes the* DUKE *by the arm, leads him toward the door.* THE DUKE *moves like a man made of wood*)

MONIPODIO Cervantes.

(CERVANTES *pauses in the doorway*)

I think Don Quixote is brother to Don Miguel.

CERVANTES (*Smiling*) God help us — we are both men of La Mancha.

(*The* DRUMMERS *and* CAPTAIN *about-face. The drums strike into their slow-march roll and the chanting resumes. The little* PROCESSION *moves across the forestage as the* PRISONERS *come forward to watch.*

The girl ESCALANTE [ALDONZA] *stands apart from the others, in her own dream.*

THE DUKE *walks stiff-legged.* CERVANTES *keeps an arm about him, guiding, lending him strength as* THEY *go.*

The arrogant Spanish march-music swells as THE LIGHTS DIM OUT.)

THE END

APPENDICES

COUNTRIES WHICH HAVE PRESENTED "MAN OF LA MANCHA"

Argentina	Italy
Australia	Japan
Austria	Kenya
Bolivia	Luxembourg
Brazil	Mexico
Chile	Nicaragua
Colombia	Norway
Costa Rica	Panama
Czech Republic	Paraguay
Denmark	Peru
Ecuador	Poland
Estonia	Puerto Rico
Finland	Romania
France	South Africa
Germany	Spain
Guatemala	Sweden
Holland	Switzerland
Honduras	Turkey
Hong Kong	Uruguay
Hungary	Venezuela
Iceland	Yugoslavia
Israel	Zambia

LANGUAGES INTO WHICH
"MAN OF LA MANCHA" HAS BEEN TRANSLATED

Afrikaans

Bohemian

Czech

Danish

Dutch

Estonian

Finnish

Flemish

French

German

Greek

Hebrew

Hungarian

Icelandic

Italian

Japanese

Latvian

Norwegian

Polish

Portuguese

Romanian

Russian

Urdu

Slovak

Spanish

Swedish

Turkish

Yugoslavian

MUSICAL ADAPTATIONS
OF WORKS BY CERVANTES

OPERAS AND BALLETS:

SAJON, CARLO (C. 1650–?)
Il Don Chisciot della Mancia

ECCLES, JOHN (1655–1735)
Don Quixote
1684

FÖRTSCH, JOHANN PHILLIP
(1652–1732)
*Der Irrende Ritter Don
Quixote de la Mancha*
Text by Marco Morosini
Hamburg, 1690

PURCELL, HENRY (1658–1695)
AND JOHN ECCLES
(1650–1735)
*Comical History of
Don Quixote*

CONTI, FRANCESCO (1681–1732)
*Don Chisciotte in
Sierra Morena*
Vienna, 1719

TREU, DANIEL GOTTLIEB
(1695–1749)
Don Chisciotto
Breslau, 1727

CALDARA, ANTONIO
(1670–1736)
*Don Chisciotte in
Corte della Duchessa.*
Vienna, 1727

RISTORI, GIOVANNI ALBERTO
(1692–1753)
Un Pazzo Ne Fa Cento
(Il Don Chisciotte)
Text by Pallavicini
Dresden, 1729

ACKEROYD, SAMUEL (C 1650–?)
*The Comical History
of Don Quixote*
London, 1729

GILLIER, JEAN-CLAUDE
(1667–1737)
*Sancho Panca, Governeur,
Ou, La Bagatelle*
Paris, 1730

MARTINI, "PADRE" GIOVANNI
BATTISTA (1706–1784)
Don Chisciotto, Intermezzo
Bologna, 1730

CALDARA, ANTONIO
(1670–1736)
*Sancho Panza, Governatore
dell'Isola Barataria*
Text by G.C. Pasquini
Vienna, 1733

SILVIA, ANTONIO JOSÉ
(c. 1670–1736)
*La Vida do Grande Don
Quixote de Mancha*
Lisbon, 1733

FIELDING, HENRY (author)
(1707–1754)
*Don Quixote in
England. A comedy.*
London, 1734

FEO, FRANCISCO (1685–1745)
*Don Chisciotte della
Mancia, Intermezzo*
Naples, 1740

AYRES, JAMES
*Sancho at the Court, or,
The Mock Governor*
London, 1741

LEO, LEONARDO (1694–1744)
*Il Fantastico od Il Nuovo
Don Chisciotte*
Naples, 1743

BOISMORTIER, JOSEPH BODIN
DE (1694–1765)
*Don Quichotte chez
la Duchesse*
Paris, 1743

HOLZBAUER, IGNAZ (1711–1783)
Don Chisciotto
Mannheim, 1755

PICCINNI, NICCOLÓ (1728–1800)
Il Curioso
1756

TELEMANN, GEORG PHILLIP
(1681–1767)
Il Curioso
1761

PHILIDOR, FRANÇOIS ANDRÉ
DANICAN (1726–1795)
*Sancho Pança, Governeur
dans l'isle de Barataria*
1762

GASSMAN, FLORIAN LEOPOLD
(1729–1774)
Un Pazzo Ne Fa Cento
(Don Chisciotte)
Text by G. Foppa
Venice, 1762

DIDBIN, CHARLES (1745–1814)
The Padlock
Text by I. Bickerstaffe
London, 1768

PAISIELLO, GIOVANNI
(1741–1816)
Don Chisciotte della Mancia
1769

PICCINNI, NICCOLA (1728–1800)
Don Chisciotto
Naples, 1770

SALIERI, ANTONIO (1750–1825)
Don Chisciotto alle Nozzi
di Gamazzo
Vienna, 1771

SCHACK, BENEDICT (1728–1826)
Don Chisciotto
Vienna, 1785

WINTER, PETER VON (1754–1825)
Der Bettelstudent oder
Das Donnerwetter
Text by Weidmann
München, 1785

BEECKE, IGNAZ VON (1733–1803)
Don Quixote
Berlin, 1788

ZACCHARELLI, — (1759–?)
Le Nouveau Don Quichotte
Paris, 1789

CHAMPEIN, STANISLAUS
(1753–1830)
Le Nouveau
Don Don Quichotte
1789

SPINDLER, FRITZ (1759–1820)
Ritter Don Quixote:
Das Abenteuer am Hofe
1790

TARCHI, ANGELO (1760–1814)
Don Chisciotte
Paris, 1791

HUBATSCHEK, — (c. 1760–?)
Don Quichotte
Hermannstadt, 1791

PITROT, ANTONIO (author)
Don Chisciotte
(Composer's name
not known)
Milano, 1792

FOIGNET, CHARLES GABRIEL
(1750–1823)
Michel Cervantes
1793

DITTERSDORF, KARL DITTERS
VON (1739–1799)
Don Quixotte der Zweite
1795

MAYR, JOHANN SIMON
(1763–1845)
*Un Pazzo Ne Fa Cento
(Il Don Chisciotte)*
Text by Giuseppe Foppa
Venice, 1796

ARNOLD, DR. SAMUEL
(1740–1802)
The Mountaineers
New York, Philadelphia,
and Baltimore

NAVOIGEVILLE, GUILLAUME E. J.
(1745–1811)
*L'Empire de la Folie
(La Mort et l'apothéose
de Don Quichotte)*
Paris, 1799

LEFÉBRE, LOUIS F. H.
(1754–1840)
Les Noces de Gamache
Paris, 1800

MUELLER, WENZEL (1767–1835)
Ritter Don Quixote
Text by Von Hensler
Wien, 1802

GENERALI, PIETRO (1783–1832)
Don Chisciotte
Libretto di Rossi
Milan, 1805

MIARI, ANTOINE COMPTE DE
(1787–1854)
Don Quichotte
Venice, 1810

SEIDEL, FRIEDRICH LUDWIG
(1765–1831)
*Die Abenteur des Ritter Don
Quixote de la Mancha*
Berlin, 1811

BOSCHA, ROBERT NICOLUS
CHARLES (1789–1856)
Les Noces de Gamache
Paris, 1815

AUBER, DANIEL FRANÇOIS-
ESPRIT (1782–1871)
Leocadie
Text by P. A. Wolff
Berlin, 1821

WEBER, CARL MARIA VON
(1786–1826)
Preciosa
Text by P. A. Wolff
Berlin, 1821

MENDELSSOHN-BARTHOLDY,
FELIX (1809–1847)
Die Hochzeit des Camacho
Berlin, 1827

GARCIA, MANUEL DEL POPOLO
VICENTE (1775–1832)
Don Chisciotte
New York, 1827

MERCADANTE, GIUSEPPE
SAVERIO R. (1795–1870)
Don Chisciotto
Cadix, 1829

DONIZETTI, GAETANO
(1797–1848)
*Il Furioso nell'Isola di
San Domingo*
Text by G. Ferreti
Rome, 1833

RODWELL, GEORGE HERBERT
BONAPARTE (1800–1852)
Don Quixote, operetta
London, 1835

MAZZUCATO, ALBERTO
(1813–1877)
Don Chisciotte
Milano, 1836

GÄHRICH, WENZEL (1794–1865)
Don Quixote
Berlin, 1840

BALFE, MICHAEL (1808–1870)
The Bohemian Girl
London, 1843

MACFARREN, GEORGE
ALEXANDER (1813–1887)
Don Quichotte
London, 1845

MONIUSZKO, STANISLAU
(1819–1872)
The New Don Quixote
Text by Count Fredro
Wilna, 1847

CLAPPISON, ANTOINE L.
(1808–1866)
Don Quichotte et Sancho
Paris, 1847

"RONGER" (HÉRVE, FLORIMOND)
(1825–1892)
*Don Quichotte
et Sancho Pansa*
Paris, 1848

LASSEN, EDUARD (1830–1904)
Le Captif
Text by E. Cormon
Brussels, 1865
(Deals with an incident in
the life of Cervantes)

ACEVES Y LOZANO, RAFAEL
(1837–1876)
El Manco de Lepanto
1867

BOULANGER, ERNEST, H. A.
(1815–1900)
Don Quichotte
Paris, 1869

MINKUS, ALOYSIUS
FYODORVICH (1827–1890)
Don Quichotte
Moscow, 1869

PESSARD, ÉMILE (1843–1917)
Don Quichotte
Paris, 1874

OFFENBACH, JACQUES
(1819–1880)
Don Quichotte
Book by Sardou
Paris, 1874

CLAY, FREDERICK (1840–1889)
*Princess Toto and
Don Quixote*
London, 1875

MENENDORFF, A. (1843–1897)
Don Quixote

ROTH, PHILLIP (1853–1898)
AND MAX RITTER VON
WEINZIERL (1841–1898)
Don Quixote
Vienna, 1879

STRAUSS, JOHANN (1825–1899)
Das Spitzentuch Der Königin
Text by H. Horrmann-
Riegen and R. Genee
Vienna, 1880

RICCI, LUIGI (1852–1906)
Don Chisciotte
Text by Fiorentino & Gallo
Venice, 1881

LUCANTINI, GIOVANNI
(1825–1902)
Don Chisciotto
Milan, 1884

CHAPÍ Y LORENTE, RUPERTO
(1851–1909)
La Venta de Don Quijote

ROTH, LUIGI (1849–C 1914)
Don Chichotte
Budapest, 1888

DE KOVEN, REGINALD
(1859–1920)
Don Quixote
Boston, 1889

JACQUES-DALCROZE, EMILE
(1865–?)
Sancho
Geneva, 1897

RAUCHENECKER, GEORG W.
(1844–1906)
Don Quixote
Elberfield, 1897

KIENZL, WILLHELM (1857–1941)
Don Quixote
1898

VAN DEN EEDEN, JAN [JEAN
BAPTISTE] (1842–1917)
La Numancia
1898

BEER-WALBRUNN, ANTON
(1864–1929)
Don Quijote
Müchen, 1908

Besi, Simone
Don Chisciotto della Mancia.
San Sepolcro, 1908

MASSENET, JULES EMILE
FRÉDERIC (1842–1912)
Don Quichotte
1910

PASINI, FRANCESCO
Don Chisciotto della Mancia
Florence, 1910

PAUMGARTNER, BERNHARD
(1887–?)
Die Höhle von Salamanca
Dresden, 1923

FALLA, MANUEL DE (1786–1946)
El Retablo de Maese Pedro
Seville, 1923

LAPARRA, RAOUL (1876–1943)
L'illustre Fregona
Text by composer
Paris, 1931

LATTUNDA, FELICE (1882–?)
La Caverna di Salamanca
Text by Piccoli
Genoa, 1938

ORBÓN, JULIÁN (1925–)
Incidental music to
La gitanilla
Habana, 1944

RODRIGUEZ ALBERT, RAFAEL
(1902–2002)
Clavileño
1948

PETRASSI, GOFFREDDO
(1904–2003)
Il Cordovano
La Scala, 1949

HENZE, HANS WERNER (1926–)
Das Wundertheatre
Heidelberg, 1949

FRAZZI, VITO (1888–1975)
Don Chisciotte
1951

FRAZZI, VITO (1888–1975)
Clavileño
1952

ORFF, CARL (1895–1982)
Astutuli
Munich, 1953

BARRAUD, HENRY (1900–1997)
Numance
1955

RIVIÈRE, JEAN (? –1987)
Pour un Don Quixote
1961

PETRASSI, GOFFREDO
(1904–2003)
Clavileño
1967

HALFFTER, RODOLFO
(1900–1987)
Clavileño
1970

NUREYEV, RUDOLPH (1938–93)
Don Quixote (Film version)
Music by Ludwig (Leon)
Minkus and John
Lanchberry
1972

LATORRE, JAVIER (1963–)
Rinconete y Cortadillo
(Flamenco ballet)
Music by Juan Carlos
Romero and
Mauricio Sotelo
Cordoba, 2002

CHAPÍ Y LORENTE, RUPERTO
(1851–1909)
La Gitanilla

OFFENBACH, JACQUES
(1819–1880)
Les Bavards
(Based on "Los dos
Habladores")

**ORCHESTRAL
COMPOSITIONS:**
TELEMANN, GEORGE PHILIPP
(1681–1767)
Don Quichotte Suite

GANDOLFO, E.
*Marche Héroique de Don
Quichotte*
1892

KIENZL, WILHELM (1857–1941)
*Don Quixote's Phantasticher
Ausritt und Seine
Traurige Heimkehr*
Berlin, 1899

RUBINSTEIN, ANTON
  GREGORIEVICH (1829–1894)
  Don Quixote
  1871

CHAPÍ Y LORENTE, RUPERTO
  (1851–1909)
  Scherzo

STRAUSS, RICHARD (1864–?)
  Don Quixote
  1898

GHERARD, ROBERTO
  Don Quijote
  London, 1945

RÁNKÏ, GYÖRGY (1907–1992)
  Don Quixote y Dulcinea
  1960

DIEMECKE, ENRIQUE ARTURO
  Camino y Vision
  2001

SONGS: VOICE AND PIANO:
OBRADORS, FERNANDO J.
  Consejo
  Madrid, 1930

RAVEL, MAURICE (1875–1937)
  Don Quichotte á Dulcinée
  Chanson romantique
  Chanson èpique
  Chanson à boire
  (3 songs)
  Text by P. Morand

HILTS, CYNTHIA
  Dulcinea Regrets
  2000

MUSICAL DRAMA:
WASSERMAN, DALE (1917–)
  Man of La Mancha
  Music by Mitch Leigh
  Lyrics by Joe Darion
  New York, 1965

DALE WASSERMAN THEATRICAL WORKS

TELEVISION

Elisha and the Long Knives
Fiddlin' Man
Eichmann: Engineer of Death
The Citadel
Brotherhood of the Bell
Drop on the Devil
Dynamite
The Fool Killer
The Bequest
American Primitive
Collision
The Time of the Drought
Boys Will Be Boys
The Monster
The Man That
    Corrupted Hadleyburg
The Lincoln Murder Case
Long After Summer
Look What's Going On
The Milwaukee Rocket
The Medallion
The Fog
The Gentle Grafter
The Forger
The Luck of Roaring Camp
I, Don Quixote

The Blue Angels
Cress Delehanty
The Grand Deception
The Commuters
Scaramouche
Circle of Death
Stranger
The Seventh Dimension
Dracula: The True Story
Burden of Proof
A Fine American Family
My Name Is Esther
The Girl from Botany Bay
Murder Among the Saints

FILM

Aboard the Flying Swan
Two Faces To Go
The Vikings
O Jangadeiro (The Sea
    and the Shadow)
Man of La Mancha
Stay Away, Joe
A Walk with Love and Death
Quick, Before It Melts
Doctor, You've Got to Be Kidding
Mister Buddwing

The First Thing We Do
The Power and the Glory
Look, We're Alive
The African
The Mary Bryant Story
Scheherazade
Red Sky
Conquest
An Arrangement of Animals
Cleopatra

THEATRE

Livin' The Life (Musical)
One Flew Over the Cuckoo's Nest
Western Star (Musical)
How I Saved the
    Whole Damn World
An Enchanted Land
Players in a Game
Montparnasse (Musical)
Shakespeare and the
    Indians (Musical)
Beggar's Holiday (Musical)
Wait for Me, World (Musical)
A Walk in the Sky (Musical)
Play With Fire
Bequest
The Shining Mountains
Man of La Mancha (Musical)

INDEX